W9-BDH-334

Culture and Customs of Sweden

Map of Sweden. (Courtesy of BookComp, Inc.)

Culture and Customs of Sweden

BYRON J. NORDSTROM

Culture and Customs of Europe

AN IMPRINT OF ABC-CLIO, LLC
Santa Barbara, California • Denver, Colorado • Oxford, England

Library of Congress Cataloging-in-Publication Data

Nordstrom, Byron J.
Culture and customs of Sweden / Byron J. Nordstrom.
p. cm. — (Culture and customs of Europe)
Includes bibliographical references and index.
ISBN 978–0–313–34371–1 (hard copy : alk. paper) — ISBN 978–0–313–34372–8 (ebook)
1. Ethnology—Sweden. 2. Sweden—Social life and customs. I. Title.
DL639.N68 2010
948.5—dc22 2010014133

ISBN: 978–0–313–34371–1
EISBN: 978–0–313–34372–8

14 13 12 11 10 1 2 3 4 5

This book is also available on the World Wide Web as an eBook.
Visit www.abc-clio.com for details.

Greenwood
An Imprint of ABC-CLIO, LLC

ABC-CLIO, LLC
130 Cremona Drive, P.O. Box 1911
Santa Barbara, California 93116-1911

This book is printed on acid-free paper ∞

Manufactured in the United States of America

Contents

Series Foreword

THE OLD WORLD and the New World have maintained a fluid exchange of people, ideas, innovations, and styles. Even though the United States became the de facto world leader and economic superpower in the wake of a devastated Europe in World War II, Europe has remained for many the standard bearer of Western culture.

Millions of Americans can trace their ancestors to Europe. The United States as we know it was built on waves of European immigration, starting with the English, who braved the seas to found the Jamestown Colony in 1607. Bosnian and Albanian immigrants are some of the latest new Americans. In the Gilded Age of one of our great expatriates, the novelist Henry James, the Grand Tour of Europe was de rigueur for young American men of means to prepare them for a life of refinement and taste. In the more recent democratic age, scores of American college students have Eurorailed their way across Great Britain and the Continent, sampling the fabled capitals and bergs in a mad, great adventure, or have benefited from a semester abroad. For other American vacationers and culture vultures, Europe is the prime destination. What is the new post–Cold War, post–Berlin Wall Europe in the new millennium? Even with the different languages, rhythms, and rituals, Europeans have much in common: They are largely well-educated, prosperous, and worldly. They also have similar goals, face common threats, and form alliances. With the advent of the European Union, the open borders, and the Euro, and considering globalization and the prospect of a homogenized Europe, an updated survey of the region is warranted.

Culture and Customs of Europe features individual volumes on the countries most studied for which fresh information is in demand from students and other readers. The series casts a wide net, including not only the expected countries, such as Spain, France, England, and Germany, but also countries such as Poland and Greece that lie outside Western Europe proper. Each volume is written by a country specialist with intimate knowledge of the contemporary dynamics of a people and culture. Sustained narrative chapters cover the land, the people, and offer a brief history; they also discuss religion, social customs, gender roles, family, marriage, literature and media, performing arts and cinema, and art and architecture. The national character and ongoing popular traditions of each country are framed in a historical context and celebrated along with the latest trends and major cultural figures. A country map, chronology, glossary, and evocative photos enhance the text.

The storied and enlightened Europeans will continue to fascinate Americans. Our futures are strongly linked politically, economically, and culturally.

Preface

As the Series Foreword indicates, this volume shares its basic content themes with a number of books that are intended to provide new and current looks at one European country—in this case, Sweden. When I was asked to undertake this project, I was initially somewhat reluctant. I am a historian. My fields of specialization are Scandinavian and Scandinavian-American history. I have been researching and writing in these fields for nearly 40 years. I am, however, neither a current affairs specialist nor a native Swede; and I wondered whether an "outsider," someone who was neither raised in Sweden nor constantly immersed in it, could really understand the place. As a result, it was only after some reflection that I decided the invitation was too enticing. Of course, what I knew about the country's history would inform many components of the book, and the challenge of developing useful and accurate descriptions of many elements of contemporary Swedish national life was irresistible.

The book is based largely around the Series' standard structure. An introductory chapter looks at Sweden's geography, climate, population, history, politics, economy, and some of the characteristics that supposedly define Swedes today. In Chapter 2, the focus is on religion, with particular attention given to the long history behind the predominance of the Lutheran Church, the emergence of other Christian denominations, the Jews and Muslims in Sweden, and the apparent secularism of many Swedes. Chapter 3 has three main themes. One is the changing nature of marriage and family. Here the focus is on what these terms have meant in the past and what they are coming to mean in the present. Another is on the status, roles, and issues facing women. The last is a look at the ongoing evolution of an educational system that offers almost literally cradle to grave opportunities for individual growth and development. Chapter 4 is about fun, special times Swedes celebrate and how they do so; customs; foods; leisure activities; and sports. Chapter 5 takes a look at the major mass media of Sweden: the press, radio, television, and the internet. It is about how Swedes are informed and entertained. Chapter 6 surveys Swedish literature—first by looking at its history, and then turning to several important genre, including crime fiction and immigrant literature, and examining what contemporary Swedes read. Chapter 7 introduces the performing arts—theater, opera, dance, music, and film. Chapter 8 surveys the past and present of Sweden's art, architecture, and design.

One of the most challenging aspects of writing this book was obtaining current information. It is one thing to reflect on one's own experiences or impressions, and quite another to make the contents useful, accurate, and up-to-date. Scholarly books and articles on many of the themes considered were, of course, very important, but they were also often years out of date. More current printed materials in periodicals or the press helped to fill some of the gaps. Conversations with Swedish friends were frequently useful, too. Not surprisingly, the internet proved to be an absolutely essential tool—one that is continuously evolving as an increasingly important aid to research. However, it also had its limitations, some of which became very clear as I worked through this project. One, of course, was the sheer glut of information. Some good, some bad. All research involves source evaluation, and applying various measures of reliability to internet sources was essential. Another downside of the internet is that many Web sites are not permanent. (Perhaps none are.) Information that was available one day was gone another.

In the end I was glad to have taken on this project. However, I was time and again reminded of the pitfalls that are inherent in an undertaking of this kind and aware of the limitations in terms of accuracy and completeness I faced. At the core of these is the assumption that there are such things as national cultures and customs or that a national group, even one supposedly as homogeneous as Sweden's, can be defined by some set of shared historical events, famous people, images, icons, festivals and celebrations, foods, cultural artifacts, politics, ideals, beliefs, everyday behaviors, etc. What is manifestly clear is that all definitions of Sweden's (and any other country's) culture and customs are going to be skewed and vary widely. Time, place, the perspectives of the observer, generation, age, ethnicity, political affiliation, religious beliefs, context, audience, and intended purpose are some of the factors that will influence these definitions. Also, trying to develop such definitions is like attempting to hit a target that seems to be moving faster and faster under the influence of both internal and externals forces. Today's Sweden is vastly different in many many ways from just a generation or two ago, and almost every aspect of life is caught up in an ongoing and endless process of transformation that makes pinning down the country's culture and customs all that more difficult.

Acknowledgments

THERE ARE MANY who deserve thanks for their help. Completion of the project would have been impossible without the fine scholarship of my colleagues in Sweden, the other Nordic countries, the United Kingdom, and the United States. Also indispensable were the many very fine Web sites used in this book, especially those maintained in Sweden by individuals, organizations, and government agencies such as the Church of Sweden, the Swedish Institute, Statistics Sweden, *Skolverket*, the Nordic Museum, or the Swedish Film Institute; and the conversations I had with a number of very helpful people I reached via these Web sites. Special thanks go to Roland Thorstensson and his students in the Gustavus Adolphus College Semester in Sweden Program for 2009 who read, reviewed, and recommended changes to many of the chapters; to Helena Karlsson, Roger McKnight, Glenn Kranking, and Brian Magnusson for help with several parts of the book; to Gustavus Adolphus College that provided me with a semester sabbatical; and to my wife, Janet, for her patience, encouragement, proofreading, and editorial comments.

Chronology

c. 10,000 BCE	Oldest evidence of human habitation in the far south
c. 4000 BCE	Evidence of earliest farming
c. 2300 BCE	Boat Axe People's In-Migration
c. 1800 BCE	Earliest evidence of bronze production
	Tanum rock carvings
c. 500 BCE	Earliest evidence of iron production
c. 400	Earliest Gotland picture stones
c. 780–1100	Viking Age. Swedish activity was mainly to the east into what is now Finland, the Baltic states, and Russia
c. 800–1100	Gradual conversion to Christianity
1164	Archbishopric of Uppsala established
1397–1523	Kalmar Union Period. Sweden, Denmark, and Norway are linked in a kind of federation
1477	Founding of Uppsala University
1489	Bernt Notke's statue of St. George Slaying the Dragon

1520s	Sweden effects a lasting break from the Kalmar Union
	An independent monarchy under Gustav I Vasa develops
	The Reformation comes to Sweden
1535	*Vädersolstavlan* painting of Stockholm
1611	Gustav II Adolf becomes king. Perhaps the best-known Swedish monarch (d. 1632)
1620–1720	Sweden's Age of Greatness or Age of Empire. For much of this century the Baltic was under Swedish control or influence
1645	First Swedish newspaper, *Ordinari Post Tijdender*
1697	Fire destroys the old Three Crowns Palace in Stockholm
1700–21	Great Northern War ends Sweden's Age of Empire
1719–72	Era of Liberty. A fascinating period when the power of the crown was subject to the rule of parliament
	A "golden age" for Swedish painting
1773	Founding of the Royal Opera and Royal Ballet
1788	Founding of the Royal Dramatic Theater
1809	Coup that led to a new constitution and a new dynasty
	Finland is ceded to Russia
1814	Sweden and Norway enter into a dynastic union
1840s	A period of emigration begins that lasts for nearly a century. About 1.25 million Swedes leave
1842	School Reform
1866	National Museum opens in Stockholm
1868	First Swedish Folk High Schools
1870s	Industrialization accelerates
1905	Dissolution of the Union with Norway
1906	Selma Lagerlöf's *Wonderful Adventures of Nils Holgersson* is published.
1907	Nordic Museum opens
1908	Universal male suffrage
1912	August Strindberg dies

1917	*Hemutställning*, The Home Exhibition in Stockholm
1921	Women's suffrage is introduced
1925	Beginnings of Swedish Radio
1927	First Volvo goes into production
1930	Stockholm Exposition featuring Functionalism
1930s	Social Democratic Party achieves political control and begins to develop the "people's home," e.g., the welfare state
1939–45	Sweden maintains a tenuous neutrality during World War II
1945	First Pippi Longstocking book appears
1945–90	Period of nominal nonalignment in foreign and security policy
1950	Pär Lagerkvist's *Barabbas* is published
1956	First Swedish television broadcast
1958	Modern Museum of Art opens in Stockholm
	Sweden hosts the World Cup soccer competition
	Church of Sweden approves ordination of women
1965–74	Million Programme undertaken to increase housing in Sweden
1972	ABBA comes together as a musical group
1973	Carl XVI Gustaf becomes king
1976	Social Democrats' 44 years in power end
1986	Assassination of Prime Minister Olof Palme
1995	Sweden joins the EU
	The free newspaper *Metro* appears on Stockholm subways
2000	Öresund Bridge opens, creating a fixed link with Denmark and the Continent
	Disestablishment of the Church of Sweden
2005	June 6 becomes Sweden's national holiday
2009	Sweden adopts a gender-neutral marriage law

1

Land, People, and a Brief History

Contemporary Sweden is often defined as a prosperous, ultramodern, democratic, capitalist, social welfare state. To be slightly more detailed, it is a place with one of the highest standards of living in the world; where citizens enjoy the benefits of one of the most generous social welfare systems in the world; where the state and private industry have formed a symbiotic relationship to encourage growth and full employment; where life expectancies are the eighth longest in the world; where women enjoy greater equality than almost anywhere else in the world; where literacy is nearly 100 percent; where the arts receive generous support from the state; where protecting the environment has long been an important issue; where cooperation and peace in the world are highly valued; where exiles and refugees from the most troubled places in the world are welcome; where ethnic, racial, and religious diversity have become some of the most important features of the contemporary Swedish landscape; and where personal modesty, moderation, cooperation, and coziness are key words governing people's behaviors. Sweden is also a country with firm ties to its long history and perhaps exaggerated fondness for its contributions to the Viking Age, to its Age of Greatness in the seventeenth century, when it controlled much of the Baltic, and to its colorful folk traditions and calendar of special celebrations spread across the year that help define its national identity.

On the negative side, some believe Sweden is a place where the welfare state is really a nanny state that has removed or stifled individual initiative, taxes are so high everyone is turned into an evader if not an exile, conformity is valued above creativity, the collective is more important than the individual, its alleged commitments to globalism and peace and cooperation are false, and the new heterogeneity of the population is actually deeply regretted and toleration is a sham.

There is certainly some truth in these lists. Bias, perspective, context, and the moment will determine which one prefers or chooses to apply. Regardless, what all of these defining elements point out is the complexity of this place and the difficulty of defining its, or any country's, identity. To complicate matters, today's Sweden is, perhaps more so than at any other time in its history, a place in the throes of change in almost every facet of its national life—not least of all in terms of its culture and customs. In the last 50 years or so, for example, the ethnic composition of the population has been radically transformed, primarily by immigration. At the same time, global influences and new technologies have acted upon Sweden, and the results can be seen in areas that include language, literature, the press, the arts, religion, popular culture, and cuisine, to name but a few.

Like every country of the world, Sweden's culture and customs have been shaped by basic, built-in factors such as geography, climate, and topography. At the same time, factors including individuals, social groups, in-migrations, contact with outsiders, external forces, and sheer accidents have determined what defines Sweden as well. Some of these are examined below.

The Place/The Land

Sweden is located in the far north of Europe. Its immediate neighbors are Norway, Finland, and Denmark. (These four countries, plus Iceland, constitute an historical region variously called Scandinavia or *Norden*/The North.) Across the Baltic lie Russia, Estonia, Latvia, Lithuania, Poland, and Germany. Sweden is a relatively large country, about the size of California. In area it measures about 173,000 square miles (450,000 square kilometers)—slightly larger than Germany but smaller than France. The southern-most point, Smygehuk, near the coastal town of Smygehamn, lies at about 55 degrees north latitude. Its northern-most point, 69 degrees north latitude, is just to the west of Kilpisjärvi in Finland and about 90 miles north of the iron mining center at Kiruna. Long and relatively narrow, the country extends almost 1,000 miles from south to north—a distance about equal to that between Los Angeles, California, and Portland, Oregon, or between Chicago, Illinois, and Boston, Massachusetts. Sweden is a little more than 300 miles across at the widest point. It shares a 380-mile (614 km) border with Finland and a 1,006-mile (1,619 km) border with Norway and has some 2,000 miles

(3,218 km) of coastline that front in the west on the passages leading from the Baltic to the North Sea (Öresund, Kattegat, and Skagerrak), to the south and east on the Baltic and the Gulf of Bothnia. The country also includes the large islands of Öland and Gotland (with its several surrounding islands) and archipelagos that extend up the west coast and north and east from Stockholm to Finland.[1]

The underlying bedrock of Sweden is several hundred million years old, and the soils that cover it are relatively thin. Wind, water, and ice have been the principal shapers of the landscape over the last 60 million years or so. During this time, Sweden has been repeatedly carved by the advance and retreat of glaciers, the most recent recession coming mainly between about 14,000 and 5,000 years ago. (Several small glaciers remain in the northern mountains.) Through these forces, mountains have been eroded, the land has been compressed and then allowed to rebound, and rivers have been carved, lakes formed, and topographical features created by deposits left behind. All of these processes have been (and continue to be) important in shaping the human history of the region. For example, the glaciers plowed up vast amounts of surface materials including rocks and gravel as they advanced; this was then left behind as glacial rubble as they receded. In parts of Sweden, these stone deposits have plagued farmers for millennia and been a primary building material for foundations, fences, and fortifications. They inspired Vilhelm Moberg, one of Sweden's best-known twentieth-century writers, to label his native province of Småland "the kingdom of stones" (*stenriket*) in his emigrant novel, *The Emigrants.*[2]

Topographically, Sweden is a country of contrasts. In one model it is divided into three regions: the southern lowlands, the central plains, and the north. There is, however, great variety within this simplistic view. In another scheme there are some 36 different landscapes, each characterized by differing landforms and vegetation. In general, the far south, principally the historic province of Skåne, begins as a relatively low-lying, flat plain. This changes to a hilly region to the north, along the provincial border with Småland. Similarly, the landscape of the west begins as a narrow coastal plain and then becomes gently rolling as one travels from west to east. On the southeast side of the peninsula the land again falls off toward the coast with the Baltic and the low-lying island of Öland. There are also the south Swedish highlands that lie along the northwest border between Småland and Västergötland. Much of the middle of the country is dominated by the central Sweden depression. There open plains and parallel valleys define the landscape. The northern two thirds of the country tilts upward, rising slowly from east to west toward the mountain spine (*Kölen*/Keel) that divides Norway and Sweden.

Almost all of these landscapes have a special place in how the country and its people are defined. Reinforcing this is how, to some degree, each is contained within one of the historic provinces or *landskap* that make up the country. The number of these grew over time. Six made up the earliest Swedish state. There were 23 in the seventeenth century. Today there are 21. Each has a history and set of defining traits including folk art, customs and costumes, economic activities, and the like, and for centuries, one's provincial origins were far more important than being "Swedish." Take Dalarna as an example. It is sometimes considered the quintessential Swedish region. Located in central Sweden, it is a strikingly beautiful area of rolling hills, vast forests, idyllic lakes and rivers, small farms, and red-painted cottages. (This color, called *falu röd*, is very much a part of Swedish culture. For centuries, it has been made from the tailings of the copper mine at Falun.) Dalarna also holds an important place in the nation's history, secured by its people's rebellions against tyranny and support of Gustav I Vasa, the "founder" of modern Sweden in the early sixteenth century. It is an area with a rich folk culture, reflected in its costumes, music, dance, unique farming economy, and, perhaps most famously, in its *dalahästar* (plural) carved wooden horses of various sizes usually painted orange with blue and white decorations.[3]

Sweden's natural resources have aided in the development of human settlement for millennia. Water is one of them. There are about 92,000 lakes in Sweden. The largest of these are Vättern, Vänern, Hjalmaren, Mälaren, Siljan, and Storsjön. There are also at least 30 significant river systems, including the Torne, Kälix, and Pite in the far north; the Ljungan and Dal in the central region; and the Klar and Göta rivers in the middle west. These and the seas that surround the country have been sources of food and essential to travel and transport of goods and people for centuries. Similarly, Sweden's forests have been and remain sources of timber, tar, wood for charcoal, paper pulp, and biomass, and they have provided homes for game and fur-bearing animals. The makeup of Sweden's forests changes as one moves across the country. In the south, deciduous trees predominate, including birch and oak. Further north conifers take over. Both forest and more open areas support a host of wild native plants including shrubs, fruit-bearing plants, and wild flowers—many of them named and documented by the eighteenth-century botanist Carl von Linné/Linnaeus. In addition, Sweden's forests have also been an important element in history, as shapers of regions and obstacles to transportation and settlement, and in the development of folklore. The country's two most important mineral resources have been copper and iron, but there are also deposits of gold, silver, lead, zinc, and uranium. Only about 6 percent of the country is good for farming, and only recently have modern agricultural techniques and machines made farming a rewarding occupation.

For centuries subsisting on farms was an endless and often futile struggle against the forces of nature.

In many ways, Sweden's climate is as varied as its landscapes, and it, too, has defined Sweden and the Swedes. While one may think that this northern country must be cursed by long, dark, frigid winters with lots of snow, followed by pitifully short but dazzlingly bright summers, such generalizations are only partially true. According to some sources, there are essentially two major climate zones in the country; a temperate south and a continental north. Things are more complicated than this, however. In the Köppen-Geiger system, there are three climate zones: a warm, maritime south (type Cfb), a predominantly Subarctic or Boreal (type Dfc) through much of the country, and small areas in the mountains of the north that have a Tundra or Ice climate (type E). Regardless of the classification system preferred, there are significant variations across the country, and prevailing winds, surrounding bodies of water, topographic features, and annual variations are important determiners of weather patterns.

In general, southern Sweden enjoys a relatively temperate climate. Summers are warm and precipitation levels moderate. Temperatures across the region vary relatively little. Malmö, on the southwest coast, enjoys an overall average July temperature of about 62°F while Stockholm's average is about 63°F. Add the long days and short nights, and one has ingredients for good farming—the growing season runs to about 200 days—and an explanation for the prevalence of deciduous trees. Southern winters are cool and damp. In January, Malmö's average temperature is right around freezing, and Stockholm's about two degrees less. The days are short and the nights long. The sun comes up in Stockholm on the winter solstice at around 8:45 AM and sets around 2:50 PM.

The climate of the northern two thirds of the country is characterized by cool, short, and dazzlingly bright summers and long, cold, and dark winters. Kiruna, for example, Sweden's largest northern city and the site of the country's largest iron mine, has an average July temperature of 55°F and an average January temperature of just 3°F. Located just above the Arctic Circle, the sun does not set for almost two months in the summer or rise above the horizon for the same length of time in the winter. Precipitation in the city is moderate, however, averaging about 31 inches (80 cm) a year.

The summer/winter extremes in the length of days and nights and the varying seasonal qualities of daylight or the lack thereof are important aspects of life in Sweden. The endless daylight (Midnight sun) of high summer, the darkness of winter, and the often quite eerie qualities of dawn and dusk that occur throughout the year are aspects of the physical environment Sweden shares with all high-latitude countries, and they have played many roles in the shaping of the country's history, economy, customs, and culture. Also, contrary to what some might believe, the lack of daylight in the winter can have its positive effects. Swedes seem well adapted to these conditions and make the most of the snow, ice, and moderate temperatures to enjoy winter sports. One good thing about the temperatures that hover around freezing is that snows tend to melt between accumulating falls, and the ice on the inland lakes and even in coastal waters freezes, melts, and then re-freezes at the surface, making for some absolutely wonderful ice skating conditions. In a good winter, Stockholmers can skate for miles on the glass smooth ice of Lake Mälaren.

Finally, it is worth noting that global climate change seems to be a factor in Sweden. Average temperatures and precipitation amounts in the years since 1991 have been above the norms set in the previous 30 years. This is especially true of winter averages. There is also evidence of warming in the advance of the tree line in the north, the recession of the few remaining glaciers, and the movement of animals formerly native to warmer areas in the south.

People

In early 2010, Sweden's population was 9.35 million. This compares with about 5 million in 1900 and around 7 million in 1950. Just a few decades ago, it was relatively easy to define this population in terms of its ethnic background, nation of origin, or cultural roots. Overwhelmingly, Swedes were "Swedes": people born in Sweden of Swedish-born parents; people who could trace their ancestry back for generations within the country. The major minorities were Finns and the indigenous Sami, plus a small number of gypsies (Romani). This does not mean, however, that Sweden had never seen an influx of foreigners or that the country's population had always been so homogenous. In-migrations have been important at a number of times in Sweden's history. Archeological evidence indicates the arrival of a new and different ethnic stock called the Boat Axe People around 2500 BC, for example. These people apparently came from deep in what is now Russia, and they brought with them an entirely new culture. Gradually, as has also been so typical of in-migration populations, they mixed with the original people. Similarly, Germans were important in the Middle Ages. Stockholm and Visby (on the island of Gotland) were virtually German cities around 1300, and much of Sweden's trade was controlled by the German-based Hanseatic League until well into the sixteenth century. In the seventeenth century, Dutch immigrants, like Louis De Geer, played important roles in economic and political developments and were central in the building and growth of Göteborg, Sweden's main west coast port. Walloon iron makers from what is now Belgium were important in developing the iron foundries of the so-called *Bergslagen* of central Sweden at about the same time. The Swedish nobility has long contained families with roots all over Europe including many of the old German states, France, the Netherlands, Scotland, England, and Russia.

Since the end of World War II, Sweden has been in the midst of another very important period of in-migration, a period during which, quite literally, the faces of Swedes have changed, and the population has become vastly more diverse in ethnic, national, cultural, and religious composition. To illustrate just one aspect of these changes, in 1960 foreign-born nationals accounted for 4 percent of Sweden's population; in 2007 they accounted for more than 13.4 percent, and if children born in Sweden but with two foreign-born parents were added in, the percentage rose to 17 percent—in all more than 1.6 million of Sweden's total population.

Who are these so-called new Swedes? The answer to this question changes with *when* and *why* immigrants came to Sweden. In the first decade or so after 1945, many were Finns pushed by border adjustments following the war and drawn by employment opportunities and a relatively open immigration policy. Others, though considerably fewer, were refugees or asylum seekers, some fleeing the Sovietization of the Baltic states. As Sweden's economy continued to expand in the postwar years, other immigrants, including many from the former Yugoslavia, were drawn to jobs with good pay. Also, as is so often typical of immigration, once cores of immigrants from particular places developed, they served as magnets for others who followed. In more recent decades, employment opportunities have become less a pull factor, while political turmoil in homelands, Sweden's immigration and, especially, asylum policies, the effects of globalization, and the continue draw of core communities have fed the flow of in-migrants. In 2007, a record year, 99,485 people from more than 160 countries immigrated to Sweden. By region, the largest number came from Asia (29,658), followed by the 27 nations of the European Union (23,694), returning Swedes (15,949), Sweden's four Nordic neighbors (10,464), Africa (8,530), and non-EU Europe (6,111). In terms of individual countries, the largest numbers came from Iraq (15,200), Poland (7,525), Denmark (5,097), Somalia (3,781), Germany (3,614), Romania (2,587), Thailand (2,548), and China (2,386). In addition, another 36,207 were asylum seekers from more than 50 countries: 18,559 were from Iraq, 3,349 from Somalia, and 2,601 from Serbia or Montenegro.[4]

This extended period of net-gain in-migration has had profound effects on Sweden. Some are good, some bad. Simply put, the country's population has become vastly more heterogeneous. In every aspect of Swedish life there is a new diversity. Ethnicity, religion, culture, customs, law, politics, social structures, neighborhood organization, residential geography (the geography of ethnic settlement), schools at all levels, cuisine, literature, the theater, the arts, consumer options, crime, and gender roles are just some of these. Some aspects of the new Swedes and their impacts will be examined in subsequent chapters because no study of Sweden's customs and culture can ignore them.

A Brief History

It may seem a statement of the obvious, but one needs to remember that Sweden has not always existed. In fact, it is only possible to write about a country as a geopolitical place since about 1000 CE, perhaps a bit later. That Sweden (*Svearige or Svearike* from which today's *Sverige* comes) was considerably different from and smaller than the Sweden of today. This is not to say, however, that people have not lived in what is now called Sweden for a very long time, nor is it to say that there is not a very long pre-history and history connected to this *place*.[5]

About 12,000 years ago when the glaciers of the most recent ice age began to recede and animals and vegetation began to return, people followed. The oldest archeological finds from this period, the so-called Old Stone Age, point to the appearance of hunter-gatherer cultures in many parts of Scandinavia including the far north and far south (Stegebro, Ageröd, and Simrishamn) of what is now Sweden. These first people were nomadic and used wood, bone, stone, and eventually flint for their implements. They subsisted on diets of game, berries, fish, and mussels. They were nomadic peoples who followed the animals off which they lived. They did not build permanent settlements, but they did return to the same areas season after season. These very early people of the region developed cultures, the evidence for which is preserved in a relatively rich archeological record. Experts use that record to define changing cultural groups based on their tools, the decorative patterns they made on items of everyday life, or the ways in which they buried their dead. Bits of evidence are scattered across the full length of the country, from Skateholm in the far south to Garaselet in the far north, and include tools, human remains, garbage or refuse deposits, and the like.

Around 4000 BCE the New Stone Age began. It is different from the preceding era in several important ways, including the development of fired pottery, systematic farming, animal domestication, and more permanent, settled village life. Overall, these changes amounted to the appearance of a peasant or farming culture that was largely limited to the southern third of the region. New grave styles were also adopted in this period, most notably the so-called megalithic or dolmen graves. As mentioned above, it was toward the end of this period, around 2500 BCE, that a new ethnic group entered the area, the Boat Axe People, so named for the shape of their beautifully formed stone axes—axes that were clearly designed for combat, not forestry.

The next period in the standard chronology for Swedish pre-history was the Bronze Age. It is usually dated to between about 2000 and 500 BCE, and may have been one of the richest periods in all of Swedish/Scandinavian history. Why? For one thing, the climate was better, with warmer year-round temperatures and longer growing seasons. For nearly a millennium, parts of Sweden enjoyed a Mediterranean climate. For another, parts of southern Scandinavia, including southern Sweden, had access to important commodities of trade, including amber, honey, furs, and, perhaps, slaves, and the means to reach distant centers of trade. Great wealth, at least for a few, appears to have been generated by the trade network involving these goods leaving Scandinavia and tin and copper from which bronze was made and other goods including gold returning. (Sweden's great copper resources in the central region around Falun were not known then.)

The period's wealth is evidenced mainly by its grave mounds: Some were made simply of turf, and some of a complex blending of wood, turf, and stone. Literally thousands of these still exist from the period, and some of them, mostly in today's Denmark, were large and their contents remarkably well-preserved. For example, the mound at Egtved on the Danish peninsula of Jutland contains the remains of a young woman laid to rest, according to the latest dating techniques, in the summer of 1370 BCE. She was buried fully clothed in an exotic costume that included a short woven top and a revealingly short skirt held at her waist with a belt with a large decorated gold disk. The mound itself measured about 22 meters in diameter and was about 4 meters high. Certainly, no ordinary person was interred there.

In Sweden, the rock carvings/petroglyphs (*hällristningar*) of the western coast, such as those at Tanum, also bear evidence of a complex and fascinating culture. Stick-figure-like images of boats, plows and oxen, naked men with spears or bows and arrows, the sun, and footprints provide mute testimony about life there 3,500 years ago. Extrapolating from these images and artifacts such as bronze lures and an intriguing tambourine-like artifact from Balkåkra, it is possible to imagine a culture in which rowed boats were used for travel and trade, farming and hunting were parts of daily life, and the weather was essential to the prosperity of all. The sun was probably an object of worship, and noisy processions may have been staged as celebrations of the harvest or successful trading ventures.

Around 500 BCE the richness of the Bronze Age yielded to a period of colder weather, harsher farming conditions, a new metal that was native to the region (iron), a new predominating culture in much of Europe and the British Isles (Celtic), and far less trade. Life for the people of the area became much more of a struggle, and graves from the period indicate both heightened violence and relative poverty as characteristics of the times.

Bronze Age rock scribbings from Tanum. These images date to around 1500 BCE and are believed to reflect the importance of hunting, farming, boats, and the sun in the religion of the people living in the area at the time.

Around the turn of the millennium (0 CE), Celtic influence waned and Roman dominance gradually spread across much of western Europe. The next 500 years brought increased trade contacts and wealth for some. Although there is no conclusive evidence that Romans ever visited Sweden, imperial coins (often turned into items of jewelry), bits of Roman glass, or silver goblets depicting scenes from *The Odyssey* have been unearthed in Sweden and Denmark and indicate links between the Roman Empire and the north that may have involved trade or mercenary military service. It is also in this period that one can first read about the region, about Scandinavia or Scadinavia, in the writings of geographers of the Roman period like Pliny the Elder (25–79 CE), Tacitus (56–117 CE), and Ptolemy (83–168 CE).

The decline of Roman power brought with it centuries of turmoil across much of Europe and was accompanied by one of the largest periods of population migration in history. Referred to in traditional chronologies as the Migration Period, the years between about 300 and 800 CE saw a kind of game of musical chairs among the ethnic groups (tribes) of Europe. The movement of the Saxons and the Angles from northwest continental Europe into England, for example, triggered an out-migration by the people already settled there (hence the movement of Celtic peoples into Wales and Ireland). At the same time, out-migrations often created vacuums into which new groups could flow.

Sweden did not experience one of these great episodes of migration (that may have happened earlier), but it was caught up in the general turmoil of the time.

One can imagine an age of tribal warfare, struggles for territorial control, looting, and piracy. Archeological evidence bears this out in Sweden where dozens of small fortifications were constructed, like Gråborg on Öland, that apparently served as places of refuge during attacks and/or as centers of emerging (and conflicting) political power. Also, a number of quite remarkable caches, collections of buried goods of enormous value, such as the elaborate gold neck collar from Färjestad, support the view that these were unsettling and violent times.

Also, evidence of a new level of enlarged political organization centered on modern-day Uppsala and running east-west across the country appears toward the end of this period. It is supported by perhaps very shaky evidence in written sources from much later, such as *Ynglingasaga* that begins the Icelandic poet Snorri Sturluson's *Heimskringla*, and in archeological evidence provided by sites such as the sixth-century grave mounds at Old Uppsala or the warrior graves at Vendel, north of Uppsala. This is not to say, however, that Sweden came into existence in this period, but one can argue that the roots of a Swedish state that happened to emerge later can be traced back to these times.

The so-called Viking Age (c. 700–1100) flows seamlessly from the Migration Period. In many ways they are one and the same—a time defined by violence, trade, great wealth for some, and continued subsistence farming for most. However, several things set this era apart from the earlier era.

One is the boats and ships people from Scandinavia, including Sweden, developed. The master boatbuilders of the region created a variety of craft able to exploit the waters that surrounded them. Some were small and easily portaged. Others were large, stable ocean-going vessels. Best known are the two great burial ships of Norway, the *Oseberg* and *Gokstad*. The latter has often been taken as the model Viking ship. Examples that illustrate the variety are those extracted from the bottom of the Roskilde Fjord and are now housed at the Viking Ship Museum in Roskilde, Denmark. (A replica of one of the larger Roskilde ships was completed around 2008, and this vessel underwent a trial voyage between Denmark and Ireland with quite fascinating results.)[6] Sweden has no recovered treasures such as these, but it does have depictions of period ships on stone carvings from the island of Gotland. They reveal the form, crews, and rigging of Viking ships with fascinating accuracy. Another important difference in this period is the extent of involvement by peoples from Sweden, Denmark, and Norway in external activities that included trade, piracy, raiding, exploring, settling, and creating some kind of political order in some of the areas they contacted, including, perhaps, what became the first Russian state.

From the Swedish perspective, the central theme of the standard history is that Swedish Vikings primarily went east, up the rivers of the eastern Baltic into the heart of modern Russia via the Dnieper and Volga, on to the Caspian and Black Seas, and even beyond to Byzantium/Constantinople. They traded with merchants from the Islamic empires of the Mideast and perhaps from India and China as well. Finds in Sweden include thousands of Islamic coins, silk, glass, and even a bronze Buddha. At the Swedish end of a vast east-west trade arc, two towns developed in succession: Helgö and Birka. Both were located on islands in Lake Mälaren and lay in the heart of what appears to have been an emerging state from which the future Sweden evolved.

One needs be very careful when dealing with the Viking period. It is one of the most highly romanticized chapters in the early histories of all the Scandinavia countries. Some experts today argue there was no such thing as a Viking or a Viking Age because there was no unified culture, no truly effective central political organization, and no consciously designed external efforts. The horned-helmeted images adopted by sports teams, action comic heroes, or illustrated versions of national romantic poems from the nineteenth century are fantasies conjured up by promoters. Why the hype? Because all nations have their national myths or partial myths that provide evidence of their achievements, successes, or importance. Sweden and its Nordic neighbors have generally been relatively unimportant in the big picture of European history, but with the Vikings there is evidence that for a few hundred years a few people from this region traveled far, traded widely, acquired great wealth and personal fame, influenced the political development of some places, made quite extraordinary boats, and produced some truly magnificent works of art. Why not celebrate these achievements, even if many of them had relatively little lasting importance?

Sweden Emerges

The Viking Age is the last of the Swedish pre-history periods. From about 1100 or a bit earlier, it is actually possible to write about a history of Sweden. Written sources, both internal and external, began to appear. The conversion to Christianity, which was a 300-year struggle in Sweden, was accomplished by the close of the twelfth century, and with this came some measure of literacy among the clergy; the Church's hierarchic structure of parishes, bishoprics, and an archbishopric (Uppsala); and monasteries. The records of the Church provide some of the key sources upon which medieval Swedish history is based. Written laws codes supply others.

In a process that spanned several hundred years, a Swedish state emerged that slowly asserted growing authority over localities and territorial entities that had operated as unique elements for centuries. It grew up around a core centered in Uppland and included the historic regions of Östergötland,

Västergötland, Närke, Västmanland, and Södermanland. The far south was most often under the control of the Danish state that was developing at the same time. The northern regions were largely unsettled.

Medieval Swedish history reflects the conflicts so typical of the period, including church versus state, localism versus centralization, and crown versus emerging nobility. To these can be added the struggles for dominance among the emerging Nordic states. At several junctures the development of the region could have been very different from what did occur. Perhaps most interesting in this regard was the formation in 1397 of the Kalmar Union—a dynastic federation dominated by Denmark but supposedly designed to assure Norwegian and Swedish autonomy. This structure *could* have survived, but did not so far as Sweden was concerned. Led by one of the country's national heroes, Gustav Eriksson Vasa, Sweden left the union in the 1520s and followed the pattern of independent state development that characterized the histories of most European countries such as England, France, and Spain.

Gustav Eriksson Vasa became Gustav I, King of Sweden, in 1523. His election and coronation began an unbroken line of succession that runs down to the present—although in a sequence of families. Under the first Vasa king and three of his sons, Sweden became Lutheran (albeit gradually) and developed the trappings of early modern government including a national army and navy, semi-representative parliament, central bureaucracy, expanded tax system, and capital city (Stockholm). Sweden also became a player in northern Europe, and its leaders engaged in the typical international relations adventures of the day, including wars of territorial expansion and/or balance of power, mainly with Denmark, Russia, and Poland.

The seventeenth century was the second great moment in Sweden's national history. Under Gustav II Adolf/Gustavus Adolphus and his immediate successors, an empire was constructed that came to include many of the territories that bordered on the Baltic: today's Finland, Estonia, Latvia, and parts of Lithuania and Germany. For most of the century, Sweden's economy grew, the effectiveness of its government increased, intellectual life flourished, and the country's role in European affairs expanded. Ignoring the horrific financial and human costs of Sweden's imperial activities, there were many achievements of which to be proud and to celebrate in later histories.

The era of importance ended, brutally, in the Great Northern War (1700–1721). Since then, Sweden has been a relatively minor player in European affairs, dabbling foolishly in some adventures in the eighteenth century, stubbornly opposing Napoleon in the early nineteenth century—a policy that first cost the country Finland in 1809 and then earned it a dynastic union with Norway (1814–1905)—and then pursuing, at least nominally, a course of noninvolvement and/or neutrality in Europe's conflicts down to the present.

Politically, the country's early modern history was punctuated by a series of irregularly spaced swings between strong and weak monarchy—much like what happened in most other European countries of the period. The actors in this play included the crown, the nobility, and the parliament/Riksdag, that represented the clergy, nobles, burghers, and farmers in separate estates. At times, such as during the reign of Gustav II Adolf (1611–32), a balance was achieved that was highly successful. At other times, the crown managed to assert its dominance, as was the case under Karl XI and Karl XII (c. 1680–1718) and again under Gustav III and Gustav IV (1772–1809). In contrast, there was the so-called Era of Liberty (1719–72) during which the parliament, dominated for much of the time by the nobility, was in control, and it looked as if Sweden were going to evolve into an oligarchy or even an early democracy.

The Great Transformations

Very important changes have taken place in Sweden in the course of the last 200 years. Sometimes referred to as "the great transformations," these included the transition to genuine parliamentary democracy, urbanization, industrialization, sweeping changes in farming, and the development of "the people's home," Sweden's version of a welfare state.

In terms of political development, Sweden followed a very common European pattern as it moved from a limited constitutional monarchy to a parliamentary democracy. The ancient four-chamber parliament became a two-chamber one in 1866 and a unicameral body in 1970. The vote was extended to all adult men in 1909 and to women between 1918 and 1921. A group of political parties based on social class and ideologies developed. The cabinet of ministers, headed by a prime minister, became truly representative of the popular vote, responsible to the parliament rather than a creature of the crown, and the main agency of policy development and executive leadership. The monarch became mainly symbolic. Importantly, all of these changes were accomplished without revolutions—although there was a good deal of public involvement, discourse, rhetoric, and demonstrating. In fact, the peacefulness with which these changes came about has led some to argue that there is something special about the ways in which the Swedes solve serious political (and social) issues.[7]

At the same time, Sweden moved from being a country in which the vast majority of its people live in the countryside to one where most live in cities, especially Stockholm, Göteborg, and the string of smaller cities in between. (Today, metropolitan Stockholm's population is about 800,000 and Göteborg's 490,000. Malmö, with about 280,000 residents, makes up a third urban population center, and, in fact, seems much larger because of its easy connection with Denmark via the Öresund Bridge that opened in mid-2000.) Overall, 85 percent of Swedes now live in cities.

The third great transformation was the shift from a predominately agrarian economy to an industrial one. The roots of this change lay far back in the eighteenth century and even beyond, and the nineteenth century witnessed important breakthroughs, especially in sectors such as mining, metal production, paper, chemicals (explosives), energy, engineering, transportation, and banking. A grand celebration of these changes was staged at the 1897 Stockholm Exposition, where dozens of manufacturers displayed their latest wares. Economic growth accelerated in the twentieth century and expanded upon these beginnings. Sweden became a major producer of high grade steel, ball bearings, paper, ships, automobiles, domestic and military aircraft, weapons, chemicals, pharmaceuticals, household appliances, communication electronics, housewares, and fine furniture. Many Swedish companies became familiar names worldwide: SKF, SAAB, Volvo, Nobel, L. M. Ericsson, Tetrapak, Electrolux, Pharmacia, and IKEA.

It was in the context of these changes that the modern Swedish welfare state was created. The "peoples' home" (*folkhemmet*) that the Social Democrats began to build in the 1930s had both contemporary and older roots. To some extent, its origins lay in the rural societies that shaped the lives of their members because they educated the young, had a hand in marriage partner selection, provided employment for all, entertained, and cared for the sick and the elderly. These traditions reinforced some of the fundamental beliefs of the Social Democrats, a moderate or reformist Marxist group whose leaders believed in the possibility of transforming society through peaceful, parliamentary means. Its leaders were also attracted to the ideas of social engineering that became popular in the years between the World Wars and remained in vogue for several decades after 1945.

Between 1933 and 1965, when the Social Democrats were able to build working majorities in the parliament, the Swedish Model took form in a system of programs intended to provide education, health care, housing, old-age security and pensions, a strong infrastructure, quality in the arts, greater leisure time, and employment for all. These programs were to be efficiently delivered by an honest bureaucracy and paid for by taxes on incomes, property, consumer goods, businesses, and inheritances. Adopting a system Marquis Childs labeled "the middle way" (a compromise between communism and capitalism, between state planned economies and the unfettered free market) in the 1930s, capitalism was retained as the norm in terms of business ownership, manufacturing, sales, and most other economic activities. Sweden never embarked on a wholesale program of nationalization, and the state owned and operated relatively little within the context of Sweden's economy—mainly pieces of the fundamental infrastructure like the railroads. As part of the compromise, the government did play an active role through tax policies, incentives, and public projects to foster goals such as economic growth, full employment and quality housing for all.

At the heart of the Social Democrats' programs was the idea of *equality*. Everyone in society was equal. Social class, gender, sexual preference, age, race, religion, ethnicity—none of these were supposed to matter. All Swedes were entitled to the benefits of the people's home, and all were expected to do (pay) their share in its creation and maintenance. The well-ordered society was an ideal, a place in which each and every individual could develop to the maximum of her or his potential. These ideas became core elements of what Sweden is and what Swedes are. Today, most Swedes believe in them and are proud of the Sweden that has grown from them. As one ought to expect, there are differences of opinion on these ideals, but they are mostly differences in degree over how far the ideal should be pursued or how much it should cost.

The People's History

Before moving on, a brief look needs to be given to a few of the pieces and people that are missing from the above review of Sweden's history—from what is a rather standard politically focused version. It worth noting at least a few bits of the people's history as well.

For nearly 5,000 years, the vast majority of the people living in what is now called Sweden have been rural farm folk. They have lived in either single-family farmsteads or farming villages. Ancient subsistence farming techniques including the use of simple plows, hand-sowing of seed, little use of manure for fertilizing, fallowing, simple crop rotations, and vast amounts of human labor went largely unchanged until the late eighteenth century or later. Rooted in the past and fundamentally conservative, this timeless agricultural society avoided and even actively discouraged innovation. There was little specialization and little surplus for market. Bad weather or other problems often led to crop failures, famine, and great suffering. Within this agrarian society men and women played mutually supportive roles. Rich rural cultures developed across the country that directed economic and social activities and produced their own material cultures, architecture, decorative arts, music and dance, costumes, and celebrations. Many aspects of these traditions were abandoned and/or in danger of disappearing in the nineteenth century because of government steps to complete the consolidation and enclosure of farm holdings, the resulting breakup of many villages, greater agricultural specialization, urbanization, industrialization, and mass migration. Fortunately, many elements of the rural culture were rescued and preserved, and they form the bases for today's popular folk cultures. The premier repositories of Swedish rural cultures are the Nordic Museum and the adjacent Skansen outdoor museum in Stockholm, both established in the late-nineteenth century. (See Chapter 8.)

For centuries Sweden's towns and cities were few in number and small in population. Most of the oldest towns were market centers such as Norrköping, Jönköping, Nyköping, and Söderköping (the ending *köping* means market) or religious centers such as Uppsala, the seat of Sweden's archbishop—or a combination of both. There was also a group of smaller coastal ports like Gävle and Malmö, naval towns like Karlskrona, or natural resource towns like Falun, site of a great copper mine. Sweden's capital, Stockholm, was founded in the mid-thirteenth century. In the mid-sixteenth century it was home to about 8,000 people, and 100 years later this figure had grown to about 50,000. It was not until after 1850 that its population exceeded 100,000. From then on, however, Stockholm grew very rapidly as its functions expanded from being primarily a capital and maritime trade center to a hub for industry, education, and the arts as well. Today the city itself numbers about 800,000, and greater Stockholm has about 1.3 million people. The eight Stockholm-based novels of Per Anders Fogelström describe these changes wonderfully. In this series, which begins with the mid-eighteenth and ends in the late-twentieth century, he described the lives of working people in a context of growth and change in the city. Two in the series have been translated, *City of My Dreams* and *City of Their Children*.[8] Sweden's second largest city, Göteborg, dates mainly from the early seventeenth century and began largely as a merchant trading center. Today its population is approximately half a million.

As was the case elsewhere, Sweden's towns were places of excitement, activity, opportunity, violence, disease, and misery. Small upper-class minorities—nobles, government officials, military officers, bourgeois merchants, and guild masters—ran them while large skilled and unskilled groups supported them. Larger towns and especially the capital developed as centers of conversation and ideas that found voice in coffeehouses, taverns, and salons in the eighteenth century. In many ways, they were important engines of change in an otherwise very conservative place.

Life Today

If Sweden is the product of its location, climate, natural resource base, and centuries of history, it is also highly dynamic and clearly caught up in processes of ongoing development and change. Some of the enduring elements of Sweden are the monarchy; a parliament that can trace its origins to the fifteenth century; the importance of law and order; lingering aspects of a hierarchic social class system; the nominal predominance of Lutheranism; the importance of agriculture, forestry, and mining; and a host of folk arts and traditions. More recent additions to Swedish life today are the centrality of participatory democracy; the extent of industrialization and urbanization; the importance of organizations in many aspects of Swedes' lives; gender equality; the growing diversity or heterogeneity of its population; nominal openness to and toleration of differences of many kinds; concern for the environment; a foreign policy that centers on cooperation and peace; creativity in the arts, sciences, technology, and business; and one of the most generous (and costly) welfare systems in the world.

Political System

The monarchy has taken on largely symbolic functions in the decades since World War II. Today's king, Carl XVI Gustaf came to the throne in 1973. Born in 1946, he may become the longest reigning king in the country's history. His oldest daughter, Victoria, is expected to be his successor. When or if this happens, she will become the first queen since Ulrika Eleonora in 1719. Governing power lies in the hands of the prime minister, who heads a cabinet composed of about 20 ministers—nearly half of whom were women in 2009. Since the election of September 2006, this post has been held by Fredrik Reinfeldt, the leader of the Moderate Party. His cabinet is a four-party coalition based on the Moderate, Center, Liberal, and Christian Democratic parties. The major opposition party is the Social Democrats, which held power for all but 11 years between 1932 and 2008.

The Parliament (*Riksdag*) has been unicameral since 1970; it has had 349 seats since 1976. Seven political parties secured seats in the assembly in the 2006 election; Moderate, Center, Liberal, Christian Democrat, Social Democrat, Left, and Green. Although there are important differences, ideological and programmatic, among these parties, there is also a strong element of agreement about the nature of the political system, the basic concepts of the welfare state, foreign policy, and the like. Differences tend to be in matters of degree or extent. Suffrage is universal, and seats in the parliament are allotted by a system of proportional representation designed to maximize representation. The government is the primary initiator of legislative proposals. These often come after a careful vetting of ideas by special commissions that represent concerned individuals, interest groups, and organizations. Members of parliament may introduce counter or substitute proposals. All bills pass through one of 15 parliamentary committees before they come up for open debate and vote in the full assembly. It is the responsibility of the government to implement legislation that is passed. Overall, the legislative process is designed to be as open as possible, and the building of multiparty consensuses is an important part of the process and one of the defining elements of the system in Sweden—at least by reputation.

There are, of course, critics of the political system that has been created over the last 70-plus years, and the political environment is certainly not a place of complete or idyllic harmony. Eighteen minor parties failed to win seats in the 2006 election, and there have been several dozen local or single-issue parties that have come and gone in recent years. Some of these are serious, others quite whimsical. One of these, the Pirate Party, is a bit of both. It has as one of its main goals making the private duplicating of copyright-protected material legal. In 2009, it enjoyed enormous notoriety because of a legal case as well as success at the polls in the election for the EU parliament. Another is the Cheaper Beer Party, whose goal is rather obvious. A few of these groups are openly critical of democracy, modernity, the industrial society, the country's growing multiethnic population, and the like. Into this group fall several neo-Nazi organizations. Two stand out. The Sweden Democrats (*Sverigedemokraterna*) came together as a political party in 1988 and have been gradually growing a following ever since. The party's program is expressed in carefully worded rhetoric that emphasizes nationalism, Lutheranism, and responsible citizenship. Behind this lies anti-immigration, anti-asylum, anti-Muslim realities and a fondness for violence. Although the party has relatively few members, it has done fairly well in recent elections. In 2006, it secured about 160,000 votes in the parliamentary election and did better in local races. The National Socialist Front (*Nationalsocialistisk front, NSF*) has been less successful. Founded as an organization in 1994 and as a political party in 1999, it was dissolved in late 2008 and replaced by a new group with the same ideals and leadership. First called The People's Front/*Folk Fronten*, in 2010 it became The Swedes Party/*Svenskarnas parti*. The group's 14-point "program" emphasizes things like social order, national defense, state control of the media, and racial-biological ideals. It is avowedly neo-Nazi in outlook and has even adopted a blackshirt uniform for its public demonstrations. It won just over 1,400 votes in the 2006 election!

Wealth and Health

Based on many different measurements Sweden is a good place to live, and Swedes live well. According to 2006 figures, they were sixth in the world in income per capita, first in gender equality, second in the number of women in parliament, second in quality of life, and fourth in most educated. Generally, they followed Norway in many of these measurements, not surprisingly given the tremendous wealth that country is able to derive from its offshore oil and gas resources.

Swedes are among the most affluent people in the world. In 2008, the median annual per capita income was about $29,000. (For native-born Swedes between 20 and 64 years of age it was about 240,000SEK or $39,000 in mid-2008 dollars.) Although their taxes are very high, what they are left with after paying them is generally largely expendable because they do not need to save to the degree Americans do for things like their children's college education, retirement, medical emergencies, or the arrival of a new dependent. Not surprisingly, they are great consumers who enjoy all of the *things* of contemporary society.

There are more than 4 million cars in Sweden, nearly one for every two Swedes. In 2007, more than 300,000 new cars were registered in Sweden, and nearly one fifth of these were classified as "green cars"—cars with very low emissions, used alternative fuels, or were electrically powered. Parenthetically, this relatively small country was able to have two native automobile makers, SAAB and Volvo, for over half a century. Both did well in the home market as well as enjoyed success abroad. However, Volvo's automobile division was acquired by Ford and SAAB's by GM in the late twentieth century, and then both brands fell victim to the troubles in the industry in the early years of this century. In 2010, the Chinese automaker GEELY purchased Volvo's car division, and the future of the brand appeared to be secure. After a number of possible deals fell through, SAAB was picked up by Spyker, a Dutch company that builds exotic and very expensive sports cars.

Cellular phone use is among the highest in the world, with 900 phones per 1,000 people. The Swedish company, L. M. Ericsson was a pioneer in the field of wireless communications and, in partnership with Sony, is one of the largest producers of cell phones worldwide. Similarly, computers are ubiquitous, and Internet use is virtually universal.

Although the country has not been inundated with the range of big box retail stores that America has and some of the best-known international giants such as Walmart have failed to make inroads there, there are chains like Åhlens department stores and ICA grocery stores, and shopping malls galore.[9] Perhaps the best-known Swedish retail company is the "flat-pack, u-assemble-it" furniture giant IKEA. Founded in Sweden by Ivar Kamprad in 1943 as a door-to-door business, IKEA gradually evolved to catalogue sales. Furniture was added to its product line in 1947, and the company moved to showroom-based marketing in the 1950s. Today it has about 250 stores in 24 countries, and Kamprad, who now lives in Switzerland, is one of the wealthiest men in the world. Other indices of the affluence of many Swedes is the number that own two homes, one for everyday and one for vacations, and the extent to which they travel, particularly to warmer climes in the winter.

Swedes are healthy. They eat fairly well and value exercise and healthy lifestyles. Their medical care is provided as an element of the welfare system. Direct, out-of-pocket costs are minimal. Although there are criticisms about the quality of the system—it is impersonal, there may be waits for elective surgeries, and the best medical personnel go elsewhere to make more money—the results of the system seem to belie these complaints. Life expectancy overall is 80.4 years (ninth in the world): more than 83 years for women and 78.5 years for men. The infant mortality rate runs around 2.75/1,000 births—the second lowest in the world according to one ranking.[10]

Foreign Relations

Another distinctive feature of Sweden today is its foreign policy. Not since the close of the Napoleonic Wars in 1815 has the country been directly involved in a war. Since then its governments have pursued a policy variously called neutrality or nonalignment. Luck, flexibility, and, at least since World War II, relatively strong defenses have been important in making this policy appear to work. True neutrality is a rarely achieved ideal, and Sweden has never been genuinely neutral in any of Europe's conflicts. In fact, the country's leaders have repeatedly violated the rules of neutrality to protect national interests or appease potential aggressors. This was clearly the case in several instances during World War II and again during the Cold War. Another factor that compromises the country's neutrality is the fact that Sweden is a global arms merchant. Many components of Sweden's defenses are domestically designed and produced, including combat aircraft, military vehicles, and a vast array of increasingly complex weapon systems. These are expensive to develop and produce, and some of the costs are offset by sales abroad.

Contrary to what one might think, Sweden's foreign policy, especially since 1945, has not meant disengagement from regional, European, or global affairs. Sweden is a very internationally minded country. In 1952, it joined its Scandinavian neighbors to form the Nordic Council, a group committed to regional cooperation and development. For much of the Cold War era, Sweden's leaders sought to avoid East-West clashes in the north and, especially, to preserve Finland's independence. As a result, Sweden did not join NATO or the early versions of the European Union (EU). It was, however, a founding member of the Organization for European Cooperation and Development in 1960 and of the European Free Trade Association in 1961. A late-comer to the EU, it became a member in 1995. On the global level, Sweden joined the United Nations in 1946, and has supported its activities including peace keeping missions. Dag Hammarskjöld served as the Secretary General from 1953 until his tragic death in 1961. Through the Swedish International

Development Cooperation Agency (SIDA), whose "objective is to help create conditions that will enable the poor to improve their lives," and many other organizations, Sweden continues to provide development assistance around the world and to maintain a dollar target of .7 percent of GNP in developmental aid. According to one evaluator, Sweden ranks first in the world, followed by Norway and Denmark, in humanitarian assistance on a global scale.[11]

In the context of these activities, many Swedes remain curiously mixed in their feelings about some international organizations, especially the European Union. For example, in a spring 2008 study, just over half of the polled Swedes thought EU membership was a good thing, while about a fifth thought it was a bad thing and another fifth were undecided. In the same study, just one half thought Sweden had benefitted from membership, while 40 percent thought the country had not benefitted. Some of the concerns Swedes have about the EU include the impact of membership on markets for Swedish goods, fear that manufacturing will leave for cheaper labor markets, concerns over maintaining low unemployment, health care quality, the costs of membership, and crime. The same study also indicated fairly strong belief in the effectiveness of EU institutions, slowly growing support for joining the common currency system, and favorable sentiments for a common EU foreign policy and some kind of common security policy. Overall, Swedes are, it seems, both nationalists and internationalists who tend to see themselves as Swedes first and Europeans second.[12]

The People

Are there discernible national character traits? There certainly are stereotypes about both the country and its people—many of which circulate in the popular press and/or in ethnic humor. In the 1960s, Sweden was commonly labeled the land of socialism, sex, and suicide—and sometimes spirits (liquor) was added. None of these tags were particularly accurate, nor are they today. For some, it is the land of a string of successful sports heroes including Björn Borg and Annika Sörenstam or great hockey or soccer teams or the home of the immensely popular pop music group ABBA—whose songs seem to be indelibly imprinted in the brains of a couple of generations. For others Sweden is the land of painted wooden horses (*dalahästar*), quaint folk costumes and the music and dance that goes with them, Maypoles, crayfish and aquavit, groaning *smörgåsbords*, or boxy but safe cars.

What about the Swedes as a people? Is there some kind of norm, some kind of stereotypical Swede whose behavior is easily predicted? In appearance they are usually thought of as tall, blonde, and blue-eyed. This description has never been particularly accurate, and the heterogeneity of today's population makes it even less so. In terms of behavior or personality, many sources describe them as taciturn, stoic, silent, quiet, reserved, cool, or aloof. A wonderful example of these stereotypes may be seen in Bent Hamer's Norwegian-Swedish film from 2004, Kitchen Stories/*Salmer fra Kjøkkenet*. Set in the 1960s, it involves a Swedish sociological study of kitchens and efficiency. The two central characters, one a Swedish researcher and the other a farmer living in neighboring Norway, epitomize these traits.

Peter Berlin in his somewhat irreverent *Xenophobes Guide to the Swedes* returns repeatedly to two nearly untranslatable words to describe his countrymen: *lagom* (moderation) and *undfallenhet* (compliancy or submissiveness). The former means that Swedes are measured, careful, modest, rational; the latter means they are compromising, cooperative, willing to negotiate, open to problem solving. Both are useful and to a degree valid. Christina Johansson Robinowitz and Lisa Werner Carr in *Modern Day Vikings: A Practical Guide to Interacting with the Swedes* are more analytical. They, too, use *lagom*, but then add *vemod* (melancholy), *duktig* (capable), *vanlig* (ordinary), and *mysig* (cozy) to flesh out their standard Swede—someone who in the dark of winter can be deeply melancholy, who in summer can be surprisingly exuberant, who is capable at whatever he/she does, who seeks the middle way in all things (work, dress, diet, appearance, personal possession, and the like), and who places great value on democracy, equality in all things, cozy settings, cooperation, and properly executed rituals and rules of behavior.

Åke Daun, professor and head of the Institute of Ethnology at Stockholm University, is also careful and analytical in the traits he singles out. He argues that Swedes do not easily show their feelings, appear relatively stiff, tend to be gloomy in the winter and exuberant in the summer, have very subtle and low-key senses of humor, and are modest and unpretentious.[13] Many of these traits are embodied by a term that appears in virtually every book about the Swedes (and other Scandinavians), one that is useful if not entirely accurate, the *Jantelagen* (the law of Jante). The expression was first coined by the Danish writer Axel Sandemose in his 1933 novel *A Fugitive Crosses His Tracks*. It is understood throughout Scandinavia and expressed in the following:

1. Thou shalt not believe thou art something.
2. Thou shalt not believe thou art as good as we.
3. Thou shalt not believe thou art more wise than we.
4. Thou shalt not fancy thyself better than we.
5. Thou shalt not believe thou knowest more than we.
6. Thou shalt not believe thou art greater than we.
7. Thou shalt not believe thou amountest to anything.

8. Thou shalt not laugh at us.
9. Thou shalt not believe that anyone is concerned with thee.
10. Thou shalt not believe thou can teach us anything.[14]

All of these attempts to define Sweden and Swedes *may* be most useful, appropriate, and accurate when considering the past and older generations of Swedes. Contemporary Sweden is a very different place from just a generation or two ago. Immigration, globalization, and the Internet have made sure of that. Younger Swedes today are more regional, European, global, mobile, secular, digital, and connected, and they do not think or behave like their parents or grandparents in many ways. An indication of this may be seen in a strong anti-*jantelagen* sentiment held by younger Swedes. This is expressed on many Web sites in Sweden, one of which argues the *Jantelagen* is "the symbol for the tyranny of the collective and the defenselessness of the individual" and another that offers this alternative:

Antijantelagen/The ten commandments to follow:

You shall believe that you are unique.
You are worth more than you think.
You can learn everything.
You are better than many others.
You know much more than many others.
You have much to be proud of.
You are capable of anything.
You should play and laugh.
Be proud of yourself.
You have knowledge to share with others.[15]

Notes

1. Good sources of information about Sweden are the CIA's FactBook at https://www.cia.gov/library/publications/the-world-factbook/geos/sw.html and *The National Atlas of Sweden*. Volume 17 indicates the country has a coastline of 7,624 km. The difference may lie in counting all the irregularities.

2. Vilhelm Moberg, *The Emigrants*, Part I, Chapter I, "King in His Stone Kingdom."

3. Historically, parts of Dalarna had a fascinating inheritance system. In contrast to much of the rest of the country, all surviving children long shared inheritance rights. This meant farms were passed to heirs in pieces, which led to a complex system of spouse selection and marriage in order to maintain farm holdings.

See Michael Jones and Kenneth Olwig, eds., *Nordic Landscapes. Region and Belonging on the Northern Edge of Europe* (Minneapolis: University of Minnesota Press, 2008).

4. Complete lists can be found at the Statistics Sweden Web site (http://www.scb.se), an excellent source for detailed statistics about Sweden. There is an English language option that can be searched.

5. A number of good, general histories of Sweden exist in English. The most detailed is Franklin Scott's *Sweden: The Nation's History* (Carbondale, IL: Southern Illinois University Press, 1988). For brief histories see Neal Kent, *A Concise History of Sweden* (Cambridge: Cambridge University Press, 2008), Stewart P. Oakley, *A Short History of Sweden* (New York: Praeger, 1966) and Byron J. Nordstrom in Bibliography.

6. Andrew Curry, "Raiders or Traders?" *Smithsonian Magazine*, July 2008, 24–30.

7. Dankwart A. Rostow, *The Politics of Compromise: A Study of Parties and Cabinet Government in Sweden* (Westport, CT: Greenwood Group, 1955).

8. Per Anders Fogelström, *City of My Dreams* and *Children of Their City*, translated by Jennifer Brown Bäverstam (Iowa City, IA: Penfield Books, 2000 and 2008).

9. Interestingly, the Swedish government has joined Norway in blocking Walmart from one of its pension stock funds because of unethical practices. The stock was blacklisted and 300mSEK/47mUSD in shares were sold.

10. On infant mortality, see http://brambledoula.wordpress.com/2007/09/09/world-wide-infant-mortality-ranking/. Accessed July 28, 2009.

11. According to Dara International, an organization based in Madrid, Sweden is the fairest and most humanitarian of the world's nations. See http://blog.foreignpolicy.com/node/7176. Accessed July 28, 2009.

12. On Sweden and the EU, see Lee Miles, *Fusing with Europe?: Sweden in the European Union* (Farnham, UK: Ashgate, 2005).

13. Åke Daun, *The Swedish Myths: True, False or Somewhere in Between* (Sweden: The Swedish Institute, 2005).

14. There are many versions of this. Google *jantelagen.*

15. Antijantelagen. See http://home.swipnet.se/marja-leena/tankvart/antijantelag.html (accessed July 17, 2009) for the quoted phrase and http://retoriksallskapet.se/Antijantelagen.htm for an alternative. Accessed July 17, 2009.

2

Religion

EXTENSIVE ARCHEOLOGICAL and historical records indicate that some kind of religious beliefs have been practiced in Sweden for about the last 10,000 years. This can be seen, for example, in a sequence of grave styles that range from simple single-person cyst graves to megalithic graves to mounds to elaborate ship burials to the familiar internments of the Christian era. Paralleling these is a changing array of images—carved in stone or wood or amber, or painted, drawn, or sculpted—that includes animals essential to the hunt, the sun, anthropomorphized deities of the Viking Age, and the Biblical and church figures of the Christian era. There is also evidence of sacred places and buildings that includes the sites where the stone carvings of the Stone and Bronze Ages were executed, the evidence of a pagan temple at Old Uppsala, and, of course, the literally thousands of Christian buildings.

Little is known of the earliest religions, but it appears that at first the people of the region worshiped the animals essential to their lives. The development of agriculture brought with it new religious practices. In some parts of southern Sweden, the sun was apparently central. By the later Iron Age and Viking Period, a complex religion had developed complete with two families of gods that watched over war, weather, the farm, families, fertility, knowledge, social behavior, and the like. Heading this pantheon were Odin, Thor, Frey and Freyja, Baldr, and Loki. This religion had its own creation myth, history, complex cast of characters, ongoing and cyclical view of time, explanation for the nature of human society, and code of ethics by which people were to live. There was, apparently, no priesthood, but there were cult leaders, sacred places, and rituals. This religion can be seen in the Icelandic sagas and in the *Hávamál*, sources written down in the thirteenth century, perhaps loaded with doses of Christian bias but probably based on long-preserved oral sources. One section of the *Hávamál*, titled "Wisdom for Wanderers and Counsel to Guests," reads:

> Cattle die, kinsmen die
> the self must also die;
> I know one thing which never dies:
> the reputation of each dead man.

Another, in the section "Maxims for All Men," includes:

> Praise day at even, a wife when dead,
> a weapon when tried, a maid when married,
> ice when 'tis crossed, and ale when 'tis drunk.[1]

Although this religion has long since disappeared, it is very much a part of the historical record in archeology and in the literature of the Viking Age, which, as was noted earlier, is a period central to the canon of Swedish history and to national identity.

Christianity in Sweden

Conversion to Christianity was a slow process in Sweden. Active missionary efforts began in the early ninth century and continued by fits and starts for almost 300 years. Although the people of Sweden became more and more nominally Christian, what they believed and practiced was probably highly syncretic, as ancient ideas and practices were absorbed into the new faith and modified. There is also evidence that the conversion was never entirely complete, as some ancient ideas and practices, such as leaving food offerings to a cast of forest creatures, continued to be practiced for a very long time—some well into the twentieth century.

Still, by the late eleventh century, Sweden was officially part of Western Christendom. An archbishopric was established at Uppsala in 1164. The country was divided into seven bishoprics (Uppsala, Skara, Västerås, Strängnäs, Linköping, and Växjö, plus Åbo/Turku in present-day Finland), and more than 2,500 parishes. Monastic orders came to Sweden as well, and eventually there were as many as 70 monasteries, abbeys, and convents in the country.

One of the best known of these was the male-female Augustinian cloister at Vadstena. Land for this religious center was willed to the Church by King Magnus in 1346, and its rules, written by Birgitta Birgersdotter, were approved by the Pope in 1370. Birgitta, who was canonized in 1391, believed God spoke directly to her, and her *Revelations* are important sources from the period.

For nearly 400 years, the Church was a dominating force in the region because it impacted almost every aspect of life including politics, law, international relations, language, learning, art, and architecture. This is also when "history" came to Sweden as written sources became more and more available.

This statue of Saint Birgitta dates from the fifteenth century. Executed in wood, it is located on the grounds of her abbey at Vadstena in Östergötland and is thought to depict her as an older woman. (Photo courtesy of Brian Magnusson.)

The Protestant Reformation reached Sweden in the 1520s, largely through young clergy who had studied in Wittenberg and preached the new ideas in urban churches. Their work, however, took place in a cauldron of political turmoil surrounding Sweden's leaving the union with Denmark and establishing a new monarchy. To a limited extent, it was also impacted by criticism of the Catholic Church in Sweden, especially with regard to the actions of the upper clergy, most notably Gustav Trolle, Archbishop of Uppsala. In the late 1520s and early 1530s, Sweden gradually broke all its ties with the Church in Rome. A national church was established under the leadership of the king (Gustav I Vasa) that was, for the most part, Lutheran. The doctrinal identity of this church was actually fairly fluid over the course of the next three quarters of a century, and there were moments when it appeared as if Sweden might swing or be swung back into the Catholic camp. In 1593, however, a meeting of church leaders in Uppsala reaffirmed the country's ties to Lutheranism and the Augsburg Confession, and this has held down to the present.

Sweden's Lutheran state church developed along familiar north European lines. All monastic orders were closed. Church property became state property, and the clergy became employees of the state and were important agents in spreading royal policies and national ideas. The hierarchy of church governance remained, with the Archbishop of Uppsala acting as the spiritual leader of the church while the king was its temporal head. Legal matters were settled in the parliament, in which the clergy had its own chamber. The role of the clergy as the record keepers was also expanded in the wake of the Reformation. Pastors were the keepers of birth, marriage, death, and mobility records—records that were important then for tax and recruitment purposes, are remarkable in their extent, and are among the most useful in all of Europe for genealogists, social historians, and other researchers.

In the context of the Reformation and the struggle for souls that developed in Europe in the sixteenth and seventeenth century, it is not surprising that this new church, like those in most of Europe, was conservative and closed to outside ideas, diversity, and toleration. The clergy was the sole authority in religious matters. Dissent by native-born Swedes was forbidden. The Conventicle Act of 1726, which was aimed at Lutherans inspired by the Pietist movement of the period and intended to preserve religious uniformity, prohibited the holding any private religious meetings without an ordained pastor present. Some religious freedom did creep in for practical reasons—mainly to encourage immigration by entrepreneurs or experts in some kind of enterprise, such as Dutch merchants or Walloon iron smiths. A 1741 law, for example, insured toleration for members of the English or Dutch Reform churches. A more expansive law from 1781 extended this toleration, but there were strings attached. In particular, non-Lutherans could not hold public offices, teach, or proselytize. In this protective context, the Church became, at least in the eyes of many, increasingly conservative and tied to its history and practices.

As Sweden was swept up in the great transformations of the nineteenth century, the Church lost its monopoly but not its place as *the* state church. Dissenters ignored the proscriptions of the Conventicle Act and held private church services, despite the fines, terms of imprisonment, or exile that could be imposed. These rebellions can be seen in the so-called Readers' Movement of the early nineteenth century, the Laestadian Movement of northern Sweden from the 1840s, or the popularity of Eric Jansson, who left Sweden with hundreds of his followers to establish a religious commune in western Illinois at Bishop Hill in the late 1840s. In 1858, the Conventicle Act was repealed, and the growth of denominational groups such as the Baptists, Catholics, Methodists, and Mormons accelerated. Importantly, however, these denominations always were in the minority among Sweden's Christians, and they remain so.

In the twentieth century two major developments affected Swedish Christianity. The first was the legislation establishing full freedom of religion that took effect on January 1, 1952, and was subsequently included in the country's new constitution of 1974. The second was the formal disestablishment (the divorce) of the state church that took place on January 1, 2000. Discussions about this issue spanned much of the twentieth century. One concern was over Martin Luther's notion of two kingdoms: one worldly and the other spiritual. A state church blurred this distinction and could be forced to compromise its role as teacher of the Word. Another revolved around the question of how one could have a state church in a democracy, especially when democracy in all aspects of life—politics, the workplace, organizations, gender matters, education, etc.—was considered an essential defining characteristic of Sweden. Although disestablishment was studied in the decades following World War II, there was not sufficient support or consensus to effect it. A more favorable political climate, coupled with the increasingly diverse nature of Sweden's population and religious cultures in the 1990s, led to careful study of the issue by several government commissions and to the legislation, passed in late 1995, that went into effect five years later.[2]

In its new situation, the Church of Sweden is a kind of first among equals. It and other registered denominations receive support from the state through a small percentage of tax income. Membership is no longer automatic, based on having at least one parent already a member, and is now a matter of choice by individuals. Faced with competition, the Church actually has had to assess its position and market its beliefs and activities, which is not necessarily a bad thing. Freed of any kind of ties to the state (except for its responsibilities as the curator of burial facilities for the country), the Church has been able to focus on the fundamental tenets of evangelical Lutheranism and openly advocate for issues its leaders and governing bodies believe important. While some criticize its views, the Church has become a strong voice for the ideals of the welfare state, environmentalism, world peace, international relief efforts, tolerance, sexual preference freedom, ecumenism, the ordination of women, and the like; and the two most recent archbishops, Anders Wejryd and his predecessor Karl Gustav Hammar, have been strong voices for a liberal and open Church that responds to the realities of the world around it.

The disestablished Church of Sweden remains the largest religious organization in the country. There are about 1,800 congregations staffed by some 25,000 people. It is the country's tenth largest employer, has an annual budget that approaches $1 billion, and manages a significant endowment in both property and financial holdings. Structurally, the church is divided into 13 dioceses (Göteborg, Härnösand, Karlstad, Linköping, Luleå, Lund, Skara, Stockholm, Strängnäs, Uppsala, Visby, Västerås, and Växjö), each headed by a bishop who is responsible for overseeing the activities of the diocese's congregations. The spiritual leader of the church is the Archbishop, who is also the Bishop of Uppsala.[3]

Although organizationally intact, financially secure, and staffed by an able and dedicated clergy, the new status of the Church of Sweden has had negative impacts. Most importantly, membership is down significantly and continues to decline. In 2005, it was just under 7 million; in 2006, slightly more than 74 percent of all Swedes were members. In 2007, the church gained about 5,000 new members, but lost more than 56,000 old ones. Only about two fifths of newborns are baptized, just over one third of all young people are opting to go through Confirmation, and about half of all marriages take place in the church. More encouraging, perhaps, 83 percent of all Swedes are buried by the church. Some of these impacts are not simply because of disestablishment. For one thing, young people seem to be turning away or turning elsewhere. Also, the new ethnic and religious diversity of the population, the popularity of some of the free churches, and alternative religious experiences works against it. Finally, secularism is a powerful factor.

The Free Churches

By one count, Sweden has at least 45 so-called free churches. All of them are Christian denominations, and their membership numbers about half a million. The largest are Catholic (92,000), Pentecostal (90,000), Swedish Mission Church (67,000), Evangelical Free (29,000), Serbian Orthodox (27,000), Syrian Orthodox (25,000), and Jehovah's Witnesses (23,000).

Others include Baptist (18,000), Alliance Mission (13,000), Salvation Army (7,000), Mormon (9,000), and—with a special place in Swedish history—Swedenborgians (150).[4] Twenty-eight denominations belong to or are observers in the Christian umbrella organization Sweden's Christian Council (*Sveriges Kristna Råd*). These are divided into four "families"; Lutheran, Catholic, Free Church, and Orthodox. This denominational variety has two bases; one in the development of European and American Christian denominations, the other in the religions of the immigrants and refugees. In terms of members, the adherents to the former groups tend to be the "old Swedes," those of the latter are mainly new Swedes.

The success of some of these groups, like the churches of the Pentecostal movement, rests in the rejection of Sweden's largely secular society, a genuine need for a meaningful spirituality, and the belief in living an active Christian life. (On religiousness of the Swedes see below.) They attract people who seek a greater spirituality in their lives and who look for it in an organized church. Although free church denominations can be found throughout Sweden, parts of the country have been more prone to this tendency than others. One area is around the cities of Jönköping and Göteborg—an area that is sometimes referred to as Sweden's Bible Belt. Another is in the north and northeast.

The strength of some of these churches has, to some extent, been the source for support of Sweden's Christian Democratic Party (*Kristdemokraterna*), formed in 1964. Although relatively weak for several decades, its success at the polls increased in the 1980s. Since then it has secured between about 7 and 11 percent of the vote. In the 2006 election, it won 24 seats in the parliament and 3 places in the non-Socialist coalition government of Fredrik Reinfeldt. The party's program is based on a set of fundamental ideals. As its Web site puts it:

> [The Christian Democratic Party] was not founded to safeguard the interests of a particular social group, but to promote concepts based on the Christian ethic. Our party name explains that we stand for democracy based on a Christian outlook on people and fundamental values. Everyone who shares our concept is welcome in the party.
>
> [The Christian Democratic Party] is a value-oriented concept party. The value-oriented social vision can be described in the following way: a realistic and sustainable outlook on people comprised of the concept that citizens create the best conditions for a good society.[5]

Among the values important to the party are right to life, the importance of every unique person within a social context, the centrality of the family, the importance of community, the responsibility we owe to the present and the future, and the solidarity we owe to one another.

Non-Christian Groups

Non-Christian religious groups make up very small segments of Sweden's population, but this does not mean they are not important. Probably most significant today are the Jews and the Muslims.

The Jewish Presence

For most of the Christian era in Sweden, Jews were prohibited from taking up residence or even visiting the country. This does not mean, however, that none ever came. There is evidence of some Jewish visitors in the sixteenth century. In the late 1600s, several families came to Stockholm, where they accepted baptism in a formal and apparently costly ceremony that symbolized their conversion. Also, there were a few Jews who were permitted to travel the countryside as pedlars. From about 1730 Jews were allowed temporary stays in Göteborg to take part in Swedish East India Company auctions, and in the last decades of the century Gustav III allowed a Jew named Aaron Isaac to settle in Stockholm and establish a small congregation there. In 1782, Gustav issued a decree that limited Jewish settlement to the capital, Göteborg, and Norrköping (later adding Karlskrona and Marstrand), and prescribed a very large fee for the privilege. Technically, their economic activities were to be restricted, and marriage between Jews and Lutherans was prohibited. They did not receive full legal rights as citizens of the state until 1870.

Despite these obstacles, many of the early Jewish immigrants were highly successful as merchants or businesspeople. For example, the Bonnier brothers, who came to Göteborg from Denmark in the early nineteenth century, established themselves in the book trade, publishing, and newspapers there and in Stockholm. From these beginnings has come Bonniers AB, a family-owned giant in publishing, broadcasting, music, newspapers, and magazines. Among the firm's best-known Swedish newspapers are *Dagens Nyheter, Expressen, and Göteborgs-Tidningen.*

Most of the Jews who came to Sweden in the eighteenth and nineteenth centuries were from Germany, Denmark, or the Netherlands. They tended to be professionals, doctors, academics, and businessmen. By about 1880, they numbered around 3,000 and were fairly easily assimilated into Swedish society. A few found their way into the elite of Stockholm, and some of the leading intellectual and cultural figures of the early twentieth century had Jewish backgrounds, including the economic historian Eli Heckscher, the writer and critic Oscar Levertin, and the artist Ernst Josephson.

Important changes to the overall composition of Sweden's Jewish population occurred in the late nineteenth and early twentieth century with the influx of about 3,500 Jews who were fleeing persecution in the old Hapsburg and Russian empires. These were so-called East Jews. They tended to be Orthodox, relatively poor, and less easy or less willing to assimilate. Many of them settled in the Nöden district of Lund or on the island of Söder in Stockholm.

By the onset of World War II, there were about 6,000 Jews in Sweden. During the war this number swelled because of the sanctuary Sweden provided to about half of Norway's 2,100 Jews and to nearly all of Denmark's 7,500 Jews when the Holocaust roundups began in those countries. Most of these returned to their homelands after the war, but some new Jewish refugees came to Sweden from war-torn Europe. Many of these did not stay. Other groups came after the Soviet action in Hungary in 1956 and from Poland in 1969.

Counting how many Jews (or members of other religious groups) there are in Sweden is often difficult because religion is considered a personal matter and questions about one's beliefs are not asked in the usual statistical surveys. Another difficulty is that many have been totally assimilated into Swedish society, while others have retained only parts of their religious and/or ethnic cultures. One count puts the number of Jews in Sweden in the early twenty-first century at about 20,000, with perhaps half belonging to active Jewish communities. The practicing Stockholm Jewish community is estimated to be around 6,000, Göteborg's is about 1,800, and Malmö's is about 1,300. There are at least six synagogue buildings in Sweden, including three in Stockholm, two in Göteborg, and one in Malmö. The Great Synagogue in Stockholm, located in the heart of the city near the King's Tree Park, was built in the late 1860s.

Göteborg's main synagogue dates from 1855. In addition, Stockholm is home to a permanent Jewish theater, museum, library, and the offices of the Central Council for Jewish Congregations in Sweden—a group founded in 1945 and dedicated to fostering Jewish religious and cultural activities.[6]

There is a dark side to story of Jewish life in Sweden that has both historical and contemporary dimensions. The country has seen and continues to see its share of anti-Semitism. In good times, anti-Semitism has tended to be subdued, often virtually invisible. But during hard economic times or times of social unrest, this horrific aspect of all of Western history has emerged. This was true around the end of the nineteenth century, during the troubles of the 1920s and 1930s, and even in recent decades. In the first instance, some Swedes were caught up in the rise of a racially focused anti-Semitism, and some of Sweden's best known intellectuals, including August Strindberg, voiced their criticism of the Jews whom they believed could never become Swedes. In the years between the World Wars, anti-Semitism ran rampant throughout Europe, fed by economic troubles, the rhetoric of political movements, and the new "science" of race biology that led to both eugenic policies and the Holocaust. Sweden was not exempt from these troubles or from anti-Semitism. A powerless but noisy Nazi movement developed, Jews were attacked in some sectors of the media, and for a time the country closed its doors to Jewish refugees from Germany and elsewhere in Europe.

Sweden's record during the later years of World War II is better. As already mentioned, the country gave asylum to Norwegian and Danish Jews. Also, several relief efforts for Holocaust victims were initiated. One of these, organized by Folke Bernadotte, involved the so-called white buses that were used to transport some 30,000 Nazi concentration camp victims to safety toward the end of World War II. Another involved the work of Raoul Wallenberg and his colleagues at the Swedish mission in Budapest to save Hungarian Jews in mid-1944.

Anti-Semitism continues to manifest itself in Sweden and has many sources. One is the small but noisy neo-Nazi groups. They hold to ideas that come straight from Hitler's Third Reich. One of these, The Swedes Party/*Svenskarnas parti*, (formerly the National Socialist Front) has as a point in its party program "the taking of vital racial biological measures to ensure the Nordic race's spiritual and biological purity."[7] Some of Sweden's Muslims constitute another source of anti-Semitism. Their attitudes arise from historical hatreds, current Arab-Israeli problems in the Middle East, and anger over the situation of some Muslims in Sweden.

Regardless of the source, this anti-Semitism takes two basic forms. The first form is physical and includes protest marches and demonstrations, the defacing of Jewish property, graffiti, slogan shouting, intimidation, and physical violence. The second involves utilization of the media—radio, television, the press, and especially the Internet, which has become a global playground for radical individuals and groups spouting their favorite "truths" for all to see. Examples of the first type can be seen in events that have occurred in Malmö in recent years. There Jewish cemeteries have been vandalized, businesses harassed, and individuals intimidated and threatened. One of the main voices illustrating the exploitation of the media is Moroccan-born Ahmed Rami, who came to Sweden in 1973 as an asylum seeker. Since then he has become one of Sweden's most outspoken critics of Jews, Judaism, and Israel; and he is a Holocaust denier. His Radio Islam began in 1987 as a program on a public-access radio station and has grown into a multilingual Web site. A banner introduction to the site reads "Living History FACTS instead of Jewish propaganda." The content is clearly anti-Semitic. An interesting sampling of what can be found there is the following:

> Since one of the more important goals of the educational system and the media is to make people believe in the story of the Holocaust and to achieve the one

> hundred percentage of believers demanded by the Jewish power, Göran Persson (then the Prime Minister) has promised to take quick steps to intensify the brainwashing of the junior high school students and citizens in general, and to shut the mouth of everybody, who spreads doubt about the reality of the Holocaust.

Behind this outburst was the reaction of Göran Persson's Government to a poll from 1997 that showed some 34 percent of Sweden's young people between 12 and 17 were "prepared to entertain the thought that the Holocaust never occurred."[8] Rami has been convicted of "hate speech" twice and served brief prison sentences. Two other examples are the short-lived conservative magazine *Samtidsmagasinet Salt*, edited by Jonas De Geer, that appeared in a number of editions between 1999 and 2003, and the Web site Indymedia, which calls itself "a democratic media outlet for the creation of radical, accurate, and passionate tellings of truth." Both are sources of blatantly anti-Semitic information, cartoons, and comments.

The Muslim Presence

Muslims form the largest non-Christian religious minority in Sweden. Again, an exact total is impossible to determine, but estimates of the number of ethnic Muslims range between 250,000 and 400,000. Although communities of Muslims can be found throughout the country, about half of Sweden's Muslims live in the greater Stockholm area, and there are significant concentrations around Göteborg and Malmö. They come from a wide range of national and ethnic homelands where Islam is the dominant religion, including Turkey, Arabic-speaking countries (mostly Iraq), Iran, Pakistan, and the Balkans, or are the children of parents from these places. The oldest Muslim groups in Sweden have Turkish or Balkan roots and came as labor migrants in the 1960s and 1970s. At first they were predominantly men who left families back home to take jobs in Sweden. In the 1970s and early 1980s, some of their families joined them. In the 1990s and early twenty-first century, the Muslim in-migrants to Sweden have been mainly refugees or asylum seekers.

An ongoing problem among Sweden's Muslims is their national, ethnic, and sectarian diversity that includes Shia, Sunni, Ahmadiyya, Turkish, Iranian, Tatar, Bosnian, Somali, and other communities. Establishing working relationships and cooperation among these often highly different and even competing Muslim populations are difficult, if not impossible. There are, however, a number of umbrella organizations like the Islamic Cooperation Council (*Islamiska samarbetsrådet*) and the Swedish Muslim Council (*Sveriges muslimska råd*) that work for these goals.[9]

Not all of Sweden's Muslims are active worshipers, and one estimate identifies about 150,000 religious Muslims, active practicers of the religion, individuals whose lives are shaped and lived by the teachings of the Koran and Islamic/Sharia law. Most practicing Muslims in Sweden apparently use what are termed "basement mosques," of which there are many—perhaps as many as 20 in Göteborg, for example. There is also a growing number of purpose built mosques including those in Göteborg (one was established in 1976), Malmö (the first built in 1984/4 and then rebuilt after a fire in 2003), Stockholm, Trollhättan (from 1985), Uppsala, Gävle, Skövde, Västerås, Växjö, Linköping, and Umeå. One of these, sometimes referred to as Stockholm's Grand Mosque, is located in an old power station on Södermalm that dates from 1903 and was designed by Ferdinand Boberg, who was inspired by Islamic architecture.

Given the legal and constitutional guarantees in place in Sweden covering religious freedom, one would assume that Muslims are free to practice their faith without interference, prejudice, ill-will, or opposition from others, especially Christians. Most often, this is the case. Most Swedes are tolerant and accepting—or at least try to be. Some, however, are not, and the situation is not very different from that facing Jews in Sweden. Anti-Semitism and

Malmö's mosque near Rosengård. This mosque, which has been the target of several arson attacks, serves some of the Muslims of the Malmö area. (Courtesy of Kurt Ive Kristoffersson.)

Islamophobia go hand in hand in many cases. There is an outspoken minority that stirs up what some call the Muslim Problem, and argues that the Swedish and Islamic cultures are fundamentally incompatible. To these people, Christian Swedish and Muslim rules, rituals, calendars, holy celebrations, how they view the family, ideas about marriage, divorce, adoption, women, and the state, etc. are so different they will never be able to live together peacefully. The result is a "clash of cultures" that makes mutual acceptance and tolerance impossible. Despite the fact that the Swedish government's policy regarding Muslims and other immigrant groups is based on the ideas of integration and education, which includes a new religious education requirement in schools that is designed to enhance students' understanding of world religions and is supposed to allow all immigrants to become Swedish without sacrificing their ethnic and/or religious cultures, this minority believes assimilation is what must really happen. They argue that in order to truly fit in and be accepted Muslims must become cultural Swedes, and this implies that they must give up their religion.[10]

Sadly, the lives of many of Sweden's Muslims are far from the ideals so often portrayed for people in this country. For example, many tend to be ghettoized in ethno-religious enclaves located in decaying, inner-ring, high-rise suburbs; their employment opportunities are limited and tend to be at the low end of the skill and pay levels despite the educations many bring with them; and they are discouraged from becoming politically involved—in part because they are generally branded as outsiders and in part because of their own ethnic and religious differences.

In addition, many aspects of Muslim culture are used against them. What is seen as their subjugation of women, interruptions in the workday for prayer, dietary practices, and conflicts between Sweden's laws and Sharia law are just a few of these. There have also been a number of specific events that have fueled the xenophobia. One of the most notable for itself and for the reactions it generated was the January 2002 murder in Uppsala of Fadime Sahindal, a 26-year-old Swedish-Kurdish woman, by her father. The action was a so-called honor killing, and had more to do with ethnic background than religion. It occurred because the young woman had refused to accept the dominance of her father, had fallen in love with an Iranian-Swede (who died in a car crash in 1998), had moved out of the home, and was well on her way to becoming "Swedish." Because she acted in these ways, it was believed she had dishonored her family and killing her was the right thing to do. Killings like this one have occurred throughout Europe. They alarm those who wish to be accepting or tolerant and provide ammunition for the xenophobes. Although Fadime's murder had nothing to do with the family's religion and was the result of customs brought to Sweden with the family from Turkish Kurdistan, it served the purposes of anti-immigrant groups who use "Muslim" as a derogatory term.[11]

The range of anti-Muslim sentiments varies from mild to rabid. At one end of the spectrum are critics who find their levels of tolerance strained. Then there are those who argue the Muslims must either become Swedes in a narrow sense of the word or leave. At the other end of the spectrum are those who advocate sending "them all" back to their homelands without any period of acculturation. Similarly, there is a range of activities that includes some sensible and moderate dialogue between Swedes and Muslims, rational and irrational publications, and then, sadly, violence and vitriolic rhetoric. In this realm, individuals have been attacked, property damaged or defaced, protest rallies held, and the media exploited at its worst to defame and belittle Sweden's Muslim populations. Again, it is the far Right and the far Left on the political spectrum that are most opposed; and, it is neo-Nazi organizations that are particularly outspoken and active.

Behind the arguments, misunderstandings, rhetoric of abuse, and defensiveness, life goes on for Sweden's Muslims. Among the many interesting examples of this life is Rinkeby, a Stockholm suburb. Its population in late 2007 was almost 90 percent foreign born, and many of its residents are Muslim. It is a place that has seen more than its share of troubles and illustrates some of the darker aspects of the lives of the new Swedes. But it also a place that shows what multicultural Sweden can be—in the faces of children of many nationalities playing together, in multicultural events, in cooperation.[12] The developments in Rinkeby may also illustrate the processes of adaptation so common for immigrant groups in new and different places regardless of time or place; processes by which the first generation has the hardest time fitting in and faces the worst reactions from the established population, while the second tries very hard to fit in, and the third seeks both to fit and to know its past. Although some Muslim immigrants and refuges do return to their homelands when the situations there improve, many do not. It is highly likely that those who stay will become Swedes, but it is also likely that what it means to be Swedish will be changed in the process.

Religiosity

Another important aspect of religion in Sweden surrounds the question: Are Swedes religious? This is far more difficult to address than questions about the Christian denominations or non-Christian minorities, and any answer is likely to be highly impressionistic. Complicating related questions include: What does one mean by "religious," what standards of measurement are there, and does one have to have an institutional or denominational affiliation to be religious?

If acknowledged membership in the Church of Sweden is the standard, then the answer to this question is yes. In 2008, about three fourths of all Swedes were registered members. About 5 percent belonged to other Christian denomination churches. (In both cases, membership is falling. In the case of the Church of Sweden at a rate of about 1% per year.) Practicing Muslims, Jews, and some other small groups perhaps add another 2 percent. If church service attendance is the measurement, then the answer is no. Very few (between 2 and 4%), Swedes attend services every week. One often used cynical comment about attendance is that the average Swede goes to church four times in her/his lifetime—to be baptized, confirmed, married, and buried. Of course, this is far from the truth. Many attend services occasionally, some do so regularly. If participation in choirs is any indication, then there is clear evidence that at least the music component of religious life is live and well. Similarly, if participation in some of the social activities of churches such as sewing circles, discussion groups, book clubs, or volunteer projects is a measure, then there is considerable vitality. The lively religious lives many Christians, Jews, and Muslims lead certainly point to a deep level of religiousness, and there seem to be other forms of religious engagement that address this question as well.

Many have tried to determine the religious dimension of Sweden's culture, and this is a hot topic in the churches and some academic settings. While it does not deal with all of Sweden, *Guds närmaste stad?*, a study from 2008 on the importance of religion in lives of residents of the city of Enköping (population 39,000), is an example of such efforts. The work of nine scholars from different disciplines and/or perspectives, the study was conducted under the auspices of the Church of Sweden. Its conclusions were based on the 1,045 responses the research team received from a lengthy questionnaire sent to a random sample of city residents, interviews with some from the sample group, and personal observations. The results shed some light on the question of Swedes' religiousness and related issues. Also important was a question that lay in the background of the Enköping study—is a religious revolution underway in Sweden akin to what Paul Heelas and Linda Woodhead (*The Spiritual Revolution: Why Religion Is Giving Way to Spirituality*, 2005) concluded was happening in Kendal, England, that is, the decline of traditional religion and the rise of a New Age spiritualism to replace it. The team borrowed the definition of religion developed by Ninian Smart. It included seven basic "dimensions": teachings and philosophy, practices and rituals, story and narrative, experiential and emotional, ethical and legal, social and institutional, and material or aesthetic.[13]

The sample group broke down as follows in terms of religious identification: Strong Christian 25.5 percent, Mildly Christian 39.3 percent, Muslim

1.1 percent, Buddhist/Hindu 1.1 percent, Atheist, 10.9 percent, Non-Confessional 19.7 percent, and Multi-Confessional 2.5 percent.[14] Some of the conclusions from the study were: although there is considerable vitality in the organized churches, all are facing declining membership, as are most of Sweden's folk movement organizations and political parties; older people are more religious than younger; women are more religious than men; there are strong generational differences in religious views and engagement; Muslims seem to be more engaged in their religious lives than Christians; as in much of the Western world, many Swedes are frustrated by the hurried pace of modern life and the lack of truly personal time; modern society is increasingly one in which the individual is isolated and must navigate life on a very personal basis (individualization); there are deep and intense needs among contemporary Enköping residents for experiences that take them away from the stresses of their lives; many Swedes in search of meaningful spiritual experiences are finding them in new opportunities within the existing church frameworks, Buddhism, athleticism, alternative medicine, dietary options, and the like; and quiet, solitude, and time for personal reflection are more important to most than rituals, words, and doctrines. Although the authors concluded there was no revolution under way, they did concede that changes were taking place, and they recommended that the Church of Sweden needed to face these developments and adapt to them if it wished to survive.[15]

Some similar conclusions appeared in *Eurobarometer 225* from 2005. As part of a larger study, the European Commission of the EU polled citizens of its member states and those of several aspiring member states about their religious and spiritual beliefs. When asked "how frequently they thought about the meaning and purpose of life," 75 percent said either often or sometimes; 8 percent said never. Among Swedes the responses were 30 percent for often, 45 percent for sometimes, 20 percent for rarely, and 5 percent for never. Swedes were near the bottom in frequency of asking this question, trailing the United Kingdom (UK) and ahead of the Czech Republic. (Cypriots were the highest.) When asked about their religious or spiritual beliefs, 52 percent in the surveyed states said they believed in a God, 27 percent believed in some "sort of spirit, God or life force," 18 percent said they did not believe in anything of the kind, and 3 percent did not know. Again, the Swedes were toward the bottom of the list: 23 percent responded they believed there is a God, 53 percent believed in some kind of spirit, God, or life force, and 23 percent did not. In this case Malta was the most believing; Estonia was the least. The preparers of the report concluded that while there was a move away from "religion in its traditional form" in some parts of Europe, there was an affirmation of traditional churches in other parts (Italy, Ireland, and Greece, for example), and that there was a tendency toward "a new kind of religion characterized by the belief that 'there is some sort of spirit or life force.' " This was particularly the case in Sweden, Denmark, the Czech Republic, and Estonia.[16]

Given all of the above, it is probably safe to conclude that while there is a growing number of religious denominations or options in Sweden, it is clear that in terms of religious beliefs Swedes are becoming less and less church-oriented with each passing generation. At the same time, minority groups both Christian and non-Christian remain intensely faithful to their beliefs, practices, and institutions. Also, while they do not go to church very much, most Swedes seem to need a spiritual element to their lives, are religious in more personal and/or spiritual senses, and find religious/spiritual experiences in several non-Christian options and in nature, music, and participation in a wide variety of activities.

Notes

1. *Hávamál. The Words of Odin the High One*, from *The Elder* or *Poetic Edda* (Sæmund's Edda), translated by Olive Bray and edited by D. L. Ashliman, at http://www.pitt.edu/~dash/havamal.html. Accessed July 18, 2009.

2. For an full review of the steps leading to the disestablishment legislation, see E. Kenneth Stegeby, "An Analysis of the Impending Disestablishment of the Church of Sweden," *Brigham Young University Law Review*, January 1999. Online at http://findarticles.com/p/articles/mi_qa3736/is_199901/ai_n8848933/. Accessed July 19, 2009.

3. The Church of Sweden's Web site is a fine source of information in Swedish or English. See http://www.svenskakyrkan.se/. Accessed July 19, 2009.

4. The following list is from the Web site of Sweden's Christian Council/*Sveriges Kristna Råd*: http://www.skr.org. Accessed July 18, 2009. Member churches and observers—The Lutheran Family: Church of Sweden & Evangelical Mission, Estonian Evangelical Lutheran Church, Latvian Evangelic Lutheran Church, Hungarian Protestant Church; The Catholic Family: Stockholm's Catholic Church; The Free Church Family—Adventist, Evangelical Free, French Reform, Salvation Army, Methodist, Pentecostal, Swedish Alliance Mission, Swedish Baptist, Swedish Mission, Vineyard North; The Orthodox Family—Armenian Apostolic Church, Bulgarian Orthodox, Estonia Orthodox, Ethiopian Orthodox, Finnish Orthodox, Coptic Orthodox, Macedonian Orthodox, Rumanian Orthodox, Russian Orthodox/Christ Declaring, Russian Orthodox/Moscow Patriarchate, Serbian Orthodox, Syrian Orthodox, Eastern Assyrian.

5. On the Christian Democrats' principles, see http://www.kristdemokraterna.se/otherlanguages/English.aspx. Accessed July 19, 2009.

6. See http://www.jf-stockholm.org/english/index.php. Accessed April 14, 2010. This Web site offers information about Stockholm's Great Synagogue and includes a link to a history of the Jews in Sweden.

7. On the neo-Nazis ideals, see http://www.svenskarnasparti.se/. Accessed March 30, 2010.

8. See Mordecai Specktor, "Sweden Confronting Its Role in the Nazi War Machine," *American Jewish World* at http://www.jweekly.com/article/full/8901/sweden-confronting-its-role-in-the-nazi-war-machine/. Accessed July 20, 2009. *Note:* This outcome was particularly shocking to then Prime Minister Persson and others, and it led to changes in Swedish school curricula to improve teaching of the Holocaust. A key to these was the Living History project and the book *Om detta må ni berätta. En bok om förintelsen i Europe, 1933–1945/Tell Ye Your Children: A Book about the Holocaust in Europe, 1933–1945* by Stéphane Bruchfeld and Paul Levine.

9. See http://www.sverigesmuslimskarad.se/insider.html. Accessed July 20, 2009.

10. Religious education is compulsory in accordance with the National Curriculum. Currently, the curriculum involves ethical discussions and a general knowledge of different religions. It is believed that an important part of the religious education is an ability to understand other people's values and ways of life, and Sweden's educational system seeks to approach all religious groups in unbiased ways.

11. Unni Wikan, *In Honor of Fadime: Murder and Shame* (Chicago: University of Chicago Press, 2008). Published in Swedish in 2003.

12. See http://www.rinkeby.nu/. Accessed July 19, 2009. Another urban area to consider is the Rosengård district of Malmö. More than 60 percent of the local population is foreign born. It is home to a major Muslim education center and mosque, and in some respects going there is like entering a Middle Eastern city. Rosengård has been the focal point of unrest and racist attacks, and its problems fodder for radical right criticisms of Sweden's immigration policies. See http://islamineurope.blogspot.com/2009_01_01_archive.html. Accessed July 28, 2009. See also http://news.bbc.co.uk/2/hi/europe/5348622.stm. Accessed July 20, 2009.

13. Kajsa Ahlstrand and Göran Gunner, eds., *Guds närmaste stad? En studie om religionernas betydelse i ett svenskt samhälle i början av 2000-talet* (Stockholm: Verbum, 2008), pp. 56–57. The title of this book derives from Enköping's nickname as Sweden's *närmaste stad*/Sweden's Nearest City because one third of all Swedes live within an hour of the city! See also Paul Heelas and Linda Woodhead, *The Spiritual Revolution: Why Religion Is Giving Way to Spirituality* (Maldon, MA: Blackwell, 2005).

14. Ahlstrand and Gunner, *Guds närmaste stad?*, p. 67.

15. Ibid., Chapter 11.

16. *Eurobarometer 225, Social Values. Science and Technology, 2005*. European Commission publication, 2005 at http://ec.europa.eu/public_opinion/archives/ebs/ebs_225_report_en.pdf. Accessed July 28, 2009.

3

Marriage, Family, Gender, and Education

As is the case with almost every aspect of Swedish culture, the themes of this chapter are ones caught up in processes of profound change. Marriage and family are being redefined. Although women have made great progress in many aspects of Swedish life, the struggle for true gender equality continues. Gender preferences in intimate relationships are increasingly matters of little concern, especially to younger Swedes. Education continues on a course set decades ago toward greater democratization and more and more opportunities. To some observers these developments are all good things. They demonstrate how Sweden is a leader in the ongoing processes of freeing individuals to live their lives as they choose. To others they are parts of the regrettable unraveling of what is good and right, and Swedes are blindly destroying sacred and immutable institutions and norms of behavior and failing to prepare new generations for the future.

Marriage and Family

Unquestionably, Sweden is a leading country in the West in terms of redefining marriage, relationships between individuals, gender roles, and the family. Statistics show that important changes are occurring in all of these areas. Marriage rates are low; the number of bisexual and same-sex partnerships is increasing; women continue to make advances against a formerly patriarchal society; what constitutes a family is becoming very different from just a generation ago in terms of size, composition, functions, and place in society; and the state is playing a ever-increasing role in the socialization of children through day care and compulsory education.

Among the striking facts that point in these directions are:

- Sweden has a relatively low marriage rate compared with other European states. In 2007, a statistically good year for weddings in Sweden, it was 5.24/1000 in the population; in the preceding decade, it had usually been around 2.2. The highest rate in 2007 was in Romania, 8.8/1000; Denmark's was 2.6/1000.
- About one third of all couples live together without being married.
- Some unmarried couples, including gay, lesbian, and heterosexual, live together in what are termed "registered partnerships." The number of these is relatively small, about 4,200 in 2007.
- The divorce rate is relatively high, and nonmarried couples can and do separate easily.
- Slightly more than half (54%) of all households are made up of a single person.
- The birthrate is relatively low, and the average number of children per woman is less than two (about 1.8).
- Almost three quarters of all households are without children.
- There are a large number of single-parent households, and about 80 percent of them are headed by a woman with one or more children.
- Just over half of all births are out of wedlock.
- About 80 percent of adult females work outside the home while 87 percent of men do.
- Day care facilities are easily available, and state support is available based on income and need.
- The nine-year compulsory education begins at 7 and continues to age 16. Most young people then go on to a three-year, postsecondary school before entering the job market or moving on to a university.

One of the most important developments in Sweden today is the change taking place in the nature of the "family," at least as it was defined from the late nineteenth century. Of course, the typical family has undergone a number of transformations in the history of every culture or national group. In early modern Sweden, down to about 1750, the typical family was a large, multigenerational, multiple-kinship unit. Its members included parents, children, grandparents, and live-in help. Among its functions were procreation, coordination of economic activities, education and training of the younger generation, welfare for the ill and aged, and organization of social activities. Beginning in the late eighteenth and continuing well into the nineteenth century, the typical Swedish family came increasingly to be composed of more closely tied kinship units. This process was encouraged by higher survival rates for children, government-imposed changes in landownership (consolidation and enclosure), greater mobility, and increasing economic opportunities both outside Sweden and in the country. In this period a kind of "peasant ideal" developed that is still harkened back to and celebrated in some contexts. Today, it is very much a part of the national romantic image of Sweden. Beginning in the later decades of the nineteenth century, urbanization and industrialization triggered changes that resulted in the emergence of a new ideal. Variously called the Victorian, bourgeois, or nuclear family, this new ideal was composed of a bread-winning father, a stay-at-home mother, and a small number of highly valued children. This model dominated much of the twentieth century and was at the center of decades of official policies and programs aimed at its encouragement. Today, however, this bourgeois ideal is giving way to something more fluid, less permanent, less formally structured, and less involved in the lives of its members.

David Popenoe, who has been looking at family development in Sweden for decades, describes this process in *Disturbing the Nest. Family Change and Decline in Modern Societies* and other publications. He, along with many others, has repeatedly argued that in one sense Sweden is in the midst of the decline of what he calls "familism"—the decline of an ideology about the family and the shared ideals contained within it.[1] Statistically, his ideas are illustrated by the low frequency of marriage, the lateness of first marriages, the number of nonmarriage partnerships, the high divorce or relationship termination rates, the low fertility rate, and the very high percentage of women who work full time rather than stay at home. They are also supported by state policies and programs that he believes are antifamily. For example, the simple difference between what the state calls its support for children, "child allowances" (*barnbidrag*) rather than "family allowances," illustrates this. First instituted as a need-based program in 1937, these became universal in 1948. Today, child allowances cover all children between birth and age 16. Thereafter, they are often replaced by other kinds of support payments. Another example of the state's supposed antifamily policies was the absence of a tax break for joint-income filers. This is no longer the case, and when it was, the differences in rates were quite small. Even the state's support of day care is seen as antifamily by some critics of the system because it enables parents to act more freely in making employment decisions or in being absent from the home for other reasons. Schools are also villains in this scenario because they take on child-raising functions. Adding to this negative view is criticism of the long-held idea that children are unique, independent units within the society as a whole and not integral parts of an important social element, the family.

Numbers do not tell all, and a very different interpretation of the situation in Sweden can be presented. For example:

- Although the level of traditional marriage is relatively low, some kind of cohabiting arrangement makes up 49 percent of all "family units" in Sweden.
- On average, about two thirds of all children live in two-parent "family" units.
- Separation/divorce rates are no higher than in most Western countries and have actually fallen since the late 1990s.
- All seven of Sweden's leading political parties advocate strong families—although they may differ on the definition thereof.
- Starting in 1974, "parental benefits" have been offered. Initially, these involved 180 days off from a job at 90 percent of pay to care for a child up to age 8. As of early 2009, the time period was 450 days, the rate of compensation varied across the term of the benefit, and, beyond a requirement that each parent take 30 days to be with the child (Mummy/Daddy Month), parents can arrange how the time is to be apportioned between them. The program was designed to encourage individuals to have children, share in parental responsibilities, and enhance the early childhood experiences of children by having both parents involved.[2]

All of this tangible evidence is useful, but it misses another perspective: what actually goes on with and in families that points to their continuing importance. Many Swedes still consider the family to be one of central aspects of their lives. Much of what they do takes place in the context of partners and children. The calendar of rituals, special moments, and celebrations points to continued family importance. Swedes have a fondness for what people might see as ritualized celebrations of birthdays, graduations, confirmations, weddings, and the like. Also, most have their own special foods, dress, and customs that may include songs, dances, and toasting (or roasting). Vacations, summer holidays, and winter getaways are often family centered.

Another issue related to the changes in the nature of the family in Sweden and elsewhere is what constitutes a marriage. Historically, it has long meant a formal union between a man and a woman for the purposes of procreation and mutual support—at least in the ideal. Since the 1960s, however, getting married in Sweden has been less and less the pursued option as more and more couples simply chose to live together (*sambo*). David Popenoe calls these unions "marriage lite." Sometimes they lead to a formal marriage; sometimes they do not. The increasing acceptance of gay and lesbian relationships has added to this trend.

In recent decades, Swedish law has been changed to give such unions more formal status and legal protections. The country's basic marriage laws date back to church codes from the late seventeenth century and a 1734 civil law.

In 1987, a specific "man and woman" element was inserted. Eight years later a Registered Partnership Act provided the same legal rights and obligations to cohabiting heterosexual couples as marriage, and this was extended to same-sex unions by the 2003 Gender Neutral Cohabitation Act (*Sambolag*). Neither of the two recent laws led to a flood of registrations. Importantly, however, the option is there and has symbolic importance. The final step in the legal redefinition of marriage in Sweden occurred on May 1, 2009, when the gender-neutral marriage law proposed by the nonsocialist coalition Government of Fredrik Reinfeldt and passed by the Parliament on April 1 went into effect. The vote was 261 to 22, with 16 abstentions, and the only members openly opposed to the measure were from the Christian Democrats. Sweden joined the Netherlands, Belgium, Spain, Canada, South Africa, Norway, and several states in the United States by passing the new law.[3]

What causes lie behind these changes in relationship patterns, family, fertility, and the like? Welfare policies, positive and negative developments arising from economic growth, expansion of educational opportunities, generational rebellion, advances in birth control, the decline of institutional religion, women's liberation, and sexual preference freedom are some of factors. It has already been noted how government policies have been intended to encourage individual development at the expense of family. The rapid growth of Sweden's economy, in the 1960s especially, led to prosperity but also to a severe housing shortage. As Richard Tomasson has pointed out, the latter resulted in more people opting to live together out of necessity, and this, in a kind of chain reaction, led to a relaxing of old taboos. Subsequently, the affluence in Sweden has continued to contribute to levels of economic independence for both men and women that negate the need for partnerships. The youth rebellion of the 1960s was also important. *Sambo* arrangements were often part of the decade's rebellion against convention (marriage) and parental control. At the same time, the birth control pill helped create a sexual revolution that encouraged both multipartner freedom and long-term intimate relationships without the fear of pregnancies.[4] In recent decades the growing acceptance of same-sex relationships has been important in driving change, too. Contributing to the context in which all this occurred was the decline of religion and/or increased secularism.

Women

True gender equality has been a goal of Sweden's leading parties at least since the late 1960s. A defining statement of this position was a central feature of On Equality/*Jämlikhet*, a 1971 publication that came from the

Working Group on Equality established by the then governing the Social Democratic Party and its labor market partner, the National Confederation of Trade Unions. In this, Alva Myrdal (one of the most remarkable women in recent Swedish history and well known as a social problems researcher, author, politician, peace advocate, diplomat, and 1982 Nobel Peace Prize recipient) and her colleagues argued that in order for each individual to achieve her or his maximum potential as a person there must be genuine equality in all aspects of life including economic situation, career opportunities, education, housing, health care, leisure opportunities, and the like. These goals are not the monopoly of the Social Democrats, however; and, although some of the rhetoric is different among the political parties, they are agreed upon by almost all of them. It is safe to say that one of Sweden's national policies is gender equality, and this is well summarized by the authors of a 2008 report on gender relations in Sweden:

> For a country to grow and develop, it is necessary to take advantage of the knowledge and competence of the entire population. Each individual, women and men alike, should have the opportunity to develop their talents within the areas they are best qualified for, regardless of sex. Gender equality between women and men is therefore an important factor for growth. To obtain results, gender equality policy must pervade in all aspects of government policy.[5]

Of course, declaring gender equality to be a national goal and actually achieving it are two very different things. The history of Sweden's women's movement goes back into the middle of the nineteenth century, and for decades progress of any kind was slow, as the following list shows:

- 1842: School reform designed to lead to a compulsory elementary "folk school" system for boys and girls.
- 1845: Equal inheritance, but women and their property remained under the control of a male guardian (father, husband, brother, etc.).
- 1846: Women gained nominal access to some skilled trades.
- 1858: Single women, 25 and older, gained legal independence, but only through a court application process.
- 1870: Right to sit for the university admissions exam and study medicine is gained.
- 1873: Sweden's universities are opened to women.
- 1884: Twenty-one becomes the age of maturity for men and women.
- 1908: Married women with property gain the vote in local elections.
- 1920: Legal and financial independence of married women is assured.

1921: Rights to the vote and to run for office in all elections are gained.

1923: Government jobs are made accessible to women.

1931: Maternity insurance is introduced.

1935: Equality in pensions for men and women becomes the norm.

1938: Lifted the ban on the spreading of information about birth control.

1946: Full employment equality in government positions, except the church and military, becomes policy.

1947: Equal pay for equal jobs in state employment becomes policy.

1950: Equal parental authority becomes the norm.

1958: Right to become a priest in the Church of Sweden is recognized.

1965: Law against "marriage rape" is enacted.

1975: New abortion law giving a woman the right to decide up to the eighteenth week in a pregnancy is enacted.

1979: Right to a six-hour workday for parents of small children becomes law.

1980: Law against gender discrimination in the workplace, education reforms aimed at gender equality through a new curriculum, a gender-neutral law on succession to the throne, and the creation of an Office of Equal Opportunities Ombudsman are enacted.

1983: All occupations are opened to women including in the military.

1984: Equal Opportunities Act (modified in 1992, 1994, 1998, and 2001) is passed.

1988: New law on violence against women is passed.

1999: A measure called the "sexual services act" against purchase of sexual favors is enacted.

2005: A stricter law on gender discrimination is passed.

2007: The Ministry of Integration and Gender Equality is created. (The head of this ministry in 2009 was Nyamko Sabuni. Born in 1969, she came to Sweden with her family from Burundi in 1980. In recent years she has been highly controversial for her out-spoken opposition to honor killings, female genital mutilation, and young Muslim girls wearing the hijab. In ways she represents one facet of the new Swedes.)[6]

Taken as a whole, the gains made are significant, and they make Sweden a world leader in terms of gender equality.

There are other indicators that support Sweden's high ranking on women's issues. For example, women play leading roles in national politics. In the 2006 election, they won 165 of the 351 seats in the Parliament. Fredrik Reinfeldt's coalition government, labeled the "Alliance for Sweden," included 10 women; they headed the ministries of Communications, Integration and Gender

Equality, Enterprise and Energy, Elderly Care and Public Health, Culture, International Development Cooperation, Trade, Social Security, EU Affairs, and Justice. Beyond the capital, women make up about two fifths of the membership of local and county governing councils, and 8 of the 21 country governors are women. They hold about 40 percent of the judgeships in the country. Seven women sat on the country's supreme court in 2009. In education, girls tend to do better in compulsory public schools, account for 60 percent of university students, have achieved near parity in the number of doctorates awarded, and are in the majority in adult education programs. Women compose about half of the workforce. About 81 percent of women are employed full time versus about 87 percent of men. In the labor market, women have made important progress in the area of income equality. Since the 1930s, state programs including child allowances, legalization of birth control, support for day-care and preschool programs, parental leaves, and support for a six-hour work day for mothers of young children have eased the personal and financial burdens of having children. They have also encouraged the involvement of both parents, whether there is a two-parent family unit or not, and they have helped offset the costs women (more than men) incur when they have children. Finally, in recent years the government has taken up the long-ignored realities of the issue of violence against women, especially in partner relationships and is committed to dealing with them.

Although the gains are genuine and important, there are many ways in which women have not achieved real equality in Sweden. Among these are disparities in occupations and career choices, postsecondary university or professional program involvement, pay equity, and time allocation. Concerning work options, the author of one 2008 internet blog summed up the situation when she wrote that Swedish women were still doing "classic women's work." By this she meant that the majority of women who work fill the same kinds of positions they have tended to fill since the late nineteenth century (nurse, teacher, clerk) and/or that involve domestic functions (cleaning, cooking, care giving) that fit traditional stereotypes of women's abilities and employment options. This reality is reflected in the following employment information from 2007:

- 85 percent or more of all social workers, assistant nurses, preschool teachers, and child-care providers are women.
- 82 percent of all health-care workers are women.
- About 80 percent of hotel and office cleaners and kitchen staff are women.
- 68 percent of all compulsory school-level teachers are women.
- About 60 percent of all sales clerks are women.

While:

- About one fifth of all systems designers or computer programmers are women.
- Only about one fourth of employed women work in "industry."
- Less than one tenth of employed women work in the construction trades.
- 2 percent of heavy truck drivers are women.
- Women hold a disproportionately small share of management positions, especially in the private sector, and only a tiny fraction of the leaders of corporations at either the management or board of directors level are women.[7]

The last of the above is particularly rankling for many, and when one looks closely the details are striking. In 2006–7, 2 women and 292 men were corporate board chairpersons, and 5 women and 289 men were "managing directors." Among companies listed on the Swedish stock exchange in 2008, 18 percent of board members were women versus 82 percent men. Of the 294 companies listed, seven had female managing directors; nine had a woman as the chairperson of their boards. (In contrast, in the public sector, women account for 58% of managers.)

The career education options women tend to pursue reinforce these patterns of employment. In universities, where women now make up about 60 percent of the student bodies, they are in the overwhelming majority in programs in the health sciences and teacher training. Their lead drops somewhat in the humanities, the medical sciences, forestry and agriculture, and law. About equal percentages study the arts. In contrast, three times as many men as women are enrolled in technical programs. A similar pattern exists among students who opt to take the vocational track through the upper secondary schools (*gymnasia*). There, programs in handicrafts, child care and recreation, and the arts involve nearly three times as many young women as men. In hotel and restaurant, business administration, and social science oriented programs a 60:40 women to men split is typical. Parity exists for programs in the natural sciences, and males dominate the programs in technology, industrial arts, vehicle engineering, and construction.

In terms of pay equity, women have done well in general, but not in all areas of work. In this sphere they are helped by the requirement of equal pay for virtually all jobs in the public sector. So, for example, men and women are paid equally as teachers, parliamentary representatives, social services personnel, and the like. There is also nearly equality in pay for store clerks, cashiers, and vehicle drivers. On the other hand, women only earn 86 percent as much as men in the military, 82 percent as much as men as finance and sales professionals, and 80 percent as much as men in the construction trades or in financial and human resources positions.

A final way to look at whether or not Sweden has achieved genuine gender equality is to consider how time use has changed in the last 20 years or so. Initially, women who worked continued to spend a significant share of their time on domestic work (what is called "unpaid work" in the statistical sources). For example, in 1990–91 an employed woman's weekday was divided into about five hours of paid work, four hours of unpaid work, less than an hour for education, about eight hours of personal time (mostly for sleeping), and four hours for leisure. In the same period, an employed male worked eight hours, engaged in about two hours of unpaid work, slept about the same as a women, and got slightly more leisure time. Ten years later, women did a little less unpaid work and had a bit more leisure time. Men, on the other hand, did less paid work, but did not offset this with more unpaid work. This data is reinforced when one looks at the amount of time men and women spend on unpaid work across various stages in their lives. Women always do more, and they do the most (between about 35 and 43 hours per week) when they are either a single or cohabiting parent of small children. Overall, women spend about one third more time engaged in unpaid work than men.[8]

Education

Sweden has been developing, reforming, tweaking, and revising its national education system since the passage of the country's first compulsory elementary school law in 1842. There were earlier schools and attempts at some kind of broader education in Sweden before then, but the former were few and often reserved for members of the social elite, and the latter tended to be irregular and uneven in both extent and quality. During the Middle Ages, the Church played a leading role in education and provided schools mainly in diocesan towns. Before the Reformation in the sixteenth century, many of the country's monastic houses also played important educational roles. Sweden's first university was founded at Uppsala in 1477, and a second opened in Lund in 1666. The Reformation brought an increased concern for literacy, and this gradually led to efforts to ensure at least a basic reading ability for most Swedes. The Enlightenment's emphasis on the importance and usefulness of education resulted in some curricular reforms in the universities aimed at introducing more practical programs of study, and there were new efforts to improve general literacy levels. It was not until 1842, however, that every parish was required to have and maintain a school (*folkskola*) for boys and girls, and it was decades before a real system with proper facilities, relatively uniform teaching materials, and teacher training institutions and programs developed.

One of the principal problems with Sweden's education system as it evolved was that it was fundamentally undemocratic. While the so-called folk schools served to provide a basic education to most Swedish children in reading, arithmetic, and a kind of national composite of history, geography, literature and the like, secondary education and the universities remained closed to the vast majority, both on the basis of social class and gender. In the first half of the twentieth century, reforms gradually democratized Sweden's education system and built curricula that served the ends of the political parties, mainly the Social Democrats.

Today, Sweden boasts an open, accessible, and highly democratic educational system that stretches virtually from infancy to the end of life. Preschool programs are open to children between one and six years of age. These are generally not free, but the fees are scaled according to ability to pay. Six-year-olds occupy a kind of limbo between the preschool and nine-year compulsory system. However, many are involved in a transition program. At seven, young people enter Sweden's nine-year compulsory school system. Enacted in 1962 and phased in over the following decade, this system is roughly equivalent to America's grades one through nine. Its bases were described in the following extract from the 1985 School Law:

> All children and young persons shall irrespective of gender, geographic residence and social and financial circumstances have equal access to education in the national school system for children and young persons. The education shall be of equal standard within each type of school, wherever in the country it is provided.
>
> The education shall provide pupils with knowledge and skills and, in co-operation with the home, promote their harmonious development into responsible human beings and members of the community. Particular attention shall be paid to pupils who need special support.

The law went on to specify that schools were to promote gender equality and discourage "insulting treatment such as bullying and racist behavior."[9]

The design of Sweden's educational system blends centralization and local independence. From the top comes the basic format for the system, sets of fundamental goals, and national curricula that embody the basic goals and ideals. At the individual school level come implementation, variety, and creativity. National course syllabi are developed by the National Agency for Education (*Skolverket*). These reiterate the basic goals and ideals of the system and, in particular, spell out what students ought to know about and do with given subjects in general and, in particular, at the end of their fifth and ninth years in the system when they are tested. These syllabi do not, however, tell schools and teachers exactly what or how to teach; there is a good deal of individual flexibility beyond core sets of basics. For example, in history students are expected to gain a "sense of history," an "understanding of the background to historical phenomena and events," a "broad and in-depth knowledge of their cultural heritage as well as that developed by different national minority groups," insight into the importance of cultural heritage to identity, "a knowledge of important historical figures, events and periods," the "ability to use history as an instrument for understanding other subjects," and "an ability to assess different texts, media and other sources." Swedish and Nordic history are viewed as especially important, as are knowledge of modern developments, especially genocide and the Holocaust.[10] As was noted earlier, a religion requirement is also part of the compulsory curriculum, and the national syllabus for it includes such goals as the development of knowledge of several world religions, the role Christianity has played in Sweden's history, the role of other religions in Sweden, and a sense for the importance of religion in shaping how people think and act.[11] At the core of all of these syllabi are statements that affirm the state's commitment to encouraging learning, fostering curiosity in a wide range of subjects, encouraging appreciation for equality and diversity, and creating an informed society capable of making democracy work. Also important here is the idea that lies at the heart of so much of what happens in contemporary Sweden, that the state can (and should) play an active role in shaping society.

Upon completion of the compulsory school years, most Swedish students move on to an upper secondary school (*gymnasium*). These schools are intended to continue the development of students' knowledge of certain fundamental subjects such as Swedish, English, mathematics, and history, and to prepare students either to enter a career path or move on to specific university programs. Each school generally offers a mix of some of the 17 mandated national programs in the arts, business administration, child care and recreation, building construction, energy, foods, handicrafts, health care, hotel and restaurant operations, industry, media, natural resources, natural sciences, social sciences, technology, and transportation (vehicles).

A reform aimed at the upper secondary schools called "Knowledge and Quality: Eleven Steps for the Development of the High School" took effect in 2007. It included such changes as replacing course exams with subject exams, improving individualized programs of study, raising the quality of job internship programs, developing apprenticeship programs in the trades, and making history one of the core subjects that all students must study. This package of changes grew from a government-initiated study and was just one more example of the seemingly constant changes that have taken place in education in Sweden over the last several decades. Schools are seen as vital in both personal development and in shaping society, and the profound changes that have taken place in Sweden, not least important the enormous demographic transformation, have been at the center of compulsory and secondary school reform developments.

Independent Schools

Since 1992, an interesting and often controversial option to the public schools in Sweden has appeared, the independent school (*friskola*). Under a law pushed through the parliament by the non-Socialist government of Carl Bildt that year, schools without direct ties to or managed by the community in which they were located could be established via an application and approval process overseen by *Skolverket*, the national school authority. In response to the new law, individuals, parent cooperatives, parishes, ideological and economic organizations, and for-profit companies got involved. Growth was quite remarkable. From relatively few in the early 1990s, the number of these schools rose to about 750 in 2008, including basic and upper secondary schools. Although concentrated mainly in Stockholm and Göteborg, they can be found throughout much of the country. About 10 percent of all of Sweden's students attend them. Based on figures from 2004 to 2005, more than half of these schools are operated by for-profit companies, primarily *Vittra* and *Kunskapskolan*/Knowledge Schools. In 2009, each was operating about 30 schools and enrolled between 8,000 and 10,000 students.

What is the attraction of these alternative schools? Several things. For some parents it is simply having a choice rather than being compelled to send their children to the local public school. For others it may be proximity, family tradition, size of the school or classes, the typically low student-teacher ratio, the teaching methods used (Montessori and Waldorf schools fall into the independent school category), the religion or ethnicity of the founders or operators, or a special program. What the rhetoric about these schools seems most often to claim is that they will do the job better than the public schools. For example, this is implied in *Vittra*'s Web site's language:

> Our aim is to strive for increased opportunities in life through knowledge and learning.
>
> Our pedagogical model stems from three fundamentals: individual development, a viable working culture, and a challenging learning environment.
>
> We give all of our students the possibility to develop as independent, inquiring individuals with all of the knowledge and preparation needed in life. At a *Vittraskola* your child will develop the motivation, desire, and judgment needed to succeed.[12]

Kunskapskolan is more direct. It claims that:

> The old school system is built on the notion that everyone learns in the same way, in classrooms with lectures and corridors. It's been like this since 1842.
>
> We have developed another approach that we call "a personalized education" because everyone is different and learns differently.[13]

Overall, the track record of these schools is quite good, and there is evidence that students do better on the compulsory tests, attend more regularly, and have better overall school experiences. Opponents, on the other hand, argue, generally erroneously, that:

- They are elitist and dominated by the upper middle class.
- They encourage segregation of young people along ethnic or religious lines.
- Because they receive exactly the same support from the state as the public schools, they deprive the public schools of resources.
- They are religiously, ethnically, or ideologically biased and shape students along the lines of those biases.
- Their teachers are less qualified than those in the public schools.
- It is inappropriate for schools to be run for profit.
- They are less subject to national standards and controls.[14]

Certainly, the independent schools have their strengths and weaknesses, their advocates and their detractors; and no doubt the debates about them will continue. However, all the discussion aside, it is clear that they have successfully established themselves in a niche alongside the public system and are not going to disappear any time soon.

Post-Secondary Education

Very rapid and extensive changes have taken place in Sweden's postsecondary education systems in the last few decades. Until the 1960s, there were relatively few universities and professional schools in the country, as the founding dates of first few institutions on the following partial list of schools indicate:

Uppsala University (1477)

Lund University (1666)

Royal School of Music/*Kungliga musikskolan* (1771)

Caroline Institute/*Karolinska Institutet* (1810)

Chalmers University of Technology (1829)

University College of Arts, Crafts and Design/today *Konstfack* (1844)

University of Gothenburg (1954)

Stockholm University (1960)

Umeå University (1965)

Royal Institute of Technology (1970)

Linköping University (1975)

Swedish University of Agricultural Sciences/*Sveriges lantbruksuniversitet* (1977)

Luleå University of Technology (1997)

Karlstad University (1999)

Växjö University (1999) (From January 2010 Linnaeus University in a merger with Kalmar University)

Örebro University (1999)

Mid Sweden University with three campuses (2005)

In total, there were forty-nine, institutions of higher learning in the country in 2009. Of these, thirty-six were public and thirteen private. Nine specialized in the arts (visual, dance, theater, music). Six concentrated on medicine. Twenty-one were accredited to offer graduate degrees. Although many were located in the greater Stockholm area, the overall distribution throughout the country was fairly good.[15] Undergraduate enrollment in 2006–7 totaled just over 322,000; graduate enrollment was slightly more than 17,000. A number of features of the student population are worth noting:

- Women outnumbered men overall, but tended to be concentrated, as noted earlier, in programs that were historically female dominated, such as health care and teaching.
- About one tenth of the students were foreign/international students, and this was viewed as a good thing because "international students reinvigorate the environment at higher education institutions and introduce new influences."
- As Sweden's population ages and given the country's relatively low birthrate, international students are vital to the higher education system.
- About half of all Swedes born since 1990 will have entered the higher education system by the time they are 31.
- Students of middle class backgrounds are overrepresented, while students from working class backgrounds are underrepresented.
- The proportion of young people from working class backgrounds is rising, but these students tend to enroll in programs that take less time to complete.
- Slightly less than one fifth of the students entering higher education programs in 2006–7 were foreign-born Swedes or had two foreign-born parents.

> Within this group Iranian, Nordic, and European backgrounds were strongly represented. African backgrounds were weakly so.[16]

In general, all of these numbers and developments point to good things. Sweden has an ample number of institutions of higher education each with its own particular focuses and strengths, the opportunities for students are extensive and have expanded in recent decades, the costs of higher education are low largely because most programs are tuition free and student allowances help pay living costs, many facilities are new and state of the art, the faculties are strong and largely the products of Swedish training, and the level of research is high—often focused on themes, major issues, or problems and engaging groups of junior and senior scholars. This is not to say that there are no problems. Some believe Sweden has overbuilt, that there are too many schools competing, especially because after 2004 the number of potential students began to decline. Others cite falling standards or a glut in various employment markets that have more graduates than places to fill. These problems and criticisms are not, however, unique to Sweden.

Folk High School and Adult Education

Finally, one cannot leave a review of Sweden's education system without including the folk high schools and the extensive adult and continuing education (*folkbildning*) programs of the country. Both are based largely on ideas formulated by the Danish pastor, N. F. S. Grundtvig around the middle of the nineteenth century. He was highly critical of schools in Denmark at the time and once referred to them as "schools for death" where a dead language (Latin) and useless subjects were emphasized. He believed education ought to be "for life," and schools ought to be places where one learned to be a citizen and a constructive member of a democratic society, and acquired skills for a productive life. Teaching ought to be based on sharing ideas, dialogue, and respect for every individual and her or his life experiences. As the Swedes have put it in the following, the underlying philosophy of the folk high schools and adult and continuing education:

> Presumes that all citizens are free and independent individuals, with the right to participate in all aspects of a democratic society. The activities should provide a comprehensive approach, stimulate curiosity and critical thinking; as well as be a part of the crucial process of lifelong learning. [This] creates the conditions necessary for people to freely pursue knowledge and contributes towards giving them the opportunity to change their lives.[17]

The first Danish Folk High School opened in Rødding in 1844, and the first folk high schools were established in Sweden in 1868. Today there are about 150.

They receive support from the state, but unlike the compulsory and upper secondary schools are free of state interference and most state controls. Two thirds of these schools are linked to so-called associations or organizations such as the trade unions, temperance societies, or women's movement groups. Almost all offer programs in general education that parallel the state's curricula, have some kind of focus (such as in the arts, industrial relations, folk traditions, or a particular craft or set of crafts), and are at least partially residential. Nearly 30,000 students are enrolled every year.

Adult education is organized primarily by a group of about 10 national associations that are related to the labor, temperance, and sports movements or to special interests groups like the Census Study Association. They generate literally tens of thousands of programs. Many are simply one-time cultural events. Others, often organized around what are called study circles, might include book clubs or long-term research projects. In 2003, more than 320,000 (!) study circles engaged some 2.5 million people in adult education experiences.

Notes

1. David Popenoe, *Disturbing the Nest. Family Change and Decline in Modern Societies* (New York: Aldine De Gruyter, 1988). (See especially Part II, "The Case of Sweden," pp. 85–258; and "Marriage and Family: What Does the Scandinavian Experience Tell Us" in *2005. The State of Our Unions*, a publication of The National Marriage Project at University of Virginia. See http://www.virginia.edu/marriageproject/annualreports.html and http://www.virginia.edu/marriageproject/. Accessed April 8, 2010.
2. On Parental benefits see Statistics Sweden, *Women and Men in Sweden—Facts and Figures 2008* (Stockholm: Statistics Sweden, 2008) pp. 46–47. This publication is available in pdf format at www.scb.se/List____117051.aspx. Accessed March 30, 2010.
3. On registered partnership laws, see *Lag om registrerat partnerskap* (1994:1117) and *Sambolag* (2003:376). Both are available online in Swedish and English at http://lagen.nu/2003:376. Accessed July 28, 2009. See the Wikipedia article "Same-Sex Marriage in Sweden" and the Web site of *Riksförbundet för homosexuellas, bisexuellas och transperoners rättigheter*/The Swedish Federation for Lesbian, Gay, Bisexual and Transgender Rights. It has a lengthy article on this issue. See http://www.rfsl.se/?p=420. Accessed July 29, 2009 in Swedish. According to a January 2008 public opinion poll, 71 percent of Swedes were in favor of such a law.
4. Richard F. Tomasson, "Modern Sweden: The Declining Importance of Marriage," *Scandinavian Review*, Autumn 1998, pp. 83–89.
5. Statistics Sweden, *Women and Men in Sweden—Facts and Figures 2008*, pp. 8–12.

6. Ibid., pp. 8–11. About Sabuni see http://en.wikipedia.org/wiki/Nyamko_Sabuni. Accessed July 28, 2009.

7. Statistics Sweden, *Women and Men in Sweden—Facts and Figures, 2008*.

8. Ibid., pp. 40–41; and Statistics Sweden 2008 publication, p. 12.

9. See Sweden's 1985 Education Act. Available online at http://www.regeringen.se/sb/d/2034/a/21538. Accessed July 28, 2009.

10. See http://www3.skolverket.se/ki03/front.aspx?sprak=EN&ar=0809&infotyp=15&skolform=11&id=2087&extraId=. Accessed July 28, 2009.

11. See http://www3.skolverket.se/ki03/front.aspx?sprak=EN&ar=0809&infotyp=24&skolform=11&id=3886&extraId=2087 for a full version of this syllabus.

12. For Vittra schools, see http://www.vittra.se/. Accessed July 28, 2009.

13. On Kunskapsskolan, see http://www.kunskapsskolan.se/foretaget/inenglish.4.1d32e45f86b8ae04c7fff213.html. Accessed July 28, 2009.

14. On the free schools in general, see the Web site of the national free school organization, *Friskolornas riksförbund*, at http://www.friskola.se/Om_oss_In_English_DXNI-38495_.aspx. Accessed July 28, 2009.

15. On the colleges and universities, see *Högskolverket*/Swedish National Agency for Higher Education. *Swedish Universities and University Colleges. Short Version of Annual Report 2008* at http://www.hsv.se/download/18.6923699711a25cb275a80002979/0829R.pdf. Accessed July 28, 2009.

16. On students in higher education, see *Högskolverket*/Swedish National Agency for Higher Education. *Swedish Universities and University Colleges. Short Version of Annual Report 2008* at http://www.hsv.se/download/18.6923699711a25cb275a80002979/0829R.pdf. Accessed July 28, 2009.

17. See http://www.folkhogskola.nu/page/150/inenglish/html. Accessed July 28, 2009. On Grundtvig see Max Lawson, "N. F. S. Grundtvig" in *Prospects: The Quarterly Review of Comparative Education* (Paris, UNESCO, International Bureau of Education), XXIII(3/4), 1993, 612–23. Online at http://www.ibe.unesco.org/publications/ThinkersPdf/grundtve.pdf. Accessed July 28, 2009.

4

Holidays, Customs, and Leisure Activities

SWEDEN'S "CALENDAR" of moments to enjoy, events to celebrate, special days, and holidays is a full one. It includes 13 official holidays—days on which most offices and businesses are closed. These are:

New Year's Day/*Nytt år*	January 1
Epiphany/*Trettondedag Jul/ Trettondagen*	January 6
Good Friday/*Långfredagen*	Friday before Easter
Easter/*Påsk*	Varies annually with the calendar
Easter Monday/*Annandag påsk*	Day after Easter
May Day/International Labor Day	May 1
Ascension Day/*Kristi himmelsfärdsdag*	The sixth Thursday after Easter
Whit Sunday/Pentecost/*Pingstdagen*	The seventh Sunday after Easter
National Day/*Nationaldagen*	June 6
All Saints' Day/*Alla helgons dag*	The Saturday that falls between October 13 and November 6
Christmas Day/*Juldagen*	December 25
Day after Christmas/*Annandag Jul/* Boxing Day	December 26

In addition, Midsummer's Eve, Midsummer's Day, Christmas Eve, and New Year's Eve are *de facto* holidays, and Twelfth Night (January 6), Maundy Thursday (*Skärtorsdagen*), Holy Saturday (*Påskafton*), and Walpurgis Night (*Valborgsmässoafton*) (April 30) are often referred to as half-holidays. Other important days in the calendar are Gustav II Adolf's death day (November 6), Charles XII's death day (November 30), and one's "name day." Then there are the celebrations of individuals, such as the much-loved, eighteenth-century poet and troubadour Carl Michael Bellmen (usually in Stockholm in the summer), seasonal events like the crayfish (*kräftskiva*) parties of late July or early August, and Saint Lucia celebrations (December 13), and special milestones in life including confirmation, graduation from high school (*gymnasium*), marriage, and birthdays, especially decade markers like 50 and 70.

Some of these special days, including Walpurgis Night, Midsummer, Halloween, Lucia, and Christmas, have histories that go far back in time and reflect the merger of Christian and pre-Christian practices; others are more recent and have their bases in modern history and especially in the processes of national identity building in the late nineteenth and early twentieth centuries. Each of the above-mentioned special days also has its own particular celebration that includes rituals, songs, dances, foods, drink, costumes, and the like.[1]

Walpurgis Night/*Valborgsmässoafton* is named after Saint Valborg, the daughter of a medieval English king, and has long involved celebrations of the coming of spring and the promise of summer. It is also a day on which university students, decked out in their student caps (caps which are becoming increasingly varied as the number of universities in the country grows), gather to celebrate their success with qualifying exams, contemplate their futures, and engage in a bit of revelry. In what is so typical of many Swedish celebration rituals, there is solemnity and frivolity, the serious and the comedic, and one must know when to do what. Speeches, songs, dancing, toasts, bonfires, and often a good deal of drinking punctuate the day and evening. Overall, the mood is carnivalesque.

The merrymaking continues on into the next day, but May 1 also has a more serious side. It has been the domain of the working class, the trade unions, and the parties of the left since 1888, when representatives of the Second Socialist International declared May 1 to be a day to demonstrate the solidarity of the movement. Sweden's earliest May Day workers' march was in Stockholm in 1890, and it has been celebrated there and elsewhere across Sweden ever since. The day became a national holiday with this focus in 1939, the first not connected with the Church's calendar. Today, it has broader participation than just the workers and followers of leftist political parties, and in recent years has included such disparate groups as members

Students, wearing their black and white student caps, celebrate graduation from an upper secondary school. The caps reflect the development of a custom that dates back to the mid-nineteenth century, was first intended to identify students from particular universities, and is practiced throughout Scandinavia. (Courtesy of Brian Magnusson.)

of the Christian Democrats Party and advocates of open access to intellectual property (music, films, etc.) on the Internet from the Pirate Party/*Piratpartiet*.

Sweden's National Day, June 6, is a relatively recent, consciously created holiday. In 1893, Artur Hazelius, the founder of Sweden's premier ethnographic center, the Nordic Museum, organized special celebrations that were held annually on June 6 in the folk park (*Skansen*) adjacent to the museum. He called this day *Gustafsdagen* (Gustaf's Day), viewed it as a commemoration of one of the most important moments in the national memory, and referred to it as "Sweden's national day." What was the date's significance? First, June 6 was the date on which Gustav Eriksson Vasa was elected king in 1523, an event that made the break with Denmark and the Kalmar Union conclusive. Second, it was the date—intentionally chosen—on which a new constitution was signed in 1809. Third, in 1974 a new constitution that embodied all of the revisions and changes that had taken place over the preceding 166 years was adopted on that date. It was, however, more than a century before the flag waving parades of school children and royal appearances in *Skansen* or the city stadium of Stockholm (*Stadion*) became part of an official holiday. Beginning in 1916, June 6 was called Flag Day (*Svenska flaggans dag*). In 1983, it became the country's national day, as July 4 is America's, and it was declared a legal holiday in 2005.[2]

There is another special date in the Swedish calendar to consider: December 10. This is when the annual Nobel Prizes in chemistry, physics, medicine, literature, and economics are awarded in Stockholm in one of the grandest of ceremonies and celebrations. (The Nobel Peace Prize is awarded in Oslo at the same time.) These events are preceded by the announcement of the winners through the fall months and by a series of lectures by the recipients in the week or so before the ceremonies. The Stockholm Concert Hall (*Konserthus*) is normally the site for the awards ceremonies, City Hall for the gala banquet that follows. Both are very formal occasions, meticulously planned and rehearsed. At the Concert Hall each recipient is given a lengthy introduction in which her/his accomplishments are spelled out. The King actually presents the awards in the form of special diplomas and gold medals. (There is also a monetary prize that goes with these, which in 2008 amounted to 10 million Swedish krona or about US $1.17 million.) Each recipient also gives a brief speech in response.

Alfred Nobel, 1833–96. Nobel was an inventor and entrepreneur. He is known best for his invention of dynamite and other explosives and for the Nobel Prizes in chemistry, physics, physiology or medicine, literature, and peace that he endowed through his will. (Courtesy of Image Bank Sweden.)

Here is a selection from the Irish author Seamus Heaney, winner of the prize in literature in 1995:

> Today's ceremonies and tonight's banquet have been mighty and memorable events. Nobody who has shared in them will ever forget them, but for the laureates these celebrations have had a unique importance. Each of us has participated in a ritual, a rite of passage, a public drama which has been commensurate with the inner experience of winning a Nobel Prize.[3]

SUMMER HOLIDAYS

In a country of long, dark winters and short bright summers, it ought come as no surprise that Midsummer's Eve/Midsummer is a very popular holiday, and many consider it to be Sweden's true national day. Historically set on June 24, it now is celebrated on the Saturday closest to that date and really involves a full weekend of ceremony and fun, preferably in some idyllic rural setting. The roots of this celebration of summer, light, fertility, love, magic, and mystery extend far back into pre-Christian times, and the solstice has been a special time ever since. Typically, the events of the day include dancing, bonfires, singing, eating special foods, and drinking.

Midsummer's most familiar symbol is the Maypole or *majstång*. Although their appearances vary from place to place, Maypoles are typically like a ship's mast with one or two cross-spars from which wreaths may be hung. They are wrapped with green branches, and some include floral elements, colorful ribbons, and the like. After decoration, they are ceremonially erected and dancing takes place around them, typically to traditional local fiddle music. This is a time when folk dance groups perform in costume. The meals that go with Midsummer usually involve an array of pickled herring varieties, dill potatoes in cream sauce, and lots of beer and snapps, that is, *brännvin* (burned wine) or *aquavit* (water of life). The former originated in the late Middle Ages and involved making a fruity liquor from wine. The latter is distilled from a grain or potato mash and is typically flavored by steeping spices such as anise, cumin, coriander, and fennel in it. (Today all these labels are interchangeable and generally refer to some kind of flavored vodka.) Keep in mind that all this occurs on the longest day/shortest night of the year, and time tends to become something of the blur.

Two other moments of summer fun and celebration are in August and center around food. The star of the first is the crayfish. A delicacy long reserved for the nobility, Sweden's native crayfish became increasingly popular in the nineteenth century and were nearly rendered extinct by overcatching. A short season in August now helps ensure their survival. Relatively few

A Maypole with a cluster of would-be dancers in folk costume at Midsummer in southern Sweden. Often decorated with fir branches and elements unique to the place it is raised, the Maypole is an icon of Swedish folk traditions and usually the center for celebrations of the year's longest day. (Photo by Bo Lind. Copyright © Visit Sweden. Courtesy of Image Bank Sweden.)

Swedes actually go out and catch their own any longer, choosing instead to rely on imports from the United States and China. In many ways this meal is the silliest of Swedish culinary customs. Because eating the crayfish is messy, the meal often takes place outside and guests don paper bibs and caps. Paper lanterns are often strung around the table. Hard bread, cheeses, and frequently beer and aquavit are also parts of the meal that can run on for hours into the lingering twilight of the fading summer.

Surströmming/sour fermented herring is the second food-focused event of the summer, one that is especially popular in northern parts of the country.

This Swedish delicacy is extracted from cans bulging from the pressures of the fermentation process and emitting a smell that can floor the stoutest of tasters. It is washed down with plenty of beer or snapps; and diners are often rewarded with special desserts.

All of these summer events say a lot about the Swedes that goes beyond what many might consider quite strange food tastes. What is really important about them is the environment of sociability and the rituals of greeting, eating, toasting, and being together. They are times when the supposedly solitary, introverted Swedes, who allegedly often have trouble making eye-contact when being introduced, become the most gregarious and expressive folk imaginable.

Winter Holidays

December is a month of many special events, beginning with the lighting of the first Advent candle on the traditional four-candle holder, then moving on to private and public Saint Lucia celebrations, and culminating in an extended Christmas (*Jul*). Although the Christian elements remain important in Sweden, so too are those that arise from the pagan past. December is the darkest month, and the longest night of the year falls just before Christmas. The winter solstice has long been an important event, both for its darkness and for the turning point, the return of the sun, that it defines. Light is a vital aspect of this time of year, and this is illustrated by the Advent candles, the candles carried by children in Lucia processions, the candles in the wreath every Lucia wears, and the candles in windows and on trees.

The adoption of Lucia, a fourth-century Christian martyr from Sicily, by much of northern Europe may seem strange, but in many ways it fits perfectly with the moment that is being celebrated. Her name means "light," and according to legend she was still able to see even after she was blinded by her captors before being put to death. (Not surprisingly, she is the patron saint of the blind.) St. Lucia's day was December 13, the same day as the winter solstice under the Julian calendar, and was widely recognized and celebrated. After the adoption of the Gregorian calendar in Sweden in 1753, Lucia's day remained December 13 rather than being advanced to December 23. Although the solstice connection continued, it also came to commemorate the beginning of the Christmas month in some areas. Reinforcing her importance are folk tales from several Swedish provinces and from Norway about her generosity and the help she would give to those in need. The origins of today's forms of celebration are usually traced back to the second half of the eighteenth century and were first centered in the western provinces of Västergötland, Dalsland, Bohuslän, and Värmland.

Lucia Celebration. Traditionally held on December 13 across all of Sweden, this scene typifies these events. Pageantry and music blend in what are often beautiful and deeply moving moments. (Photo by Johnny Franzén. Courtesy of Image Bank Sweden.)

The day may be celebrated at home or in a church or community setting in what is called a Lucia Morning (*Luciamorgon*). In homes, young girls play special roles as Lucia and her attendants. White robes, candles, and a special wreath with candles for the Lucia, and white robes and tall conical hats decorated with stars for the boys (*stjärngossar*) are essential costume elements. The actors proceed around the house, wake a sleeping father, sing one of the songs every Swede knows, "*Natten går tunga fjät*," and breakfast on *lussekatter* (Lucia cats/saffron buns).

Natten går tunga fjät	Night walks with heavy step
runt gård och stuva:	Round farmyard and hearth
kring jord som soln förlät	As the sun sets around the earth

skuggorna ruva.	The shadows lurk
Då i vårt mörka hus,	While in our darkened home
stiger med tända ljus,	Standing with candles lit
Sankta Lucia, Sankta Lucia	Santa Lucia, Santa Lucia
Natten går stor och stum.	The night passes great and silent.
Nu hör det svingar	Listen to the rustling
I alla tysta rum	In all the silent rooms
sus som av vingar.	Like the sound of wings
Se på vår tröskel star	See standing in our doorway
vitklädd med ljus i hår	Dressed in white, with candled hair
Sankta Lucia, Sankta Lucia	Santa Lucia, Santa Lucia
Mörkret skall flykta snart	The darkness will quickly leave
ur jordens dalar	The earth's valleys
Så hon ett underbart	As she a wondrous
ord till oss talar.	Message to us delivers
Dagen skall åter ny	Day will be renewed
stiga ur rosig sky	Rising from a rose-colored sky
Sankta Lucia, Sankta Lucia	Santa Lucia, Santa Lucia.[4]

Church commemorations involve a procession, arrival at the church in the dark of early morning, costumed children and a white-clad Lucia, the singing of a familiar litany of songs, and a breakfast smörgåsbord. Yes, with those *lussekatter.*[5] Community celebrations echo many of these elements, but often with the added element of a Lucia contest. The first of these appears to have been organized in the late 1920s in Stockholm by one of the city's newspapers, *Stockholms Dagbladet.* Many lament this development, seeing it as a crass commercialization of a beloved folk tradition.

In a sense, Christmas (*Jul*) is the season that reaches from Lucia's Day to January 6, but it is more generally considered to be the days between Christmas Eve and January 6. The most important days of the season are Christmas Eve, Christmas Day, and Boxing Day, the day after Christmas. Preparations begin before the holiday season, especially decorating and cooking. Several decorations are essential, including straw ornaments in the shape of hearts, stars, birds, and angels, and a straw goat (*julbock*). Straw has many connections with the agrarian roots of most "old" Swedes because it was used in a variety of ways in the peasant culture and was an element in Biblical accounts of the birth of Jesus. The goat may actually go back to the pagan god, Thor, whose chariot was pulled by a pair of goats. Christmas trees became part of the tradition in the nineteenth century and are often only sparingly decorated. Everything in moderation. Cooking has meant preparing cookies, rolls and the like.

Foods are important to many Swedish celebrations. Here, in a setting brightly lit by candles, we see a variety of cookies, Lussekatter, and cups for coffee set out for guests on December 13, Lucia Day. (Photo courtesy of Brian Magnusson.)

The Christmas Eve meal itself is usually based on ham or, for many, *lutfisk*. *Lutfisk* is another of those culinary oddities that many would find disgusting. It starts with sun-dried cod the consistency of shoe leather. Through a series of soakings, including one in a lye solution, the fish is restored to an edible state. Cooking involves either boiling or baking. It is generally served with boiled potatoes and one kind of condiment or another (melted butter, mustard, pepper, or ginger) depending on where in Sweden you are. Done properly, it is quite tasty, once one gets past the appearance and the odor. Here again, it is probably a very ancient peasant dish, and there are others that come out at Christmas such as potato sausage (*potatiskorv*), fried blood pudding (*palt*), and rice porridge (*risgrynsgröt*).[6] In the past, all of these were made on the farm. Today they are generally purchased at the local market. The Christmas beverage of preference is *glögg*. The alcohol version is made by heating red wine spiced with cloves, cinnamon, and ginger, fortifying it with a bit of vodka, and then adding almonds and raisins. Similar ingredients go into an alcohol-free version.

One of the more delightful aspects of Christmas Eve is a family dance that begins with family members joining hands and circling the tree, and then passing through much of the house or apartment, all the while probably singing *Nu ar det Jul igen* (Now It Is Christmas Again):

Nu är jul igen	Now it's Yule again
och nu är jul igen,	And now it's Yule again
och julen vara skall till påska	and Yule lasts until it's Easter
Det var inte sant	That's not true
och det var inte sant	Oh, that's not true
För däremellan kommer fasta.	'Cause in between comes fasting.

Gifts are also a part of the celebrations, and the Swedes have theirs delivered by the Christmas Elf or *Jultomte*, a figure that developed in the late nineteenth century out of much older traditions. In some depictions, he looks much like a miniature version of the North American Santa—bearded, white-haired, dressed in red and white, but he is considerably thinner and does not ride around in a sleigh. Instead, he is apparently an ongoing resident of the home or farm that must be well treated. Supposedly, he appears at the dwelling door bearing gifts and must be rewarded with some kind of tasty goodies lest one wants to incur his mischievous wrath in the coming year.

One particularly curious aspect of Swedish Christmas celebrations is the inclusion of an hour of television that seems wholly out of context in this tradition-loaded event. At 3 PM on Christmas Eve, literally millions of Swedes stop what they are doing to tune in to "*Kalle Anka och hans vänner önskar God Jul*"/Donald Duck and His Friends Wish You a Merry Christmas, a program of Disney cartoons that was first aired in 1960. Since then it has been one of the most-watched programs on Swedish Television. Nearly 3.5 million viewers tuned in in 2007! What does this popularity mean? That television has a pervasive influence on culture? That the Disney corporation is a very effective marketer of its products? That Sweden, too, is vulnerable to the Americanization? All of these and more?

In the Church's traditions, the Christmas season extends until January 6 or *Trettondedag Jul*. For some the season ends a week later with the twentieth Day of Christmas (*Tjugondedag Jul* or *Tjugondag Knut*), when children "plunder" any remaining goodies from the tree, and it is taken (in some instances "danced") out of the house. The roots of this extended season may lie in what was called the Christmas peace (*julfreden* or *julefrid*), the origins of which are medieval and involved the legal stipulation that crimes committed during the period of Christmas carried extra punishments.

Winter traditions include relatively subdued New Year's celebrations, Fasching parties, eating *semlor* or *fettisdagsbulle*/Fat Tuesday Buns (a Swedish pastry that according to legend contributed to the death of the country's king,

Adolf Fredrik on that day in 1771) on the day before Ash Wednesday, fasting during Lent, trips to sunnier climes, preparing their tax returns, longing for Spring, and Easter. The last is less involving than the Christmas season. Although this has not always been the case, Easter's relative unimportance today may be evidence of the growing secularism. There are, of course, church services at which attendance is better than usual, and some old customs including the decorating of eggs and having children dress up as witches and go knocking on doors for treats much like on Halloween. Among all of these dark season moments, the spring equinox may be as important as any, as it signals the return to summer, and it is always interesting to see the transformations that occur as the weather improves and the sun rises further in the sky each day. For example, one can observe people intentional crossing a street to be in the sun, and park benches in sunny spots are prime targets for pale people clearly needing to increase their levels of vitamin D.

Food and Holidays

As ought be clear from the number of examples mentioned above, foods play important parts in many Swedish celebrations. But they are also important on a more day-to-today basis. Like people everywhere, Swedes like to eat and have some virtually iconic favorites. These include the ubiquitous meatballs (often spiced with nutmeg), boiled potatoes (with dill), lingonberries, cloudberries, strawberries (preferably served with heavy cream), open-faced sandwiches, cheeses, a seemingly endless variety of herring, *gravad* lax/dill-cured salmon, Janssons *frestelse*/Jansson's temptation (a kind of scalloped potatoes with anchovies), *korv*/hotdogs sold by street venders and at kiosks across the country, and a wonderful array of desserts and pastries (often taken with coffee at a *konditori*/pastry shop). Outsiders seem to think that Swedish cuisine is limited and unimaginative, but they are wrong. Contemporary Swedish chefs have become increasingly creative. Consider, for example, Marcus Samuelson. Ethiopian-born, he was raised in Sweden, where he received his training at the Culinary Institute in Göteborg. Although he lives mainly in New York, where he is the chef at Aquavit, he returns to Sweden often and his reputation is international. One commentator has written the following about his cooking:

> Never one to rest on his laurels, Samuelsson continually revolutionizes Aquavit's menu, crafting innovative interpretations of classic Scandinavian cuisine that marry the traditional with the contemporary. His menu offers dishes that embody, complement, and revitalize the foundations and building blocks of Swedish cuisine. Focusing on texture and aesthetics, Samuelsson incorporates

the traditional seafood, game, and pickling and preserving techniques that have been adored and savored for years by Scandinavians.[7]

Then there is the success of Tina Nordström, the perky chef of Swedish Television fame whose program "New Scandinavian Cooking" is featured in the United States on a number of public television stations. To some degree the dynamics in Sweden's cuisine can be attributed to creative personalities, but they are also the result of globalization and the presence of the new Swedes. In general, today's standard fare might include its typical dose of meatballs and boiled potatoes or creative new recipes involving fish, but it will also include pizza, kabobs, tacos, and hamburgers.

Having written all of the above, some words of caution are needed as well. Special events, holidays, and festivities are, inherently, human creations. So, too, are the ways in which these moments are remembered or celebrated. Odd, artificial, curious mixtures of elements of the local turned into national or the private made public, consciously fabricated and commercialized are just some of the ways to describe both events and practices. As Swedish journalist Johan Tell and others have noted, for example, Midsummer is a blend of pre-Christian summer solstice celebrations, a decorated pole with its origins in Germany, foods that are not uniquely Swedish, and music with a widely varied roots.

Leisure Activities

Swedes are active people, be it in the pursuit of unorganized recreational exercise, working around the home or a country retreat, keeping up their toys, or taking part in some organized sporting group. Among their favorite athletic activities are jogging, hiking, cycling, cross-country and downhill skiing, swimming, sailing, fishing, golfing, tennis, and orienteering. Popular team sports include soccer (*fotboll*), hockey, and bandy. Of course, much of the participation in many of these is personal and private. However, Sweden has literally thousands of sports organizations, and there are professional leagues in several of the team sports. The largest number are locally focused and sport-specific, but each major sport has its own national organization. There is also the national umbrella group, The National Sports Union or *Riksidrottsförbundet*, in which 68 sports are represented.[8]

In many ways, the development of organized sporting activities is part of the history of the popular movements of the nineteenth century, which included the growth of national (and international) labor, the free churches, temperance, literacy and reading, women's rights, mass politics, and folk culture groups. Gymnastics stood at the center of the earliest organizational efforts, and a national association was founded in 1875. At that time the label covered many other activities such as hiking, rowing, and swimming.

Soccer is usually listed as Sweden's most popular sport. It was introduced from England in the late nineteenth century, and a national organization was established in 1904. Its popularity grew relatively slowly for several decades, but today the country has about 3,000 teams and as many as half a million Swedes are active players. There are organized programs for youth development and several divisions of organized team competition, the highest of which is the *allsvenskan* level for men and the *damallsvenskan* for women.

A professional men's league of elite players was founded in 1924 and currently has 16 teams, and the elite women's league that emerged between 1978 and 1988 has 12 teams. In each league the competition leads to a national championship. In 2008, the men's title was held by IFK Göteborg, the women's by Umeå IK. Sweden also competes in the European, world, and Olympic soccer competitions and has medaled in them all, with an Olympic gold in 1948, a silver in the World Cup in 1958 (held in Sweden), and a bronze in the 1994 World Cup competition, held in the United States.

Hockey is number two in popularity. Its numbers, organization, and history are very similar to those for soccer. Men's hockey became increasingly organized in the 1920s, following the founding of the Swedish Ice Hockey Association (*Svensk Ishockeyförbundet*). Today, men's upper level professional team competition is organized into three categories, Elite (12 teams), *Allsvenskan* (16 teams), and Juniors. Women's hockey began to emerge as an organized sport in the late 1960s. Although it has not grown as much as men's, it has become both popular and successful. Swedish men's teams have competed in the Olympics since 1920, and the national team, called *Tre Kronor*, won the gold at Winter Olympics and the international championship in 2006. The Swedish women's team took the silver in the 2006. An extensive youth program that starts players at a very early age involves thousands and produces elite players. Not surprisingly, the Swedish media avidly follow the careers of the many successful Swedish players in the NHL.

The third most popular sport is bandy. Introduced in the late nineteenth century, it is a game played on an ice sheet the size of a soccer field by teams of 11 skaters. The object is to score by putting an orange ball the size of a tennis ball into a goal using curved sticks. In the early decades of the twentieth century it was a sport of students and the middle class played by both men and women. The working class became more involved in the years leading up to World War II. As with soccer and ice hockey, there are several levels of league play, culminating in the elite *Allsvenskan* level. Internationally, Sweden has won seven men's world championships, most recently in 2009.

A world championship competition was introduced for women in 2004, and Sweden's women have won all these through 2008.[9]

A brief look at a very new sport, floorball or *innebandy*, also provides a window into Swedish athletic life. This game was actually invented in Sweden in the late 1970s by a group of young men in Göteborg. Much like ice hockey in terms of rules, but without the checking, it is played indoors by teams of six per side on a 40 m × 20 m surface enclosed by boards. In recent years its popularity has exploded. It is estimated that about half a million Swedes are involved at various levels, and there are more than 1,200 team organizations spread across the country in both male and female leagues. The sport has been taken up by some 30 other countries, Sweden holds the world championship title for both men and women, and promoters hope the game will become an Olympic sport in the next decade or so.

A sidebar to all of these sports is that a kind of culture goes along with each of them. Participants at all levels become members of a kind of fraternity. Engagement in youth programs means more than just having a child on a team. Parents are deeply involved, and the time commitments are enormous. In-season there are practices, games, and traveling. Off-season there are special camps, and there are secondary schools with sports emphases.

Watching sports involves more people than actually playing them, and Sweden is no exception in having a large and enthusiastic spectator culture that involves adoration of some of the leading players, team loyalty that sometimes borders on the extreme, and all of the clothing and paraphernalia that goes along with team-fan identity. All of the major sports have their arenas—outdoor for soccer and some bandy, and enclosed for hockey, bandy, and floorball. Some of the outdoor stadiums are quite exceptional. Stockholm's *Stadion*, which dates from the 1912 Olympic Games, is widely used for everything from soccer and bandy matches to track and field events, and, of course, concerts. Its capacity varies depending on the venue. The largest sport spectator crowd assembled there was for a 1959 bandy match—nearly 30,000. Ullevi Stadium in Göteborg, completed in 1958 for the World Cup soccer competition that year, is the largest in Sweden, with a seating capacity of 43,000. (Upwards of 60,000 can be accommodated for concerts.) It is home to the IKF Göteborg soccer team, the site of European and world championship competitions in track and soccer, and even the location for an American National Football League exhibition game in 1988 between the Chicago Bears and the Minnesota Vikings, which drew a crowd of just over 33,000. (The Vikings won 28–21.) An interesting feature of the stadium is the array of solar panels on part of its "roof," which, it is claimed, generates enough electricity to power the facility's artificial lighting system. A third large facility is Malmö Stadium, also completed in 1958. It is home to

Malmö FF soccer team and has a capacity of 26,500. The Globe (*Globen*) in Stockholm is an interesting and controversial venue. By some accounts it is the largest spherical structure in the world at 110 meters/361 feet in diameter. Fully enclosed, it is an obstruction-free facility that holds between 14,000 and 16,000 people. It is home to AIK and Djurgårdens IF hockey teams and the focal point of a large shopping and leisure area in south Stockholm on the island of Södermalm.

Other Leisure Activities

What else do Swedes do to combat the midwinter blahs or take advantage of the nearly endless days of summer? Given what has already been said in this chapter and elsewhere in this book, it ought be clear that many are inclined to shop, read, study, seek out a religious experience in nature, pursue additional education opportunities, or attend meetings of the multiple organizations to which many Swedes belong (labor unions, study groups, political parties, craft associations, etc.). They are also interested in film, theater, dance, and music (which are discussed later).

Then there are vacations. Almost every employed Swede is entitled to five weeks of paid vacation every year, in addition to the 12 official holidays mentioned earlier. Usually, several of these weeks are taken in succession. July has long been the traditional month for vacations, but June, August, February, and March are also popular. (Be very careful what you plan to do in Sweden, because if you go in July you could find some businesses and other venues closed! And do not expect letters to be answered or calls returned then either.) Until relatively recently, most Swedes tended to stay in-country for much of their vacation time, with favorite destinations being cabins (*stugor* often painted Falun red with white trim) in the woods or mountains, on lake shores, or on an island in one of the coastal archipelagos. Camping or caravan vacations were also popular. As noted earlier, boating is very popular, and the number of motorboats and sailboats in Sweden is very high. The archipelagoes provide particularly nice areas in which to sail, with protection from the open seas and ample harbor opportunities. The Swedes' interest in sailing also includes regular and successful competition. In the Olympics Swedes have won 9 gold, 12 silver, and 12 bronze medals over the years. In 2004–5, Volvo took over organization and sponsorship of the extremely challenging Whitbread Around the World Race for single-design (VO70). Eight boats were in the 2008–9 competition, won by *Ericsson 3*, which was skippered by a Swede with a mainly Nordic crew.[10]

Relatively inexpensive international air travel and ocean cruises have changed the nature of vacations, especially among younger people. Package tours to warmer climes have become particularly popular, with destinations including Spain, Portugal, the islands of the eastern Atlantic, and southeast Asia, especially Thailand. This new global tourism is making the Swedes far more international in experience and outlook, but it has had its downside as well. One is that travel has its risks, as illustrated by two tragedies that struck Sweden particularly hard. In September 1994, the ferry *Estonia* sank in the Baltic on a crossing from Tallinn to Stockholm. Of the 852 people who died, 501 were Swedes. Ten years later came the loss of at least 540 Swedish tourists, mainly in Thailand, from the December 26, 2004 tsunami that swept the coastal regions of the nations bordering on the Indian Ocean. Although this number paled in comparison to the total losses from this tragedy (estimated to have been more than 200,000), Swedes were stunned.

New Swedes

What about the new Swedes? Where do they fit in all this? For that one fifth of the population that is foreign born or the children of foreign-born parents, much of this makes little sense. It is not what they identify as their cultural heritage or behavioral norms and may be what they either seek to adopt or protect themselves from depending what generation of immigrant they are. Sweden's national holidays, Falun red cottages in the forest, fermented herring, *lussekatter*, and the like may mean many different things to them. Also, many find themselves in relatively low paying jobs and, although eligible for the standard vacation time, do not have the resources to spend on trips or rental cabins or strange foods, some of which may violate their own religious practices. Also, many of the new Swedes have their own special days based on their religion or national/ethnic origins. For practicing Muslims, for example, all of the special days associated with the Christian calendar have little importance, and their religious holidays are linked to a lunar calendar, not the West's Gregorian. Ramadan, Id al-Fitr (the day after Ramadan), and Ashura are among the most important, and so too is meat butchered according to halal standards.[11] One interesting aspect of these differences is that some of the new Swedes would prefer to work on holidays that are outside their own cultures. How ought one deal with that issue in a society that prides itself on being so democratic?

The current differences aside, it is probably safe to predict that some of the customs of the new Swedes will disappear with time, others will be transformed, and some will survive for generations. The diversity of American ethnic customs is likely to be repeated in Sweden. Swedish customs will continue, perhaps with some accommodating changes, while some—by no means all—of the ethnic or hyphenated Swedes will hold on to aspects of their homelands in what will likely be a dizzying and fascinating variety.

NOTES

1. Lorna Downman, Paul Britten Austin, and Anthony Baird have described most of these in a marvelous little book from the mid-1960s, *Round the Swedish Year.* Per-Öyvind Swahn's studies are longer and more detailed. The Nordic Museum's virtual museum Web site has a section that deals with all of Sweden's special days. (In Swedish.) See http://www.nordiskamuseet.se/Publication.asp?publicationid=11701&cat=148&topmenu=148. Accessed July 30, 2009.

2. See http://www.sweden.se/eng/Home/Lifestyle/Traditions/Reading/Swedish-national-day-takes-shape/. Accessed April 14, 2010.

3. At http://nobelprize.org/nobel_prizes/literature/laureates/1995/heaney-speech.html. The Nobel Foundation's Web site is excellent and includes information on ceremonies, winners, the history of the prizes, etc. in English. See http://nobelprize.org/index.html. Accessed July 30, 2009.

4. Translated by the author. The tune for *"Natten går tunga fjat"* is based on a Neapolitan folk song, although one source claims the tune was written by a Swedish poet, Gunnar Wennergren, while visiting Sicily. In Italian it has very different lyrics and is familiar as "Santa Lucia." The Swedish lyrics were written by Arvid Rosén in 1928.

5. *Lussekatter* recipe

1/3 cup milk
1/4 cup butter or margarine
1/4 cup warm water
1 package yeast
1/4 cup sugar
1 egg
1/2 teaspoon salt
1/4 teaspoon saffron
2 3/4 cups flour
vegetable oil
1 egg
1 tablespoon water
raisins

Put the milk and butter or margarine in a small saucepan. Heat until the butter or margarine melts. Mix the warm water and yeast in a large bowl. Add the warm milk and butter or margarine mixture. Add the egg, sugar, salt, and saffron. Add 1 1/2 cups of flour. Mix well. Add more flour gradually until the dough is stiff. Knead the dough on a floured surface for 5 to 10 minutes. Coat the bowl with cooking oil and put in your dough ball. Cover with a towel and let the dough rise until it is doubled in size. Punch down the dough and divide it into 12 sections. Roll each section into a rope. Cross two ropes in the middle and curl the ends into circles. Carefully place the buns on a greased cookie sheet, cover, and let rise until they are doubled in size. Mix and egg and water and brush the tops of the buns. Decorate with raisins. bake at 350°F for 15 to 20 minutes or until golden brown. At http://www.cookingcache.com/dessert/lussekatterstluciabuns.shtml?rdid=rc1.

6. *Risgrynsgröt*/Christmas Rice Pudding recipe

1 cup of rice

2 tbsp butter

1 cup water

1/2 tsp salt

4 cups milk cup whipping cream

1 whole almond

Bring water, butter, and salt to a boil, add rice, and cook until the water is absorbed. Add milk and cook on low (or in a double boiler) until milk is absorbed. Remove from heat, stir in the cream, and add the almond. Serve with cinnamon and sugar.Note that according to tradition the person who finds the almond in her or his bowl will be married within the year, assuming, of course, that she or he is not already married.

7. See http://www.starchefs.com/chefs/MSamuelsson/html/bio.shtml. Accessed July 23, 2009.

8. *Riksidrottsförbundet*/The National Athletic League is an excellent source for information. See http://www.rf.se/. Accessed July 29, 2009.

9. See http://www.bandycup.se/vm_dam_2008/. Accessed July 30, 2009.

10. See http://www.volvooceanrace.org/. Accessed July 29, 2009.

11. Ashura is a Sunni holy day, tenth of Muharram in the Islamic calendar. It moves around in the Western calendar. There was a procession in Stockholm in January 2008.

5

Media

THE MEDIA in Sweden (newspapers, magazines, radio, television, and the Internet) have histories of varying lengths and importance. Naturally, print media monopolized this aspect of Swedish life until the advent of the radio in the third decade of the twentieth century. Television effected its own media revolution beginning in the 1950s; and today Sweden, along with the rest of the world, is in the midst of new revolution centered on the Internet and wireless communication devices.

NEWSPAPERS

Printed media, which encompasses newspapers, broadsheets, pamphlets, and magazines, have their origins in the introduction of printing in the early 1500s. By most accounts, Sweden's first newspaper was *Ordinarii Post Tijdender*/ The Ordinary Post Times, a government-sponsored source of national and international news printed in Stockholm and circulated in very small numbers via a developing national postal system beginning in 1645. This publication later took the name *Post- och Inrikes Tidningar*/Post and Internal Times (or The Gazette), and ownership was turned over to the Swedish Academy in 1791. Publishing rights were transferred to *Bolagsverket*/the Swedish Companies' Registration Office in 2007. Called the oldest newspaper in the world, it is now "published" only on the Internet, a sure sign of the times. In its present form it is describes as:

> *The Post- och Inrikes Tidningar (PoIT)* is an official state agency on the Internet. In *PoIT* government authorities and others publish information that is, according to law, to be brought to the public's attention.[1]

The development of a press free of governmental control began in the second half of the eighteenth century, during a special period in Swedish history called the Era of Liberty (1719–72), a time when royal power was low and the power of the parliament (*Riksdag*) high. During the final two decades of this period, a particularly lively political culture developed that included two rival political "parties" called the Hats and Caps, heated election campaigns, and intense political conversations in the press and the taverns and coffee houses of Stockholm, especially. A Freedom of the Press law, enacted in 1766, contributed to these developments, and a number of papers were published, mainly in the capital, that were important voices in the debates of the time. Among these papers were *En ärlig svensk*/An Honest Swede, founded in 1755, *Dagligt Allehanda*/Daily General News, founded in 1767, and the provincial paper *Norrköpings Weko-Tidningar*/Norrköpings Weekly Times from 1758. The circulation of papers like these was small, largely because of cost, but their readerships were probably larger because they tended to "circulate" in public settings such as coffee houses and taverns. Sadly, many of the freedoms of this period and the political trends that defined it were ended by a royal coup in 1772, and nearly 40 years went by before writers and publishers were at least partially free to express their opinions openly.

The newspapers of the early nineteenth century, although colored by the political debates of the period, were often linked to an individual. Such was the case with what is frequently mentioned as Sweden's first truly modern newspaper, *Aftonbladet.* It was founded in 1830 by Lars Johan Hierta, an outspoken Liberal. (Interestingly, he was often too outspoken, and the paper was shut down by the government a number of times.) This was by no means a mass circulation publication, however. Large-volume papers only developed slowly over the course of the later nineteenth century, driven by entrepreneurial zeal, the growth of an educated public, urbanization, political reforms, and technological developments like the rotary press and cheap newsprint. Milestones here were the founding of *Dagens Nyheter*/The Daily News (1864), *Svenska Dagbladet*/The Swedish Daily (1884), and *Stockholms-Tidningen*/The Stockholm Times (1889). Each was a Stockholm-based morning daily that featured an expanded variety of contents and was less expensive than older papers. The circulation of the last of these was around

100,000 in the 1890s (in a city of about 250,000), which reflected how newspapers had become affordable and appealing to a mass readership.

During the early twentieth century, the number of newspapers blossomed in Sweden, eventually reaching more than 200, and this prosperity continued until about 1950. Major cities like Stockholm and Göteborg might have half a dozen or more major newspapers, and most small cities and towns could boast at least one. It was during this period that Swedes became avid and habitual readers of newspapers. Many subscribed to or purchased both a morning and an evening paper. In part, this expansion and the development of a loyal reading public was driven by the multiparty political system that emerged in the early years of the century. Many papers expressed clear political biases, and some were owned by a particular political party or popular organization. These organizations encouraged reading, and their leaders believed the press was an essential medium for shaping the society's political views. In terms of political opinion, for example, *Dagens Nyheter* was Liberal, *Stockholms-Tidningen* and *Aftonbladet* were Social Democratic, *Svenska Dagbladet* was Conservative, *Göteborgs Handels- och Sjöfartstidning* was Liberal, *Ny Dag* was Communist, and *Skånska Dagbladet* was Agrarian. As the list below indicates, some of this party press remains today.

The peak for the number of daily papers was reached around 1950, and for weeklies in the mid-1980s. A decline in the number of newspapers set in after World War II. Believing that democratic policies in education, knowledge, citizen participation, and a well-informed society are essential to a functioning democracy, the ruling Social Democrats instituted a number of measures, beginning in the early 1970s and mainly in the form of subsidies, grants, and tax breaks designed to stave off this process. These helped the smaller circulation local papers primarily. Interestingly, while the number of newspapers fell, readership grew. In part this was because of a growing population that largely carried on older cultural habits, but it can also be attributed to a new kind of newspaper, the tabloid. For example, *Expressen*, published by the same company as *Dagens Nyheter*, first appeared in 1944. It adopted the new format that was easier to handle, contained expanded coverage of sports and entertainment, was intentionally aimed at a younger audience, included more visual material, was distributed nationally, and was readily available at kiosks and shops. Many other companies followed suit, and today most printed papers are tabloids or compact format. Another trend that began in this period was the concentration of ownership of Sweden's newspapers and other media. Among the most successful participants are Bonnier AB, Schibsted (a Norwegian company), The Stenbeck Group including Modern Times Group/MTG, Egmont, Allerts, KF Media (the Cooperate Association's media branch), and Stampen AB.[2]

Metro, the leading "free" paper in Sweden. This daily has been published since 1995 and began a print newspaper revolution in Sweden that has spread to much of the world. (Courtesy of Metro Nordic Sweden AB.)

In the mid-1990s a global revolution affecting virtually all media forms began, and it continues today. For newspapers, this involved content and format options, distribution choices, the Internet, and even a choice of what technology to use to read-watch-listen to a newspaper. Illustrating the print side was the introduction of a new generation of free newspapers, or *gratistidningar*. The leading example of this was *Metro*, the first issue of which appeared in February 1995. Retaining the tabloid format, this newspaper was distributed via the Stockholm subway system and was designed to be read in the time it took to commute to work. It embodied the concept of news (local, national, international, sports, and entertainment) delivered in brief, readable, appealing form. Articles were short, analysis was minimal. There was no op-ed section and, as one student of the paper has written, no effort was made to form an emotional attachment with the reader.[3] The infrastructure of the paper was kept to a minimum. The staff of professional journalists was comparatively small. Much of the news was taken directly from *Tidningarnas Telegrambyrån/TT*, Sweden's main press bureau. Printing was contracted out. Essential to the profitability of the paper was advertising, which had to pay all of the costs. The success of *Metro* was quite phenomenal. Readership climbed to more than a quarter of million. Parallel papers were established in Göteborg and the Malmö region, and, subsequently, *Metro* went international. In early 2008, the paper's parent company, Metro International SA, rightly called *Metro* the "world's largest international newspaper." Specifically tailored national/local versions were being published in 19 countries and daily readership was around 17 million in early 2010.

When other major owner ownership groups including the Bonnier group (*Dagens Nyheter*) and Shipsted (*Aftonbladet*) tried to imitate *Metro*, a competition ensued that has been called "the gratis war" (*gratiskriget*). Millions of dollars were spent, and the losses these companies incurred were huge. Ultimately, most either dropped the effort or cut print runs and adjusted their free papers to fit particular niches.

One thing that did not happen as a result of the coming of the free paper(s) was the demise of established newspapers. Although a few have gone out of print in recent years and there is a slow decline in the readership for all printed papers, the picture generally remains positive for this media option. According to the Swedish Newspapers Publishers Association (*Tidningsutgivarna*), there were 165 daily newspapers in Sweden in 2008. Among the largest were:

Aftonbladet	Stockholm	388,500	Independent/Social Democrat
Dagens Nyheter	Stockholm	339,700	Independent/Liberal
Expressen/GT/Kvällsposten	Stockholm	303,100	Independent
Stockholm City	Stockholm	255,300	Independent
Metro	Stockholm	271,000	Independent
Svenska Dagbladet	Stockholm	196,000	Moderate
Göteborgs Posten	Göteborg	245,000	Liberal
Sydsvenskan	Malmö	121,900	Independent/Liberal
Helsingborgs Dagblad/ NST/Landskrona-Posten	Helsingborg	78,800	Nonpolitical
Lokaltidningen Mitt i Södermalm	Stockholm	70,700	Nonpolitical
Nerikes Allehanda	Örebro	65,300	Liberal
Nacka Värmdö Posten	Nacka	64,900	Nonpolitical
Kvällsposten	Malmö	55,800	Liberal
Uppsala Nya Tidning	Uppsala	55,500	Liberal
GT	Göteborg	53,300	Independent/Liberal[4]

Most of these follow a fairly standard format with sections devoted to international, national, and local news, sports, culture, the arts, travel, op ed, and the like.

The Internet and the technologies that have accompanied it form the second major area in which the Swedish (and global) press is being revolutionized. Almost all of Sweden's newspapers maintain open and free Web site versions. These provide up-to-the-minute coverage of the news and are organized in the same section structure as their print editions. They are well illustrated, carry a modest amount of advertising, and offer all of the latest digital options including extensive searchability of past issues, a range of audio and video choices that include interviews, and blogging opportunities of much debated quality. In many ways, Sweden's newspapers have become truly multimedia. In addition, steps are being taken toward developing e-papers to be read on a digital device.

The Internet press is not limited to just Swedish-language sites. It is a perfect medium for many of the new Swedes. *Al Muhajer News*, for example, is a Swedish and Arabic language news source based in Malmö. For English language readers there is *The Local*, an online daily.[5]

In the context of these developments, readership has remained strong, and printed newspapers are still preferred overall. Nearly 4 million newspaper copies are printed every day—making Sweden fourth in the world in terms of number of newspaper copies relative to population. More than 80 percent of Swedes between 15 and 79 years of age read (at least part of) a paper every day. On the other hand, a study from 2008 about reader use of newspaper Internet sites revealed a trend that does not bode well for the printed news format. Three fourths of 16- to 24-year-olds and nearly that fraction of 25- to 34- and 35- to 44-year-olds primarily read Internet newspaper versions. It was not until the age of readers reached 64 or older that a majority used print versions. Overall, 59 percent of Swedish-born, 61 percent of European-born, 56 percent of those born outside of Europe, and more men than women regularly used Internet newspapers.[6]

PERIODICALS

A related print medium is the *tidskrift* or magazine/periodical. The roots of these extend back into the nineteenth century, and today the number and variety are extensive. One catalogue lists more than 400—most of which are in Swedish and not imports. Some of the categories into which these are grouped include Antiques, Architecture and Design, Art, Automotive, Beauty, Boating, Business, Children and Young People, Construction, Fashion, Games, Health and Beauty, Knowledge, Leisure, Minorities, Nature, News, Photography, Sports, and Travel. The leading publisher is the Bonnier Group, which produces more than 50 periodicals including (for women) *Amelia, Damernas värld, M Magasin*, and *mama;* (for men) *DV Man* and *Teknikens värld;* (about the home, food, and gardening) *Allt i hemmet, Allt om mat, Allt om resor*; (for children) *Kamratposten/KP*—established in 1873 and Sweden's oldest magazine for children; (about business and the economy) *Privat affärer* and *Veckans affärer*; (about crime) *Misstänkt*/Suspect.

In addition, there are periodicals about minorities and ethnicity (I&M/ *Invandrare och minoriteter*); literature and the Swedish language (*Språktidning*—until 2004, *Bonniers litterära magasin*—or *00tal*); history (*Populär historia* and *Allt om historia*); sports (*Golfbladet, Stopper Fotbolsmagasin*, and *Bilsport*); journals that span the academic disciplines and professions; and for children of various ages (*Kalla Anka Kamratposten*, and *Glitter*). Among the best selling periodicals in Sweden are *Bilsport, Sköna hem, Populär astronomi, Sveriges natur, Hemmets journal, Året runt, Bra korsord, Allt I hemmet*, and *Leva.*[7]

Radio

Occasional radio broadcasts came to Sweden around the time of the First World War, but regular radio programming did not arrive until January 1925 when *Radiotjänst* began broadcasting on one frequency for a few hours each evening. This company, which was state regulated but not state-owned and expected to provide news, educational, and entertainment programming, enjoyed a virtual monopoly on the medium until the 1990s. Managed by a board with representatives from several newspapers, the news bureau *TT*, and the commercial radio set industry, it was reorganized in 1957 under the name *Sveriges Radio*/Sweden's Radio. It was then that the management board was changed to include members from popular movements and commercial interests, while the press's share and influence were reduced. Further restructuring occurred in 1979, and again in the early 1990s.

Today there are two central entities: *Sveriges Radio* and *Utbildningsradion* (Educational Radio). Each is managed by a governing board. UR develops its own programs, but uses SR as its broadcaster. Throughout its history *Sveriges Radio* has been a commercial-free system. Until 1990, operating costs were paid through a licensing fee (*avgift*) charged to radio set owners. Since then, the fee has been levied on televisions and income shared between the two media. The fee is set annually. In 2009, it was 2076SEK or about $255 (early 2009 conversion).

Initially, Sweden's radio broadcast on a single AM station. FM was introduced in the late 1940s. A second station, P2, was added in 1955. The third and fourth stations, P3 and P4, were added in 1964 and 1987, respectively. (The last was designated for local broadcasts.) Gradually, the extent of each day's programming increased, as educational elements, musical, dramatic, and literary programs, and Sunday church services were added. As early as the 1930s, the system was offering a full array of programming across the day. A small group of familiar announcers became well established, and, depending on one's generation, some programs were very popular. Among these were *Barnens Brevlåda*/The Children's Mailbox, which ran from 1925 to 1972 and was hosted for its entire history by Sven Jerring (1895–1979) (known as Uncle Sven); kids' adventure series like *Dickie Dick Dickens*, hit parade music shows like *Tio i topp*/Ten on Top (1961–1974) and

Svensktoppen/Swedish Tops (1962–present), and *Radioteatern* that broadcast a wide range of dramas including Swedish classics by Strindberg and Lagerlöf.

Aided by the advent of the inexpensive transistor units and the introduction of 45 and 33 rpm recordings that enhanced music radio, the 1960s may have been the heyday of traditional radio. It was also then that several so-called pirate radio stations like *Radio Nord* came on the air. Local or community stations with limited broadcast range began to be licensed in the late 1980s, and private commercial stations were allowed into the system in the mid-1990s. The results included an unprecedented growth in the number of stations and program options.

As in the case of the press, the computer/digital/wireless age, along with the removal of regulations that had prevented the development of private commercial stations, revolutionized radio in Sweden. In 1995, the first web broadcasts were aired. Digital broadcasting arrived in the late 1990s, and wireless application protocol (WAP) broadcasting in the early years of this century.

Today the choices seem almost limitless. *Sveriges Radio* remains a leader, and its offerings can easily be explored at its award-winning Web site: http// :www.sr.se/. There are the 4 national stations (P1–4), 26 regional stations, and an ever-growing number of Internet stations including at least five for minority groups or minority languages. There is something for every one: international-national-local news, children's programs, humor, educational, and every genre of music imaginable. In addition, there are about 90 private license holders that air one or more individual stations and a spectrum of local or community radio stations. The latter are maintained by organizations, such as church congregations or popular groups, and by educational institutions. Their broadcast range is limited and their service mission narrow.[8]

Television

Television came slowly to Sweden in the mid-1950s. The official beginning is usually listed as September 4, 1956, and occurred under the auspices of *Sveriges Radio*. For several years airtime was limited to a few hours a day on a single channel. A second channel was added in 1969. Like radio, television in Sweden was originally a monopoly and commercial free—supported by license fees on users. Developments outside of Sweden's control forced this situation to change. Chief among these were satellite and cable transmission systems. The earliest satellite channel, *TV3*, began operation in 1987 as a Scandinavia-wide medium and later split into separate operations for Denmark, Norway, and Sweden. *TV4* and *Kanal 5*, both commercial channels, were added in the 1990s. *TV4* offered a mixture of serious news and light

This is the logo of Swedish Television's *Kanal2*/Channel2. Sweden's second broadcast channel dates to 1969. Today the national system has six channels plus one for the web and offers a wide range of programming. (Channel logo used courtesy of *Sveriges Television*/SVT.)

entertainment that included quiz shows (for example, a Swedish version of *Jeopardy*). The latter channel was a venture launched by Jan Stenbeck who went on to start the free newspaper trend in Sweden with *Metro* and to establish the Modern Times Group. It was intended to be strictly an entertainment channel. Its motto was *roligare tv*/more entertaining tv, and its programming included films, soap operas, crime series, and sitcoms.

Rather than resist the internationalization of television, Sweden embraced it. Today, half of all Swedes are cable connected, about three fifths use antenna, and two fifths use a satellite system. There were 38 registered broadcasters in 2006. In addition to *Sveriges Television*, they included media companies that reflect many aspects of Sweden's increasingly heterogeneous society *AB Sportexpress, Nordic Shopping Sverige AB, Babylon Media Förening, Bahro Suryoyo Media Förening, Europeiska-Sydamerikanska KIF Rio de la Plata*, and *Three Angels Lifestyle Television.*

What do Swedes like to watch? Naturally, the answer varies and depends on age, gender, education, personal interests, and the like. News programs are popular. The most watched is *TV2*'s *Rapport*, a daily, evening program; and *Kanal 1* and *TV4* offer competitive options. Popular children's programs include *Bolibompa* and *Lattjo Lajban*. Swedish and international sports including soccer, hockey, and auto racing have great drawing power. Quiz programs like *Tiotusenkronorsfrågan*/10,000 Kronor Question, *Fråga Lund*/ Ask Lund (University), and, most recently, the bizarre *Boston Tea Party*—a blend of quiz program and comedy—have had strong audience support. A genuine phenomenon in the industry is the adventure reality or docu-soap program. Sweden has both created and copied its share of these. Borrowing on a British idea, *Sveriges Television* initiated an enormously popular and extensively copied series called *Expedition Robinson* in 1997. (The U.S. series *Survivor* and many others around the world are takeoffs on this idea.) The program ran for nine years and was scheduled to return in 2009. *Big Brother* is another enormously successful program in this genre. Based on the Dutch original, it ran from 2000 to 2007 on *Kanal 5*. It focused on the dynamics of making about a dozen very different people live together in a single dwelling and then voting people out until only one remained—the "winner." Documentaries and made-for-TV films, often of very high quality, have been produced by *SVT* and independents, and enjoyed good audience support. The advent of cable and satellite has, of course, internationalized the viewing habits of Swedes. From the beginning American series enjoyed great popularity. Programs like *Bröderna Cartwright*/*Bonanza*, *Dallas*, the more recent *CSI* iterations, and sitcoms like *Everybody Loves Raymond* and *How I Met Your Mother* have been hits, and their stars have enjoyed great popularity. As noted earlier, Disney's Donald Duck Christmas program developed into a kind of folk tradition, and *Julkalendern*/The Christmas Calendar appears to have a similarly wide appeal, especially among young people. A glance at the program listings at http://tvplaneten.tv4.se/ presents a good picture of what is offered on 62 channels. (The Swedish channels include: *SVT1, SVT2, TV3, TV4, TV4PLus, Kanal 5, TV6, TV7, TV8, Kanal 9, TV4 Film, TV400, TV4Fakta, TV4Guld, TV4Comedy, TV4Sport*, and *TV4ScienceFiction*.)

One thing that television in Sweden does not represent well, aside from some local programming, is the growing ethnic diversity of the population. An interesting and controversial exception to this was the 2008 program *Halal-TV*, aired by Swedish Television and featuring three devout Swedish-Muslim women; Cherin Awad, Dalia Azzam Kassem, and Khadiga El Khabiry. Seven of eight programs in which the women explored various aspects of Sweden and Swedishness with guests were broadcast. The final was cancelled amidst a storm of protest from public and private individuals opposed to the women's orthodox and apparently un-Swedish views on topics like law, gender, sex, and even public courtesies like shaking hands.[9]

Notes

1. See https://poit.bolagsverket.se/poit/PublikPoitIn.do. Accessed July 29, 2009.
2. An excellent survey of Sweden's press history is Hadenius and Weibull's 1999 article in *Nordicom Review*. Their 2008 book is an extended and updated version of this article.
3. Ingela Wadbring, *En tidning i tiden? Metro och den svenska dagstidningsmarknaden*/A Paper for Its Time? *Metro* and the Swedish Newspaper Market.
4. See http://www.tu.se/tidningarna.asp#. Accessed July 30, 2009.
5. On *Al Muhajer News*, see http://www.almuhajer.se/. Accessed July 30, 2009. On *The Local* see http://www.thelocal.se/. Accessed July 30, 2009
6. See *Statistiska centralbyrån: Pressmeddelande från SCB*. December 17, 2008. Nr. 2008:361; and *Svensk dagspress 2008: Fakta om marknad och media*. Tidnings

Utgivarna at http://www.tu.se/document/Svensk_dagspress_2008.pdf. Accessed July 30, 2009.

7. For a comprehensive list by category, see http://www.magazino.se/. (Subtitled: *Din guide i tidningsdjungeln*/Your guide in the periodical jungle.) Accessed July 30, 2009. A good for statistical information on the media in Sweden is http://www.nordicom.gu.se/eng.php?portal=&main=. Accessed July 30, 2009. Nordicom also publishes a number of periodicals, including one in English.

8. The history of radio in Sweden is well covered in "*Radiohistoria: Sveriges Radio i allmänhetens tjänst i över 80 år*" at http://www.sr.se/sida/artikel.aspx?programid=3113&artikel=1971599. Accessed July 30, 2009. Also see the Bengtsson volume in the Bibliography.

9. For a history of Swedish television, see http://svt.se/svt/jsp/Crosslink.jsp?d=29768. Accessed July 30, 2009.

6

Literature

CONTEMPORARY SWEDISH literature is rich, diverse, and innovative. Some works are clearly place bound in Sweden and deal specifically with issues unique to the country, but many are set in more regional or even global contexts and/or address issues that are more broadly "human." As a result, a significant number of Swedish books are translated into a large number of languages.

Broadly speaking, contemporary Swedish literature includes an extensive thematic array of poetry; theater and screen drama that ranges from the deeply serious to the absurd; prose fiction that focuses on themes such as the darker sides of Sweden's past, gender and sexual preference issues, problems in contemporary Swedish society, global issues, the lives of the new Swedes, and the telling of good stories; highly popular crime fiction that often is used as a vehicle for social criticism; and serious and frivolous children's stories aimed at a wide range of ages. In addition, biography, history, and cooking are genres well represented among current publications and are highly popular.

The number of authors writing today is dizzying, and the system encourages their work. Government- and organization-sponsored writing prizes and subsidies, the lure of royalties, and a library system that compensates authors based on book use are some of the ways this is done.

And Swedes read! Publishing is a good business to be in, and one list includes nearly 200 publishing companies. The largest national publishers' association has about 70 members—although a few large companies dominate the industry: Bonnier, Norstedt, Pirat, and Natur och Kultur. Bookstores are everywhere, both new and used. Bokus.com is one of several large and successful Internet book sources; while antikvariat.net provides easy access to many of Scandinavia's used bookstores.

In recent reports from the Swedish Publishers' Association (*Svenska Förläggareföreningen*), what they refer to as fine literature was the biggest selling sector of the market and showed continuous growth. Works by Swedish authors in this genre were doing better than translations of foreign authors in late 2008, which says something about the quality and popularity of Swedish writers. A sector that was doing less well was children's and young people's books, which had been in decline since 2004. The explanations for this seem to include changes within the publishing industry tied to profit motives and the growing popularity of other entertainment or time-use options among young people caught up in the digital age.

Before turning to look at a few of the best-known writers in Sweden today, it is important to give some attention to the canon, to a brief introduction to some of Sweden's greatest authors from the past and a few of the works that are vital to the national identity and important to the context in which contemporary literature is written. No attempt will be made here to be either inclusive or extensive.[1]

Classic Swedish Literature

How old is Swedish literature, and where do its beginnings lie? These are oft-debated questions without clear answers. Also, the academic answers include authors and works that many Swedes have either never heard of or never read. How might ordinary Swedes answer these questions? Certainly, they would accept the idea that the terse runic inscriptions of the Viking Age, the thirteenth century's *Ynglingasaga*/The Saga of the Ynglings (written in Old Norse by the Icelander, Snorri Sturlusson) that in part describes much earlier "events" surrounding the development of very early kingship in Sweden, provincial law codes from the Middle Ages, the *Revelations* of St. Birgitta, the *Gustav Vasa Bible* (1541), and Olof Rudbeck's *Atlantica* (1679) were parts of the oldest historical canon of Swedish literature. Would they be enthusiastic or highly familiar with any of these? Probably not.

If you mentioned Carl Michael Bellman (1740–95), however, the reaction would likely be more enthusiastic. He is the earliest and, for many, the best loved in a sequence of national poets every Swede reads and can recite or, in the case of Bellman, sing. The son of a Stockholm bureaucrat, Bellman earned a living (barely) through a sequence of minor official positions. His real life, the life he loved and lived to the fullest, was spent in the taverns of Stockholm, where he performed songs about local life and personalities or about a cast of fictional characters engaged in lives of debauchery and merrymaking—all set to familiar local tunes or melodies of his own composition. As James Massengale writes in a recent history of Swedish literature, his *Fredmans epistlar*/Fredman's Letters, a book containing some of his best-known work that was first published in 1790, "is arguably the most important songbook in Swedish literary history and probably Sweden's most popular single collection of poems in general."[2]

Bellman was followed by a sequence of nineteenth century writers whose works also belong on the list of books or writings familiar to most Swedes. In fact, the century witnessed quite stunning growth in both the number of fine writers and the volume and variety of their work. These developments were caused in part by the falling costs of book production, greater educational opportunities and a growing reading public, the rise of new and often competing ideologies, and conscious efforts to create a Swedish national identity and public consciousness of that identity. The period began with the Romantics and ended with Realism, analyses of social problems, and psychological explorations of the so-called modern breakthrough.

Among the leading Romantic writers were Erik Gustaf Geijer (1783–1847) and Esaias Tegner (1782–1846). Geijer was a historian, university rector, poet, and songwriter. Tegner was a pastor, bishop of Växjö, and poet. Both were caught up the conservative-liberal debates of their time. Geijer's poem "The Viking" and Tegner's epic *Frithjof's Saga* idealized the Viking Age and became pieces in the fabric of Sweden's emerging national identity. Also important were Carl Jonas Love Almqvist (1793–1866) and Fredrika Bremer (1801–65). Both were perceptive and outspoken critics of certain aspects of the conservative society in which they lived. In the late 1830s, for example, Almqvist attacked traditional notions of marriage in the novel *Det går an* (translated as *Sara Videbeck* or *Why Not?*), while Bremer did the same in *Hemmet* (The Home). These works and many others also reflected the success of prose fiction, primarily the novel, as the most popular literary genre, especially for Sweden's growing middle class.

The international giant in the history of Swedish literature in the late nineteenth and early twentieth century was August Strindberg (1849–1912). In terms of sheer volume and variety, the output of this brilliant and complex man was remarkable. One edition of his plays, short stories, novels, poems, and essays runs to 55 volumes. In his early work, he tended toward the realistic and the historical; his last works were deeply psychological and loaded with symbolism. In almost all there were elements of the personal, of his own life. *Det röda rummet*/The Red Room from 1879, with its combination of realism and attention to contemporary societal problems, has been called Sweden's first modern novel and embodied what was termed "the modern breakthrough" by the Danish critique Georg Brandes a few years later. Among his best-known plays are *Master Olof, Miss Julie, The Father, Easter, A Dream Play,* and *Ghost Sonata.* His well-known novels include *Getting Married, Son of a Servant,* and *Natives of Hemsö.*

THE TWENTIETH CENTURY

The twentieth century was a rich and varied period for Swedish literature, and this remains true in the early twenty-first century. Six Swedes from this period have won the Nobel Prize in Literature since its introduction in 1901: Selma Lagerlöf (1909), Verner von Heidenstam (1916), Erik Axel Karlfeldt (posthumously in 1931), Pär Lagerkvist (1951), and Eyvind Johnson and Harry Martinson (jointly in 1974). Many more have been or still are members of the *Svenska Akademien*/The Swedish Academy, an organization founded in 1786 by King Gustav III to "work for the Swedish language's purity, strength, and greatness, or its clarity, expressiveness, and reputation." Its membership or "chair holders," which includes some of Sweden's finest writers, is limited to 18. In 2009, the members were: Sten Rudholm, b. 1918 (elected 1977), (deceased November 29, 2008); Bo Ralph, b. 1945 (elected 1999); Sture Allén, b. 1928 (elected 1980); Anders Olsson, b. 1949 (elected 2008); Göran Malmqvist, b. 1924 (elected 1985); Birgitta Trotzig, b. 1929 (elected 1993); Knut Ahnlund, b. 1923 (elected 1983); Jesper Svenbro, b. 1944 (elected 2006); Torgny Lindgren, b. 1938 (elected 1991); Peter Englund, b. 1957 (elected 2002); Ulf Linde, b. 1929 (elected 1977); Per Wästberg, b. 1933 (elected 1997); Gunnel Vallquist, b. 1918 (elected 1982); Kristina Lugn, b. 1948 (elected 2006); Kerstin Ekman, b. 1933 (elected 1978); Kjell Espmark, b. 1930 (elected 1981); Horace Engdahl, b. 1948 (elected 1997), Permanent Secretary; and Katarina Frostenson, b. 1953 (elected 1992).[3]

To make order of all that has been and continues to be written in Sweden in the last century or so, many scholars have divided the period into decades, so there are the writers of the century change (*sekelskiftet*), the 1910s *(tiotalister*), the 1920s *(tjugotalister*), and so on. Also, writers and their works have been typed by specific genre labels that include neo-romantic, modern, postmodern, working class, regional, epic narrative, feminist, historic, autobiographic, documentary, political, social criticism, crime fiction, and immigrant. The lists of authors who have made it into literature histories, the syllabi of the public schools and universities, best-seller lists, and the hearts of Swedish readers are long, and only a small sampling will be attempted here.[4]

No survey of the late nineteenth and twentieth centuries would be complete without Selma Lagerlöf (1858–1940). She and Astrid Lindgren (see below) are two of Sweden's best-known women writers. Lagerlöf was the first Swede to win the Nobel Prize in Literature, and the first women to receive a chair in the Swedish Academy. A keen observer of reality and the human psyche, she was above all a superb teller of complex and multileveled stories. Two of her best-known works are *Gösta Berlings Saga* (1891) and *The Wonderful Adventures of Nils Holgersson* (1906/7). The former, set in nineteenth century Värmland, is classified as a neo-romantic novel and focuses on the redemption of the degenerate Pastor Berling and those around him.

Selma Lagerlöf, 1858–1940. The first Swedish woman to win the Nobel Prize in Literature (1909), Lagerlöf remains one of Sweden's best-known and most widely read authors. (Photo by the Hansen & Weller Studio, Copenhagen, © 1889. Image found on the Web site of Royal Library/*Kungliga Biblioteket*, Stockholm. Reprinted with permission.)

The latter grew out of a request from the country's national education board for a book for school children that would help them learn about their country. The story revolves around a rather naughty little boy, Nils, who is turned into a *tomte* and carried off by geese who take him on a tour of Sweden's provinces. It offers lessons in geography, history, folklore, the realities of life, how to treat and not to treat this world, and growing up. Among her outstanding contemporaries were Gustaf Fröding, Oscar Levertin, Verner von Heidenstam, Hjalmar Söderberg, and the poet Erik Axel Karlfeldt.

Pär Lagerkvist (1891–1974) is another of Sweden's greatest modern writers. His work spans more than half of the twentieth century. His first novel, *People* (*Människor*), appeared in 1912; his last, *Marianne*, in 1967. Throughout his life he, like many other writers of the century, was preoccupied with the deepest and most profound questions of human existence: with the meaning or meaninglessness of life, the anxiety created by not *knowing* life's meaning, the prevalence of evil and violence, man's cruelty to man, the existence of God, and the efficacy of individual actions. His writings, most of which have been translated, include the 1916 collection of poems entitled *Ångst*/Anguish (1916), *The Guest of Reality* (1926), *The Hangman* (1936), *The Dwarf* (1945), and *Barabbas* (1950). Among the Swedish writers who shared some of Lagerkvist's themes are Hjalmar Bergman, Karin Boye, Stig Dagerman, and Eyvind Johnson.

Working Class Writers

One of the more important groups from the last century were the so-called working class writers. Historically, most of the authors before them had come from the upper classes, which is hardly surprising given the limited educational opportunities, poverty, and the employment options available to the lower classes. By the 1930s, however, much of this was changing. Basic schooling was well established, job opportunities had improved, labor unions were legitimate players in the job market, and from 1932 the Social Democrats were the leading party in politics and pursuing policies designed to improve the lives of ordinary people. (With the exception of the summer of 1936, the party headed Sweden's governments from 1932 to 1976.) It was then that the first generation of working class writers emerged. This included Vilhelm Moberg, Ivar Lo-Johansson, Jan Fridegård, and Moa Martinson. Each came from poverty. Moberg was the son of a soldier-crofter, Lo-Johansson and Fridegård were sons of landless farm workers, and Martinson was the illegitimate daughter of factory worker. Many of their works focused on the lives of the rural and urban poor and were often autobiographical. But these writers were capable of dealing with much more than the miseries of poverty.

Moberg illustrates this well. He was a novelist, dramatist, journalist, social critic, and historian. Among his books are the autobiographical *Raskens* (1927); *Rid i natt*/Ride This Night (1941), a critique of the Swedish government for its un-neutral neutrality in World War II; his epic four-volume novel about emigration to North America, *The Emigrants, Unto a Good Land, The Settlers*, and *The Last Letter Home* (1949–59; and two volumes in what he envisioned would be a longer series he titled *Min svenska historia*/My Swedish History (1970–71).[5]

Per Anders Fogelström (1917–98) was in the second generation of important working class authors. He grew up and lived most of his life in the working class district of Söder in Stockholm and in many ways can be identified with that part of the city. Among his works are eight novels about the working poor of Stockholm from the early eighteenth century to the contemporary era. Written between 1965 and 1987, the best known and most popular is *Mina drömmars stad*/City of My Dreams—the story of Henning Nilsson, a poor lad from the countryside who arrives in Stockholm around 1860 filled with dreams of a new and better life. The harsh realities he encounters never break his spirit, and the life he builds around friends and family show how success can have many definitions.[6]

Post–World War II

Several new themes developed in Swedish prose fiction in the years following World War II. Among these were assessments of the growing the welfare state, intensified interest in women's issues, concern for global problems, and the lives of the immigrants to Sweden. At the same time, genres of the novel such as documentary, historical, crime fiction, and immigrant were employed to address these and other themes. Some of the leading authors in this period belonged to the older generation, active from before and during the war, but new generations were also important.

One of the foremost writers to work in the historical or documentary novel genre of the last half century has been Per Olof Enquist. His *Legionärerna: En bok om baltutlämningen*/The Legionaires: A Book about the Baltic Refugees (1968), *Musikanternas uttåg*/The March of the Musicians (1978), and *Livläkarens besök*/The Royal Physician's Visit (1999) are three examples. In the first, he critically examined how former freedom fighters from the Baltic states fled to Sweden and then were deported as Soviet forces overran their countries at the close of World War II. In the second, he looked at working conditions in northern Sweden's timber mills in the early twentieth century. In the third, he explored the life of J. F. Struensee during a remarkable two-year period in Danish history in the early 1770s, when this enigmatic

German doctor was the private physician and confidant of the Danish king, lover of the queen, and enlightened reformer of the country. Enquist is more than just a teller of good history stories, however. A journalist and dramatist as well, his work often deals with the complexities of truth, reality, morality, and doing the right thing.

While on this theme, it is important to note that history is also a very popular genre. Works on events and people in Sweden's past sell well and are widely read. Peter Englund (1957–) is good example of an historian with a large reading public, and his election to the Swedish Academy in 2002 bears witness to his importance. His best-known works, which are intentionally written for a popular audience, are superb examples of what is called "mentality history" or the history of what people thought and believed and why. Illustrating this is the following description of his epic work from 1988, *Poltava*, about the great battle between Russia and Sweden in 1709 that proved to be the beginning of the end for Sweden's Baltic empire:

> The intense, empathetic and perspicacious portrayal—hour-by-hour—of the Battle of Poltava in the Ukraine of June 1709 was an enormous sales success and may be said to have contributed in great measure to the wide interest in history among the Swedish public. History regained a narrative form, but now anti-heroic, down-to-earth and spiced with analytical acumen.[7]

The first two volumes in what is supposed to be a trilogy, *Ofredsår*/Years of War (1993) and *Den oövervinnerlige*/The Invincible (2000) and subtitled *Om den svenska stormaktstiden och en man I dess mitt*/On Sweden's Period as a Great Power and a Man at Its Center, continued in this style. In a description of his work, an author for the Swedish Academy included the following:

> Not infrequently the past appears as if it were an object under water: it is there but remote and incomprehensible, its outlines vague and elusive. Will we ever understand fully the people who lived in it? Perhaps not. Yet the attempt must be made. How otherwise can we ourselves hope to be understood by posterity? For what we are, they once were, and what they are, we will soon be.[8]

Another very popular author of history is Herman Lindqvist (1943–). He differs from Englund in at least two ways. First, he is an experienced journalist and foreign correspondent, not an academically trained historian. Second, his focus tends to be on the individual rather than the culture or society. To a large extent, he is an old-fashioned great person historian, as the subjects of many of his more than two dozen books reflect—the queens of Sweden, Napoleon, Axel von Fersen, and Madame de Pompadour. (The last, from 2008, was another best seller for him.) Like Englund, he is a popularizer of history, not someone who believes it is only the domain of scholars. His multivolume history of Sweden has sold very well and been serialized on Swedish television.

Swedish Crime Fiction

One of the most enduringly popular genres in contemporary Sweden is crime fiction, an area of literature that includes works that revolve around espionage, investigative procedures, particular crimes, and the criminal mind. Many authors repeatedly use the same investigator or other central figure(s) in a series of works; and some use the medium as a vehicle for serious looks at contemporary issues and problems. There is a constantly renewing group of very fine writers, and even some of Sweden's best authors—who are better known for their work in other genre (Kerstin Ekman, for example)—have published here. As is so typical in Sweden where there seems to be an organization for every activity, there is a crime fiction society, *Svenska Deckarakademin*/The Swedish Detectives Academy. Established in 1971, the group now centers on 24 "seated" members. It serves to promote the medium and awards a number of prizes annually including ones for the best first crime fiction novel by a Swedish author, the best young people's crime novel, and the prestigious Martin Beck Prize for the best foreign crime novel in Swedish translation.[9]

Who are some of Sweden's better known crime fiction writers?[10] Dagmar Lange (1914–91), who wrote under the pseudonym Maria Lang, has often been referred to as "Sweden's Agatha Christie" or "the queen of crime." Her first novel, *Mördaren ljuger inte ensam*/The Murderer Doesn't Lie Alone, appeared in the 1949; her last, *Se Skoga och sedan*/See Skoga and Then, was published in 1990. In between she produced mysteries for children, essays, and nearly 40 adult mysteries. Many of the last featured her female narrator, Puck Ekstedt, and Inspector Christer Wyck. Often her stories were set in Skoga, a fictional town based on her own hometown of Nora, involved a small set of characters, and centered on crimes of passion. She was one of the founders of The Swedish Detectives Academy.

Nearly as productive but more controversial is Jan Guillou (1944–). A popular journalist, television personality, and celebrity, he gained particular notoriety in the early 1970s for a series of articles he co-authored about the then secret Swedish intelligence agency, *Informationsbyrån/IB*. For what he revealed, he was convicted of violating Sweden's national secrets laws and spent nearly a year in prison. His experiences were subsequently important in influencing him to write a series of 11 spy novels between 1986 and 2006 in which the main character was Carl-Gustaf Hamilton, "*Coq Rouge*."

These books, which dealt with themes that include the Cold War, weapons of mass destruction, Mideast conflicts, and America's Secretary of State, place him alongside John le Carré and Len Deighton. Like the books of his British counterparts, many have been made into feature films. Guillou is also one of the founders of the author-centered publishing house *Piratförlaget*.

One of the more interesting women writers of crime fiction is Mari Jungstedt (1962–). She, too, is a television journalist. Her first novel, *Den du inte se*/The Unseen, was published in 2003, and she has added four more since. Her most recent book is *I denna ljuva sommartid*/In High Summer. All of her novels are set on the island of Gotland. For the first four books, her lead characters were Visby Police Inspector Knutas and journalist Johan Berg. In the fifth she put Knutas on vacation and turned the investigation over to his closest assistant, Karin Jacobsson. Location is always important, and the choice of Gotland is relatively unusual. Her explanation, however, is compelling:

> Gotland is a perfect scene for crime novels; it is isolated, the setting is defined by the island and the coastline that encircles it. Evil comes nearer, becomes clear in the small society where places and people have clear relations to each other. The milieu on Gotland is also wonderfully obliging with its wild, wind-blown and barren landscape, long stretches of beach, tall caulk cliffs that drop right down into the sea, mist-shrouded swamps, and twisted pines.[11]

Four other virtually household names in Swedish crime fiction are Maj Sjöwall (1935–), Per Wahlöö (1926–75), Henning Mankell (1948–), and Liza Marklund (1962–). Between 1965 and 1975, Sjöwall and Wahlöö co-authored a series of 10 mysteries set in Stockholm and featuring Martin Beck as the lead detective. Among the titles were *Roseanna, The Man Who Went Up in Smoke, The Man on the Balcony, The Laughing Policeman*, and *The Terrorists*. Each of their books was a meticulously crafted procedural detective story; but each was also a vehicle for dissecting and critiquing Sweden's social welfare society—a society they believed could be defined by its growing impersonalization, ballooning bureaucracy, conformity, bourgeois values, and blindness to its darker realities. All of their books have been made into films, mainly in Swedish. An exception is *The Laughing Policeman*, which was filmed in America and starred Walter Matthau.

Henning Mankell, perhaps Sweden's best-known crime fiction author in the early twenty-first century, is a man of many interests and talents. Since his first book appeared in 1973, he has authored crime novels, a group of serious adult novels, books for children (some argue he is nearly as well known as a children's book author as a crime fiction writer), and plays. Among his most popular books are the nine (plus a volume of short stories) Kurt Wallander mysteries.

Best sellers in both Sweden and abroad, all have been made into films by Swedish Television, and a new series from BBC Scotland, starring Kenneth Branagh, appeared in 2008. In addition, he is a founder of the Leopard publishing house, was the managing director of Växjö's Kronoberg's Theater, and is the founder and director of Teatro Avenida in Maputo, Mozambique—where he lives for part of every year. As with so many other writers, his crime novels are good mysteries *and* vehicles for unveiling society's problems—be they Swedish, European, African, or global. Mankell has said that he wants to make the world a better place, and his books are one way in which he tries to do so. Hence, they cover issues such as senseless violence, neo-Nazism, suffering, child abuse, imperialism, organized crime, weapons trafficking, drugs, terrorism, and the vulnerability of our modern society to disruption.[12]

Liza Marklund is a writer and journalist. Her eight crime (published between 1999 and 2008 feature Annika Bengtzon, a 30-something lead reporter on the crime desk of a Stockholm tabloid newspaper whose life is endlessly complicated by the crimes she reports (and investigates), the pressures of her job, and the conflicts that arise in her marriage and family life as a result. Among the titles in this series are *Språngaren*/The Bomber (which won her several prizes), *Nobels testamente*/Nobel's Will, and *En plats i solen*/A Place in the Sun. Marklund is also the author of the highly controversial *Gömda*/Buried Alive, published in two versions from 1995 and 2000. One of the largest selling books in Swedish history, the book told the story of a young woman, Maria Eriksson, who is stalked and threatened by a violent ex-boyfriend, forced into hiding, receives little help from Swedish authorities, and ultimately leaves Sweden to find safety elsewhere. (The controversy over the book revolved around to what degree the story was based on fact.)[13]

No overview of Swedish crime fiction would be complete without mention of Stieg Larsson (1954–2008), a graphic designer, journalist, and deeply committed opponent of white racist organizations in Sweden who published three novels before his sudden death in 2008: *The Girl with the Dragon Tattoo*/Män som hatar kvinnor, *The Girl Who Played with Fire*/Flickan som lekte men elden, and *The Girl Who Kicked the Hornet's Nest*/Luftslottet som sprängdes. Known collectively as the *Millennium Trilogy*, the books follow a tangled web of plots that include strange disappearances, murders, financial scandals, a murderous Soviet defector, and a branch of Sweden's secret police that operates above and outside Swedish law. The central characters are an investigative journalist, Mikael Blomkvist, and a brilliant and exceedingly unconventional young woman, Lisbeth Salander. In 2008, Larsson was the second best-selling author in the world. His trilogy had sold more than 27 million copies worldwide in early 2010. The first of these books was made into a very successful film in 2009, and film versions of the others are expected to follow.[14]

New Swedes and Literature

One of the most interesting genres in Swedish literature in the late twentieth and early twenty-first centuries is formed by the collected works of the new Swedes, of the immigrants and their children.[15] Often this is called "immigrant literature" or "multicultural literature" because many of the works that fall under these labels are written by and/or deal with issues faced by the immigrants and their subsequent generations, including isolation, rejection, longing for the homeland, rootlessness, racism, poverty, assimilation, cross-generational conflicts, and split identities. When these labels are used for works that actually do deal with such issues, they are useful. But they also can be misleading and have often been regarded as offensive by some of the authors who have been so categorized. Interestingly, almost all write in Swedish, which is relatively typical for ethnic minority group writers across Europe. However, this language choice sets them apart, for example, from Swedish-American authors of the late nineteenth and early twentieth centuries, many of whom wrote in Swedish rather than English, as they sought to retain their language and create a literature for a relatively closed group rather than adopt the language of their new homeland. More important than the language in which they write is the fact that many deal with issues that are not unique to the new Swedes or to immigrants.

Beyond their popularity and the volume of work they have produced and continue to produce are two interesting indicators of their importance. The first is an organization, *Sveriges internationella författarförening* (Sweden's International Authors Union), a group founded in 1974 and dedicated to providing information and organizing symposia and forums for authors with international backgrounds throughout Sweden. The second is an ongoing effort by the Immigrant Institute in Borås to identify and provide a bibliography of the works by authors with international backgrounds. As of January 2006, the institute's author list included more than 1,200 individuals with multicultural identities writing fiction in Sweden! In addition, they had separate information on the authors of children's books and nonfiction works.[16] A brief look at four writers who fall, at least at times, into the categories of immigrant or multicultural authors ought help clarify a sense of the nature of this group.

The author of nearly three dozen books between 1969 and 2008, Theodor Kallifatides (1938–) is one of Sweden's best-known and most productive contemporary writers. Born in Greece in 1938, he came to Sweden in 1964. A gifted linguist, he rapidly mastered the language, received a degree in philosophy, and went to work teaching and writing. From 1972 to 1974, he was editor of the prestigious *Bonniers litterära magasin*/Bonniers Literary

Magazine. His first novel, *Utlänningar*/Foreigners (1971), was a compelling, semiautobiographical account of a Greek leaving his homeland, immigrating to a Sweden that was in many ways far from welcoming, and wrestling with the processes of adaptation. It was a story about stepping out of one "world" into another, of the struggles involved in holding on to one's native culture and becoming part of a new culture. He has returned to these and related themes time and again, as, for example, in his 2001 novel, *Ett nytt land utanför mitt fönster*/A New Land Outside My Window. Among other central themes in this book, he dealt in compelling ways with the differences between the Swedish and Greek languages and the cultures from which they developed and how one can say things (and be understood) in one language that one cannot say in another. Not all of Kallifatides'work is about immigrants, however. Most importantly, he has written extensively on post–World War II Greece. (See, for example, *Bönder och herrar*/Peasants and Masters, *Plogen och svärdet*/The Plow and the Sword, and *Den grymma freden*/The Cruel Peace.)

Fateme Behros (1944–) came to Sweden as an exile from Iran in 1983. She had studied Swedish and earned a university degree in Persian literature in her home country, and once in Sweden she played an important role in providing educational materials about the Persian language and literature for Swedish schools. Among her early publications were books on Iran, Iranians, Persian for Swedish schools, and a Persian-Swedish dictionary. (See, for example, *Jag minns: om traditioner, seder och bruk i Iran*/I Remember: On Traditions, Customs, and Practices in Iran from 1988.) Her first novel, *Som ödet*/Fate (1997) echoes her own story of flight from Iran and the difficulties of adaptation. These themes are repeated in her later works, *Fångarnas kör*/The Prisoners' Choir (2001) and *I skuggan av Sitare*/In the Shadow of Sitare (2004). The former tells the story of Shabtab, who comes to Sweden from Iran in response to an offer of marriage from a man already there and whom she has never seen or met. The two have very different expectations of the union. He wants a traditional dutiful wife; she wants love and freedoms she expects to have in Sweden. The paths she travels to build her new life lie at the center of the novel. In *In the Shadow of Sitare,* Behros tells two stories; one about a missing young Iranian-Swedish woman who has apparently disgraced her family and been murdered in an honor killing, and the other about Narges, another Iranian-Swedish woman living as a second wife in the home of Nima and her search for a life and identity.

A third multicultural author is Li Li (1961–). He was born in Shanghai and studied Swedish in Beijing, where he translated some of Tomas Tranströmer's poetry into Chinese. He came to Sweden in the late 1980s as an exchange student. Following the killings in Tiananmen Square in the spring of 1989, he chose to remain in the country. Between 1989 and 1999, he published five volumes of poetry in Swedish and established himself as a leading poet of the new Swedes. After eight years of silence, he published a new collection, *Ursprunget*/The Source, in 2007. In it he dealt with his former life in Shanghai, the life and death of his mother, the pain of exile, the rootlessness of the immigrant, and the sorrow over the losses one endures. One reviewer described the collection, which has been viewed as both descriptive and deeply existential, as a compelling exchange between "a son and a mother, Stockholm and China, snowflakes and cotton, McDonald's and the Ming dynasty, minutes and hours."[17] As with so many of the writers in this group, Li Li is repeatedly praised for his use of the Swedish language—for his clarity, economy of expression, and depth. Interestingly, in comments to an interviewer with the Stockholm newspaper *Svenska Dagbladet*, he described how he worked out much of the new book in Chinese because that was the language in which he could express himself most fully and, echoing Kalifatides, remarked on the differences between languages and cultures and how things can be said in Chinese that just cannot be said in Swedish and vice versa.

Finally, there is Jonas Hassen Khemiri (1978–).[18] Born in Stockholm, his mother is Swedish; his father is Tunisian. He represents the second generation of multicultural Swedes, and he grew up in a capital that was alive with the dynamic, good and bad, of the rapid and often deeply troubling cultural changes Sweden was going through. His first book, *Ett öga rött*/One Eye Red, was published in 2003, when he was just 25. It is the story of a boy, Halim, caught up in his own identity struggles and a witness to and victim of many of the ills besetting the new Swedes, including racism, isolation, suburban ghettoization, and failed integration schemes. The title and much of the content is intentionally in grammatically imperfect immigrant Swedish, what some call *Rinkebysvensk*/Rinkeby Swedish, and this triggered a noisy and often rather hostile debate. Anyone who is familiar with immigrants in transition knows that the development of a unique kind of mixed language is common; and Khemiri, who is above all else a passionate observer and user of language, played with this fact of immigrant life. The book was a tremendous success and was made into a film that opened in 2007. His second novel, *Montecore: En unik tiger*/Montecore: A Unique Tiger, was published in 2006 and won the P. O. Enquist Prize that year. Here, too, Khemiri played with language and with the dreams of immigrants and their lives in a Sweden that is supposedly tolerant and accepting and is often quite the opposite. These themes were also at the core of Khemiri's 2006 play, *Invasion*. His second play, *Fem gånger gud*/Five Times God, opened in 2008 and was one of the National Theater's (*Riksteatern*) touring plays. It involved a cast of students who put their own dreams into a reading of August Strindberg's *A Dream Play.* Drawing upon a Swedish classic, it was a "Khemiri dreamplay" about words, meanings, and truth.

Children's Literature

Another vital genre to explore briefly is children's literature. Here, too, the number of fine writers is large, the output impressive, and the popularity high. The history of children and young people's literature in Sweden (and the West) dates at least to the development of printing. Sweden's oldest children's book is said to be a translation of a German instruction book for aristocratic girls called *The Maiden's Mirror* that dates from 1591. In ways, it illustrates a pattern that lasted for centuries of books aimed at curbing the natural unruliness and sinfulness of children and guiding their social and religious development. Naturally, the cost of these books was high, the number of readers small, and their reach limited largely to the nobility and the urban merchant elites. During the Enlightenment (eighteenth century), the focus of books for children shifted to more practical ends and more useful content. The period even witnessed the publication of the earliest children's magazines. Romantic themes dominated many of the nineteenth century's children's books in the form of ancient sagas, fairy tales, folk tales, and the like. In part, these served to activate the creative and the playful in children, but they also worked to spread national myths, history, and important elements of national identity. Many of the books available for children were translations, such as the stories of Hans Christian Andersen or Lewis G. Carroll. But there were original Swedish works as well, including the silly, lighthearted books of Sigfid Flodin, such as *Ack, så roligt!*/Oh, How Funny!, and the nursery rhymes collected and illustrated by the artist Jenny Nyström.[19]

The 1890s brought a shift in emphasis and a rapidly expanding market. In large part the growth was the result of the educational reforms of the nineteenth century that raised literacy to a very high level, the falling costs of books because of technological improvements in papermaking and printing, greater use of reading and books as learning tools in the primary grades, and the importance of children in the ideal bourgeois family. Among the important works of this period were the children's magazine *Jultomten* and the beginning of the classic series, *Barnbiblioteket Saga.* Both were the creations of Emil and Amanda Hammarlund. Another important children's author from the period was Selma Lagerlöf, discussed earlier. Her *Wonderful Adventures of Nils Holgersson* from 1906/7 epitomized the merger of the playful and the instructive in one of the most popular children's books of all time.

The years between 1914 and 1945 were relatively dry times for children's literature in Sweden. Perhaps this is not surprising given the two world wars and the deeply troubled decades of the 1920s and 1930s. The same cannot be said for the years since 1945. The last half century has been wonderfully productive. Astrid Lindgren (1907–2002) aptly symbolizes this. By some measures she is Sweden's most widely read author—at home and abroad. The daughter of a tenant farmer, she grew up in the southern province of Småland. After school, she moved to Stockholm, where she worked as a copy editor, secretary, and stenographer. She also took time away from work to be a stay-at-home mother in the years just before World War II. From 1947 until her retirement in the early 1970s, she was children's book editor for Rabén & Sjögren Publishers. Her first children's book, *Britt-Marie lättar sitt hjärta*/Britt-Marie Unburdens Her Heart, appeared in 1944. Real success, however, came with the publication of the first of the three full length Pippi Longstocking books in 1945. Over the next four decades she published more than 100 children's books. Her works have been translated into more than 80 languages, and several have been made into films. The number of her books sold worldwide is estimated to be nearly 150 million. Recognition of the significance of her work can be measured by the many prizes she won, including two from her publisher, a Swedish Academy gold medal, a Swedish Detectives Academy's prize in children's literature, awards from several of Sweden's leading newspapers, the Karen Blixen Prize from the Danish Academy, and numerous honorary doctorates. Following Lindgren's death in 2002, the Swedish government established the Astrid Lindgren Memorial Award (*Litteraturpriset till Astrid Lindgrens minne* or ALMA), a prize worth 5 million Swedish crowns that is awarded annually to a writer, illustrator, or children's storyteller in a competition that is worldwide in scope. It is, to quote from ALMA's Web site, "in many ways, a prize from the Swedish people to the world. In part because its costs are paid from the public treasury and in part because generations of Swedes have a broad and deep attachment to Astrid Lindgren and her works."

There is a magic about Lindgren's children's books. Why? Perhaps it is because she took children seriously. What they thought, how their minds worked, and how they played were important. Also, Pippi and Lindgren's other characters are children's ideals. They are strong, independent, intelligent, valuable, curious, and often somewhat shocking to parents and other adults.

An interesting postscript to this brief glance at Lindgren's life and work is the furor that arose in the mid-1970s over the income tax bill she received from the government and her responses. According to the Swedish tax law of the time, a flat rate was imposed on a certain portion of one's annual

Pippi Longstocking volume. Translated into more than 80 languages, this particular edition is in Arabic. (Photograph courtesy of Image Bank Sweden.)

income and then a rising percentage on portions of income above the base. The latter portion was called the "marginal tax," and it ran as high as 83 percent! Because she was self-employed as a writer, she was a business and, therefore, owed other taxes. When these were factored in, the bill came to 102 percent of her income. In response to this absurdity, she wrote a little fable, *Pomperipossa i Monismanian*/Pomperipossa in Monismanian, which appeared in the Stockholm daily *Expressen* in March 1976. An imaginary character first extolled the virtues of and her love for an imaginary land where the taxes were high but social services were excellent, where, she believed, it was right for those with wealth to share it. But then the ridiculous happened, her taxes exceeded her income, and this was too much for Pomperipossa. She pilloried the law and the situation. The piece was widely read and at the center of a debate in the parliament. It also gave ammunition to the nonsocialist opposition parties and may have played a role in the Social Democrats' defeat in the parliamentary election of that year.[20]

A second much beloved author and illustrator of late twentieth century children's books is Tove Jansson (1914–2001). This Finnish-Swedish author, illustrator, artist, and winner of the 1992 Selma Lagerlöf Prize, produced 10 books in the charming *Moomin* series between 1945 and 1970. In them, her main characters, a cast of miniature trolls, live in a fantasy universe where they face potential disaster, cope with misfortune, or explore something new or different around them. The early books were more playful than the last in the series, when she became more psychologically introspective.

A number of parallel themes and forms have run through Sweden's children's literature since the late 1940s. Some of these echo earlier patterns; others have arisen from the history and developments of the new period; many deal with the same topics or ideas as adult fiction. Contemporary Sweden's children's literature is populated with books that serve as instructions for life; are built around adventure, pure fantasy, science fiction, crime, biography, and psychological themes; or have at their cores critiques of the social system or address global issues. The winners of the Nils Holgersson Prize (awarded annually by *Svensk Biblioteksförening*/Swedish Library Association since 1950 and comprised of a plaque and 10,000 Swedish krona) over the last few years illustrate this variety. The winner in 2003 was Åsa Lind's *Sandvargen*/The Sand Wolf. A fantasy story for young children about a little girl and a golden wolf, it was described by the prize committee as "a philosophical, thoughtful, playful, and life affirming reading adventure" that was always told from a child's perspective.[21] The 2004 prize went to Douglas Foley for his *shoo bre*/Hello, a serious story about two boys from different backgrounds and with very different lives growing up in today's Sweden that is leading to a seemingly inevitable bad end. The title derived from *shobresvenska*, another of the labels used for the variants of Swedish that are developing in many places, but especially in the high-rise communities of the suburbs built in the 1960s and where many of the new Swedes live today. Collectively, the new mixed dialects are referred to as *förortsvenska*/Suburb Swedish. Petter Lidbeck's *En dag i prinsessan Victorias liv*/A Day in Princess Victoria's Life took the prize in 2005. This was another illustrated children's book, in this case about a much loved little girl with Downs Syndrome. In 2006, Kajsa Isakson, a well-known Stockholm playwright and theater artistic director, won the prize for *Min Ella*/My Ella, a story about the life at school for two teenaged girls. In language that captured the voice of young people, she dealt with problems common to this stage in life including fear, anxiety, lack of confidence, and bullying. For 2007, Cannie Möller won the prize in recognition for all of her work. Her first book, *Kriget om källan*/War over the Spring, appeared in 1983, and since then she has produced a variety of books that deal with alternative futures, the problems of Sweden's multicultural society, relationships, gender roles, the collective and the individual, and conflict resolution. The Swedish Library Society has described her work as "nuanced, consistently realistic, believable, and anchored in a strong love of humanity and belief in the future."[22] Finally, in 2008, the prize went to Mikael Engström for *Isdraken*/The Ice Dragon, a book aimed at teenaged readers about Mik, a boy struggling to survive in settings dictated by an impersonal and close-minded bureaucracy that controls his placement in a sequence of foster homes, two of which are abusive. Through the book, Engström addressed such problems as chronic alcoholism, child neglect, teen violence and crime, and isolation. As is traditional in this genre, however, all is not bad in his story. There are good relationships and good environments, and the overall tone of the book is optimistic.[23]

Drama and Poetry

Before moving on, the leading exponents of drama and poetry need to be mentioned. In the former the most important figure for the last several decades has been Lars Norén (1944–). The author of more than 50 plays and one of Sweden's most internationally recognized and produced dramatists, he began his writing career as the author of what have been described as tortured, difficult, and surreal poems. He published his first play in 1973, but went largely unnoticed until the appearance of *Natten är dagens mor*/The Night is Day's Mother—a semibiographical drama of troubled family life. In the stream of plays that followed, often grouped in series, he explored the dark sides of capitalism, the decline of the welfare society, personal loneliness, social exclusion, the disintegration of morality, and death—always, he has said, with the aim of understanding human beings. One of his most controversial plays was *7:3* from 1999, about neo-Nazism in Sweden and the nature of hatred. (The outburst of criticism over this play arose in part because two of the Swedish neo-Nazis who acted in the production of the play were subsequently involved in a bank robbery in Kisa and the murder of two policemen.) Less controversial, but equaling troubling was *Krig*/War, a play from 2003 about a broken soldier's return to his family after years away at war and the changes that have taken place in his absence. In it Norén sought to show how "war is a brutalizing business that systematically destroys whatever is noble about humanity by reducing men and women to their animal nature."[24] It played at the Rattlestick Playwrights Theater off-Broadway in 2008, and was not received well by critics. His most recent piece is *A la mémoire d'Anna Politkovskaïa*, the last part of a trilogy built loosely around the Russian journalist, d'Anna Politkovskaïa, who was murdered in 2006. One reviewer described it as follows, "The central action focuses on a drug-addict prostitute, her pimp, dealer *sambo*, and her son by another man. To say that the story is dark is an understatement."[25] The play opened in Sweden in 2008. In addition to writing, Norén is equally well known as a director, and he served as an artistic director with the National Theater Company, *Riksteatern*, from 1999 to 2007. (See Chapter 7 on Performing Arts.)

The best-known contemporary Swedish poet, both at home and abroad, is Tomas Tranströmer (1931–). Born and raised in Stockholm, he has had a life interestingly divided between being a writer and a practicing psychologist. His first collection of poems appeared in 1954, and since then he has published some 13 volumes. Variously described as a Modernist, Expressionist, and Surrealist, Tranströmer makes extensive use of deceptively simple images and a variety of poetic forms to describe places, ideas, concepts, feelings, and the like as he explores the human psyche.[26] Widely translated, a major compilation of his works is available in English in *The Great Enigma: New Collected Poems* (2006).

Another important poet from this period is Ann Jäderlund (1955–), one of contemporary Sweden's foremost feminist writers. Her 1988 collection, *Som en gång varit äng*/What Once Was a Meadow, unleashed a heated debate in Swedish literary circles over gender differences in poetry and whether or not there is a distinctly feminine version of the language for poetry. About her work, her publisher, Bonnier, notes:

> In the wave of innovative feminist poetry that we have seen in Sweden over the last ten to fifteen years, she is a central figure, and her poetry has been in the center of the on-going discussion of the genre.[27]

Like many of her contemporaries, she is also recognized and occasionally criticized for "breaking the rules" in terms of her use of Swedish and for her very contemporary vocabulary.

What Swedes Read

An extended look at what the Swedes were reading in late 2008 reveals a number of things about them including their enthusiasm for world literature, an interest in their own writers, and a broad range of tastes and preferences. An overall bestseller's list at bokus.se, one of Sweden's largest Internet booksellers, was headed by a new Swedish cookbook, followed by an Italian mystery, a Swedish terror thriller, and a book about Africa. Last on the list was a new children's book, *Mamma Mu och Kråkans jul*/Mamma Cow and Kråkan's Christmas. Of the bestsellers in fiction, half were by Swedish writers, including Viveca Lärn's *April väder*/April Weather—the seventh novel in a series about life on Saltön, an island in the western archipelago; Helena Henschen's *Hon älskade*/She Loved—a novel about a bourgeois daughter caught up in the revolutionary ideals of the early twentieth century; Lena Ebervall and Per E. Samuelson's *Era Majestäts olyckliga Kurt*/His Majesty's Unlucky Kurt—a work of historical fiction about the relationship between

King Gustav V of Sweden and Kurt Haiby; Erik Andersson's *Den larmande hopens dal*/The Valley of the Noisy Crowd—"an original and genial picture of Swedishness" by Sweden's translator of the Tolkien series; and Linda Olsson's *Sonat till Miriam*/Sonnet to Miriam—a novel about the importance of interpersonal communication, the dangers of silence, discovering the past, and love by a Swede now living in New Zealand. The other five books were by foreign authors including Brazilian Paulo Coelho, American-French writer Jonathan Littell, Norwegian Anne Ragde, Englishman Conn Iggulden, and American Joyce Carol Oates. Among the best-selling nonfiction works were P. O. Enquist's autobiographic *Ett annat liv*/Another Life, Maria Eriksson's *Emma, Mias dotter*/Emma, Mia's Daughter), Caroline Engvall's *14 år till salu*/Fourteen Years for Sale, C. M. Palm's *ABBA—the Story*, Herman Lindqvist's *Madame de Pompadour*, and biographies of Hitler by Bengt Liljegren and Mussolini by Göran Hägg. Enquist is the only author in this list who is generally identified as a major writer in Sweden. However, a closer look at the others reveals winners of major writing awards including the August Prize from the Swedish Publishers Association.

The online and print publication of the Swedish Book Dealers Association and the Swedish Publishers Association (*Svenska Bokhandlareföreningen och Svenska Förläggareföreningen*) *Svensk Bokhandel* presents a slightly different best-sellers picture. Its top 10 (from first to tenth) included seven Swedish, two American, and one English author:

- Liza Marklund's *En plats i solen*/A Place in the Sun—the eighth in her crime series featuring Annika Bengtzon.
- Mark Levengood's *Hjärtat får inga rynkor*/The Heart Doesn't Wrinkle—in which the author creates a strange world of fascinating pairings including a Chinese Elvis impersonator dancing with the queen of Denmark.
- Conn Iggulden's *Bågens mästare*/The Bow Master—the second historical fiction work in his series about Ghengis Khan.
- Jan Guillou's *Men inte om det gäller din dotter*/But Not If It Means Your Daughter—a new volume in his Carl Gustaf Gilbert Hamilton spy series.
- Åsa Larsson's *Till dess din vrede upphör*/Until Your Anger Ends—the fourth novel in her crime series set in Norrland and featuring Police Inspector Anna-Maria Mella.
- Mary Ann Shaffer's *Guernseys litteratur- och potatisskalspajsällskap*/The Guernsey Literary and Potato Peel Pie Society. Shaffer, an American author who died in 2008, sought to capture the experiences of the people of Guernsey during World War II via the correspondence between a fictional English author and a group of the island's residents.
- John Theorin's *Nattfåk*/Night Snow—a murder mystery set on Öland.

- Bodil Malmsten's *Sista boken från Finistère*/Last Book from Finistére—another book in her fictional Finistére island series.
- Jens Lapidus's *Aldrig fucka upp*/Never Fuck Up—a crime novel set in Stockholm and written from the criminal's perspective.
- Ken Follett's *En värld utan slut*/World without End—a work of historical fiction set in the late fourteenth century and a sequel to his earlier *The Pillars of the Earth.*

A third way to get at the question of who are the leading writers of contemporary Sweden is to look at the list of winners of the annual August Prizes, awards given annually by the Swedish Publishers Association to the best in fiction, nonfiction, and children's literature.

The winners in fiction over the last few years have been:

- 2008: Per Olav Enquist's *Ett annat liv*/Another Life. It was described by the selection committee as "an autobiographic chronicle with an element of personally-lived literary history and personal revelation in tragic-comedy form: he bores down on a point of pain in the self and takes us along on a diabolic journey that, despite all, has a happy ending." (The winner for children's literature was Jakob Wegelius for *Legenden om Sally Jones*/The Legend of Sally Jones—the story of gorilla.)
- 2007: Carl-Henning Wijkmark's *Stundande natten*/The Next Night (or) The Coming Night, which was described as "an existential chamber play" on death and dying told by Hasse, a patient in the last stages of his life and waiting for death. Rather than wait silently, Hasse explores what death means to him, to those with him in the ward, and to society.
- 2006: Swedish-Finnish writer Susanna Alakoski's *Svinalängorna*/The Pigsties. The book was set in an immigrant and working class district in the south Swedish city of Ystad that acquired the nickname "The Pigsties." Built around the troubled lives of Finnish immigrants, parents, neighbors, and friends, and of the means children use to survive, the story is told by 10-year-old Leena. In what was Alakoski's first novel, she blends the happy, humorous, sad, and deeply troubling. The book has been made into a feature film.
- 2005: Swedish-Finnish writer Monika Fagerholm's *Den amerikanska flickan*/ The American Girl. This is the story of the drowning of a young American girl near Helsinki and the impact she and this event had on the lives of several area teenagers.
- 2004: Bengt Ohlsson's *Gregorius*. In this the author takes Hjalmar Söderberg's classic *Dr. Glas* and tells the story through the eyes of the aging minister, Gregorius, who is ultimately murdered by Glas who has fallen in love with the pastor's much younger wife. It is described as deeply psychological and realistic.

- 2003: Kerstin Ekman's *Skraplotter*/Remnants is the last in a trilogy titled *Vargskinnet*/The Wolf Skin about three generations of women that began with Hillevis, then moved on to her daughter, Myrten, and finally to her granddaughter, Ingefrid. Set in twentieth-century Jämtland, it deals with secrets, closing the circles of stories within the story, and what is known and unknown.
- 2002: Carl-Johan Vallgren's *Den vidunderliga kärlekens historia*/The Remarkable Love Story is set in the nineteenth century and centers on Hercule Barfuss, a deaf dwarf born in a whorehouse in Königsberg who can read people's minds. Vallgren blends the historic and the fantastic, love and hate, kindness and cruelty in a kind of survival tale.
- 2001: Torbjörn Flygt's *Underdog* is another growing up story, this time set in a housing development in Malmö in the 1960s and 1970s. The narrator, Johan, tells the story from two perspectives that are randomly interwoven throughout the narrative—as a child growing up and as an adult looking back. Overall, he wonders why some do well and some do not, some go wrong and others do not, and why life takes people down such different paths, often for no clear reason.
- 2000: Mikael Niemi's *Populärmusik från Vittula*/Popular Music from Vittula is another growing up novel. Set in the far north of Sweden in the 1960s and 70s, it deals with the struggle between the world of the older generation and the modern world—symbolized by the rock and roll music of the area's teenagers. This book also became a 2004 feature film.[28]

An interesting point about these authors is their generational differences. Flygt, Vallgren, Ohlsson, Fagerholm, and Alakoski were all born in the early 1960s. Ekman and Wijkmark were born in the early 1930s. The earlier generation deals with death and/or generational issues. Three of the younger authors, perhaps not surprisingly, focus on growing up in environments beset by problems; two of them deal with larger, more psychological issues. As a group, they address many of the themes common to early twenty-first century Swedish (and world) literature.

Notes

1. One of the most recent and best general works on the history of Swedish literature is Lars Warme, ed., *A History of Swedish Literature* (Lincoln, NE: University of Nebraska Press, 1996).
2. Warme, History of Swedish Literature, p. 129.
3. See http://www.svenskaakademien.se/web/De_Aderton.aspx. Accessed July 22, 2009.
4. Warme, History of Swedish Literature. See also *Nordisk forfattereatlas* at http://www.nrk.no/kultur/forfatteratlas. Accessed July 30, 2009.

5. For a complete list of his writings, see http://www.blekingemuseum.se/lansbibl/forfattare/mobeverk.asp. Accessed July 20, 2009.

6. Two of his Stockholm novels have been translated. See P. A. Fogelström, *City of My Dreams*, translated by Jennifer Brown Baverstam (Penfield Press, 2000) and *Children of Their City* (2008).

7. See http://www.svenskaakademien.se/web/Peter_Englund_2.aspx. Accessed July 21, 2009.

8. See http://www.svenskaakademien.se/web/Peter_Englund_2.aspx. Accessed July 30, 2009. It is unclear at this site who said or wrote these words. They seem to be Englund's. See his own Web site, too. http://www.peterenglund.com/. Accessed July 21, 2009.

9. See http://www.deckarakademin.se/. Accessed July 21, 2009. This is a fascinating group! The members in 2008 included Tomas Arvidsson, K. Arne Blom, Thomas Böös, Ulf Durling, Jan-Olof Ekholm, Jan Ekström, Karl G. Fredriksson, Lilian Fredriksson, Inger Frimansson, Anders Hammarqvist, Dag Hedman, John-Henri Holmberg, Anna Jansson, Maria Neij, Per Olaisen, Marie Peterson, Ulla Trenter, Helene Tursten, Gunilla Wedding, Sven Westerberg, Bibbi Wopenka, Johan Wopenka, and Ulf Örnkloo; and honorary members Johan Asplund, Ted Bergman, Jean Bolinder, Jan Broberg, Bo Lundin, Iwan Morelius, Maj Sjöwall, Staffan Westerlund, and Bertil R. Widerberg.

10. See http://homepages.gac.edu/~fister/scandcrime/. Accessed July 21, 2009. This is a site on Scandinavian crime fiction maintained at Gustavus Adolphus College.

11. The Swedish version of Jungstedt's comments reads: *Gotland är en perfekt scen för kriminalromaner; det instängda, det slutna I och med att det är en ö med kustlinjen som en cirkel runt omkring. Ondskan kommer närmare, blir tydlig I det lilla samhället där platser och människor har en relation till varandra. Miljön på Gotland är också oerhört tacksam att skildra. Det vilda, vindpinade och karga landskapet, de långa stränderna, de höga kalkstensklipporna som stupar rätt ner i havet, de ångande myrmarkerna, de förvridna martallarna.* This was at http://www.marijungstedt.se/, a Web site that is no longer active.

12. See Mankell's Web site http://www.henningmankell.com/. Accessed July 21, 2009.

13. See her Web site at http://www.salomonssonagency.com/authors.php?id=54. Accessed July 21, 2009.

14. For general information about Stieg Larsson, see http://www.stieglarsson.com/ and http://www.vanityfair.com/culture/features/2009/12/hitchens-200912. Accessed April 5, 2010.

15. See Ingeborg Kongslien, "Migrant or Multicultural Literature in the Nordic Countries," *Eurozine*. At http://www.eurozine.com/articles/2006-08-03-kongslien-en.html. Accessed July 21, 2009. Published originally in English in Jenny Fossum Grønn (ed.), *Nordic Voices. Literature of the Nordic Countries* (Oslo: Nordbok, 2005).

16. See the Web site of *Sveriges internationella författarförening*/Sweden's Association of International Writers at http://sviff.immi.se/. Accessed July 21, 2009. See also Immigrant-institutet/The Immigrant Institute at http://www.immi.se/. Accessed July 21, 2009.

17. See http://dagensbok.com/2008/01/27/li-li-ursprunget/. Accessed July 21, 2009.

18. On Khemiri, see http://www.khemiri.se/english-info/jonas-hassen-khemiri. Accessed July 21, 2009.

19. An excellent overview history of children's books in Sweden, Sonja Svensson, *Four Centuries of Children's Books in Sweden* is available as a pdf download at the Web site of *Svenska barnboksinstitutet*/The Swedish Institute for Children's Books athttp://www.sbi.kb.se/default.aspx?id=312&epslanguage=EN-GB/ For a history of children's literature in Sweden see http://www.sbi.kb.se/en/Research/History-of-Swedish-Childrens-Literature/. Accessed April 4, 2010.

20. For a Swedish language version of this story, see http://www.expressen.se/noje/bocker/1.924415/pomperipossa-i-monismanien?standAlone=true&viewstyle=print. Accessed July 21, 2009.

21. See http://www.biblioteksforeningen.org/press/2003/030917.html. Accessed July 21, 2009.

22. See http://www.biblioteksforeningen.org/utmark/holgersson/2007.html. Accessed July 21, 2009.

23. See http://www.biblioteksforeningen.org/utmark/holgersson/2008.html. Accessed July 21, 2009. The Swedes also award the *Litteraturpriset till Astrid Lindgrens minne*/The Astrid Lindgren Memorial Prize. The competition is international. Among the winners are: 2008, Sonya Hartnett (Australia); 2007, Banco del Libro (Venezuelan organization); 2006, Katherine Paterson (USA); 2005, Ryôji Arai (Japan) and Philip Pullman(Great Britain); 2004, Lygia Bojunga (Brazil); 2003, Christine Nöstlinger (Austria) and Maurice Sendak (United States). See http://www.alma.se/en/. Accessed July 21, 2009.

24. From a review by Marilyn Stasio in at *Variety*'s Web site, February 11, 2008. See http://www.variety.com/review/VE1117936172.html?categoryid=33&cs=1. Accessed July 21, 2009.

25. For general news about theater in Sweden, See http://www.nummer.se/Default____616.aspx. Accessed July 21, 2009. For a review of Noren's latest play, see http://nummer.se/Templates/Review____7185.aspx. Accessed July 21, 2009.

26. See also Tomas Tranströmer, *The Half-Finished Heaven*, translated by Robert Bly (Greywolf Press, 2001), 90. Many of his works are available in English translation.

27. This is quoted from Bonnier's description of the author. The original Swedish is: *I den våg av kvinnlig nyskapande poesi som vi har upplevt i Sverige under de senaste 10-15 åren är hon en av de centrala gestalterna och hennes dikter har befunnit sig mitt i den diskussion om poesin som pågått.* See http://www.albertbonniersforlag.se/Forfattare/Forfattarpresentation/?personId=6504. Accessed July 21, 2009.

28. See http://www.forlaggareforeningen.se/. Accessed July 21, 2009. (English option.) For 2008, as an example, Enquist won from a field of 148 nominated books including *Men hur små poeter finns det egentligen* by Eva-Stina Byggmästar, *Tal och Regn* by Katarina Frostenson, *Reglerna* by Sara Mannheimer, *Edelcrantz förbindelser* by Malte Persson, and *Svart Som Silver* by Bruno K Öijer.

7

Performing Arts

THE PERFORMING ARTS in Sweden—theater, opera, dance, music, and film—are vital, varied, original, multicultural, and internationally important. In part the richness they reflect arises from history. All, except film and related contemporary digital arts, have existed in Sweden for centuries. At the same time, government policies and (often) financial support, the relative prosperity of contemporary Swedish society, recent demographic changes, globalization, and technology have been important in fostering these elements of Swedish culture, especially since the end of World War II. The Social Democrats were in power for much of this time, and, as has been noted elsewhere, they pursued policies intended to democratize every aspect of Swedish life, including culture, as part of building the people's home/*folkhemmet*. Their goals, embodied in a package of legislation enacted in 1974 and modified slightly in 1996, included:

- Freedom of expression for everyone.
- Equality for all to participate in cultural opportunities.
- Encouragement of cultural and expressive diversity.
- Independence from institutional or governmental interference.
- Preservation and utilization of Sweden's cultural heritage.
- Cultural participation as a way of learning.
- International cultural exchange and interaction.[1]

In ways, these policy goals helped lead to another "Swedish model," this time for the arts, as Sweden developed a reputation as an ideal place for both the creators of art and culture and for their audiences. Of course, this model had its critics, and there were those who argued that instead of getting variety, richness, and independence, Swedes were subjected to a period remarkable for its conformity and lack of the very things intended.[2]

After coming to power in 2006, the non-Socialist coalition government, led by Fredrik Reinfeldt, sought to pursue policies that would trim some aspects of state involvement (and expense) in many aspects of life in Sweden. Not surprisingly, the performing and visual arts came under scrutiny. In 2007, a cultural commission (*Kulturutredningen*) was established to review policies and prepare proposals for new legislation. Its report was brought back to the government in early 2009. Interestingly, it did not mention sweeping budgetary cuts or attack earlier governments' policies. It listed four principal goals: the elevation of regard for culture and the arts in society, greater engagement of local and county agencies in cultural planning, a democratic and nonbureaucratic system of administration, and reduction in the degree of central direction. Among the specific goals it set forth were:

- to foster a multifaceted cultural pluralism and international interaction.
- to support artistic creativity in the broadest and least restrictive sense and create places for artistic abilities to develop.
- to ensure the preservation, interpretation, and use of Sweden's cultural heritage.
- to see that cultural competence and creativity be used in socially, environmentally, and economically sustainable ways.

Some believe that all of this was just rhetoric, and that the real goal was to reduce state financial support and encourage greater privatization—a direction that has been taken in other areas of public policy in Sweden and might be called "trimming the welfare state." In response, a shadow commission was preparing its own report that would oppose the turning over arts development to the whims of the market, which is seen as inevitable with privatization. An interesting and important discussion is likely to ensue.[3]

Theater

As in so many other aspects of Swedish life, the roots of the country's contemporary theater scene lie far back in history. In Lars Löfgren's recent history of the theater in Sweden, one meets the storytellers of the Viking Age (eighth to eleventh centuries), enactments of Biblical tales in the medieval church, and the entertainments of the royal court in the sixteenth, seventeenth, and eighteenth centuries as precursors of the modern theater. As Stockholm increasingly became the center of the country's political life, it also developed as a cultural center. Traveling companies from Germany, France, the Netherlands, and England came to the city to stage productions of plays and operas. For more than two centuries, the most important location for these was *Stora Bollhuset*/The Great Ball House, an indoor ball game center near to the royal palace. It also was the home of Sweden's first royal theater company (1737–54) and the location for many of Gustav III's theater activities in the late eighteenth century. Another popular site for theater was *Lejonkulan*/The Lion's Den. An interesting moment in its history occurred in the late seventeenth century when students from Uppsala University, tired of the predominance of foreign or imported theater (including the plays and the actors), intentionally put on dramas *in Swedish* that were written by Swedes. (Parenthetically, today's national theater, *Dramaten* has named its children's theater center *Lejonkulan*.)

Most important for today was the founding of the *Kongliga Svenska Dramatiska Theatern*/Royal Swedish Dramatic Theater in 1788 by Gustav III, a king who loved the theater and wrote, directed, and acted in plays. (Some believe his entire reign was a sequence of acts in a play of his own design.) For decades this company had a virtual monopoly on theater in the capital, staging performances at Makalös Palace until it burned in the 1820s and then in facilities it shared with the Royal Opera. It purchased a theater on *Kungsträgårdsgatan* in the 1860s and remained there for nearly 50 years. Driven by the increasingly lively theater environment, new literature, and the competitive entertainments climate of the late nineteenth century, a campaign for a new theater was launched in 1901. This resulted in the company's present home on *Nybroplan*, in the heart of the city. Designed by Fredrik Lilljekvist in an elaborate Vienna Jugend style, it opened in February 1908 with a production of August Strindberg's *Master Olof.*

The history of the royal theater has not been entirely one of easy success. Internal turmoil, politics, and competition have all affected it. During the nineteenth century, for example, its costs were criticized by the farmers, who enjoyed considerable power in the parliament. In the 1880s, "royal" was dropped from its name—hence today's title, *Dramaten*—the crown's financial backing ended, and central state support became a plaything of conflicting factions in the parliament. Mission was an often-debated issue, and this translated into the question of repertoire. Just what should the theater offer as productions and why? The debate has long revolved around two poles: produce what the public wants or produce great theater—past and contemporary. Behind this debate lay issues of social equality, democracy, and how culture is defined and by whom. Along with funding, this debate has occupied the attentions of virtually all of *Dramaten's* managing directors, and, not surprisingly, the latter mission has generally been the preferred. Currently, the company offers the following as a statement of mission: "*Dramaten* is Sweden's national theater responsible for presenting classical dramas, new Swedish and foreign plays, and theater for children and young people."

Dramaten is, in many ways, the most important fixed-site theater company in contemporary Sweden. Its managing directors, who are consistently leaders in the field of performing arts, have included Lars Löfgren (1986–97), an author and director who headed Swedish Television's Theater for many years and worked with Ingmar Bergman; Ingrid Dahlberg (1997–2002), an author, radio and television personality, and now director of *Svensk Scenkonst*/ Swedish Performing Arts (an organization representing the interests of arts employers); Staffan Valdemar Holm (2002–9), an experienced director who some believe is second only to Bergman in ability; and Marie-Louise Ekman (2009–), best known as an artist (painter) and film director. The acting company includes many of Sweden's finest performing artists. Presented on seven stages,

Dramaten, Stockholm's flagship repertoire theater. The building was designed by Fredrik Liljekvist and opened in 1908. Today the theater presents productions on seven stages and is deeply involved in both public outreach programs and education. (Courtesy of Brian Magnusson.)

Dramaten's annual schedule is rich and varied, and in a typical year as many as 30 different productions are staged. The 2008–9 season included:

- *Kasimir and Karoline* by the early twentieth-century Hungarian, Ödön von Horvath
- Shakespeare's *The Merry Wives of Windsor*
- Chekov's *Uncle Vanja*
- Schiller's Don Carlos: *Crown Prince of Spain*
- Twentieth-century British writer Joe Penhall's *Dumb Show*
- Twentieth-century French writer Eric-Emmanuel Schmitt's *Little Infidelities*
- Twentieth-century German writer Mariuis von Mayenburg's *The Ugly*
- Tolstoy's *The Power of Darkness*
- Yasmina Reza's *The God of Carnage* (She is French of Iranian and Hungarian Jewish parents.)
- Nineteenth-century Swedish writers Victoria Benedictsson and Axel Lundegård's *Final*
- Contemporary Norwegian Jon Fosse's *Death in Thebes*
- Contemporary Swede Sara Stridsberg's *Medealand*
- Martina Montelius's adaptation of Lennart Hellsing's *Spaghetti—You Got that Right* for children
- Nina Wester's *Love and the Circus Birds*

Total attendance in 2006 was about 260,000.

In addition to its production role, *Dramaten* is a center for education about theater arts for both the public and future professionals. From its founding until 1964, it operated a drama school, and it remains connected with *Teaterhögskolan*/College of Performing Arts, the country's leading theater arts school.[4]

Also very important and certainly having a larger reach than *Dramaten* is *Riksteatern*, The National Theater. This is Sweden's primary touring and theater outreach company. It was established in 1933–34 under the leadership of Arthur Engberg, then Minister of Church Affairs, Education, and Culture in Per Albin Hansson's first Government—the government that initiated the development of Sweden's *folkhemmet*. Its mission has been to bring the performing arts, in all their variety, to all of Sweden. Today's *Riksteatern* is based on 21 county (*län*) and more than 200 local theater associations, and has more than 42,000 members. It defines itself in the following ways:

> *Riksteatern* is a folk movement that arranges and promotes theater arts and is a touring national theater for everyone.

> *Riksteatern* seeks to give everyone the opportunities to experience varied and quality theater arts, regardless of where one lives, or one's gender, age, education, or social or ethnic background.
>
> *Riksteatern* seeks to stimulate thoughts and feelings by presenting mental paradoxes in a variety of languages.
>
> *Riksteatern* shall through its ventures contribute to every citizen becoming involved in, having an influence on and feeling a part of the society.
>
> *Riksteatern* shall be a forerunner for the implementation and development of innovative forms of involvement, participation and influence to create the democracy of tomorrow.[5]

Riksteatern is a constantly evolving institution in Swedish cultural life. Among the important developments that have helped define it have been the addition of the Cullberg Ballet Company, the founding of the country's first theater program dedicated specifically for children and young people in 1967, the inclusion of the *Södra Teatern* (Söder Theater) in Stockholm into its repertoire in 1972, the addition of the hearing challenged company, *Tyst teater* (Silent Theater), in 1977, starting *Plural* as a medium for youth culture in 2003, and important increases in its multicultural programs. A three-year cooperative effort with *Dramaten* was initiated in 2009. In recent years it has developed 80 or more productions of its own and sponsored literally thousands of performances and special events. Attendance totaled more than 1 million in 2007. The schedule offered at *Riksteaterns* Web site is dizzying and includes something for everyone—including dance, musicals, comedy, serious drama, the classics, children's theater, and programs by touring international companies and ensembles.

Södra Teatern occupies a special place in theater life in Sweden, and especially Stockholm. First, because it is one of Sweden's oldest theaters (built in 1858), albeit repeatedly remodeled; and second, because it is the center for alternative cultural experiences in virtually every genre. The vision it holds is summed up in the following: "We are particularly interested in the great cities of the world, where hybrid cultural encounters occur and other subcultural expressions develop. On our stages we will show alternative pictures of the world than one usually encounters."[6] So, for example, it has hosted

- a series of concerts and debates on identity called "Etno-Porno-Gender-Bender-Multi-Kulti-Queer Party!" in 2000,
- a series of concerts and readings that focused on the political radicalization of music in 2002,
- appearances by Egypt's pop idol Hakim and the highly controversial Turkish star Bülent Ersoy (who underwent sex change operations in 1981 to become a woman) in 2003, and

- some of the first performances of hip hop theater (that includes or celebrates rapping, DJing, graffiti writing, and breakdancing) in Sweden in 2004.

The two state-supported giants in the theater world are not, however, the only contributors to the country's theater life. Stockholm's *Stadsteater*/City Theater, located almost literally in the center of the capital in *Kulturhuset*/The Culture House on Sergelstorg, has the largest attendance figures of any theater in Sweden—more than 460,000 in 2006. It, too, tends to offer something for everyone in terms of program variety. For example, in January 2009 Jonas Hassen Khemiri's *Fem gånger gud*, Chekov's *Three Sisters*, an adaptation of Spanish writer Pedro Almodovar's *Allt om min mamma*/Everything about My Mother, a marionette theater production, *Kärleksöperan—Fröding Naked*, Edward Albee's *Who's Afraid of Virginia Woolf*, and Selma Lagerlöf's *Charlotte Löwensköld* were some of the productions being offered.

Finally, this survey would not be complete without mentioning two historically important theaters. The first is one of the oldest in world, the Palace Theater (*Slottsteater*) on the grounds of Drottningholm Palace outside Stockholm. The current building dates from 1766 and saw its greatest use during the last years of Gustav III's reign (1771–92). Following the king's death the theater languished, but it was restored, modernized, and reopened in 1922. Familiar to many as the location for Ingmar Bergman's film version of *The Magic Flute*, it is used today for several summer productions. (In 2010, Mozart's *La finta giardiniera* and *Don Giovanni* were scheduled.) The second is *Strindbergs Intima Teater*/Strindberg's Intimate Theater, established in 1907 by the author and the actor August Falck as a smaller, more intimate venue (fewer than 200 seats). It was dedicated to staging Strindberg's plays and shaping actors and performances in his mold. Following his death in 1912, the theater became a center for the activities of the Graphic Arts Association. Efforts to restore the theater began in the 1980s, and in 2002 a remodeled theater reopened, dedicated to carrying on Strindberg's vision but also to offering variety in its productions and audiences. Among the offerings on the theater's schedule in 2009 and 2010 were two plays by Strindberg, *Brott och brott*/Crimes and Crimes and *Dödsdansen*/*Dance of Death; Ett litet drömspel*/A Small Dream Play, an original work by contemporary director and writer Staffan Westerberg; a concert by Carl Michael Bellman imitator Mikael Sammuelsson; and *Widows* by Joyce Carol Oates.

Clearly, the theater is live and well in contemporary Sweden, and there is something for every taste. The offerings of the giants, *Dramaten* and *Riksteatern*, make this evident. But so, too, do other important venues such as the fine city theaters of Göteborg, Uppsala, Helsingborg, and Malmö, and the county and regional theaters like those in Örebro, Växjö, Västerås, or Sundsvall.

In addition, there are many smaller and/or less well-known venues such as Sami, circus, ethnic, Jewish, and *avant garde* or bistro theaters. Finally, there are the literally thousands of productions and readings by local dramatic study groups and similar organizations.

BALLET AND OPERA

Ballet and opera also occupy places of importance in Sweden's cultural life. At the top of the list for both are the national companies based in Stockholm. Their histories parallel closely that of the theater. It was Gustav III who established Royal Opera and the Royal Ballet in 1773, and he encouraged and was directly involved in their activities. Ironically, he was fatally wounded in March 1792 at a masked ball being held in the opera house that had opened for these groups a decade before, and this event served as the basis for Verdi's opera *Un ballo in maschera*/A Masked Ball. That original house was the home for opera and ballet in the capital until it was razed in 1892 to make room for Axel Anderberg's neoclassical building, which opened in 1898 and remains home to both companies today.

Some of the other companies that have developed include those for both ballet and opera in Göteborg, *Skånes Dansteater* based in Malmö, *Norrlandsoperan* based in Umeå, and *Värmlandsoperan* based in Karlstad. All of these recognize the need to present a variety of programs, so a review of any of their season schedules would reveal both classical and contemporary works. In addition, many serve as centers for training future singers and dancers, such as the Royal Swedish Ballet School in Stockholm and the Swedish Ballet School in Göteborg.[7]

Productions range from the classical to the very contemporary. One of the most popular is a uniquely Swedish work, *Värmlänningarna*/The Värmlanders, a "sorrowful spoken, song, and dance drama" by Fredrik August Dahlgren with music by Anders Randel. It debuted at the Royal Opera in 1846 and has been performed there more than 800 times! It has also been made into a film five times and produced repeatedly on Swedish radio (directed for many years by Ingmar Bergman) and television. Laden with nineteenth-century social class and parental power elements, as well as tunes from Swedish folk music, the plot revolves around the love affair between Erik, son of a well-to-do iron works owner, and Anna, daughter of a simple crofter, and the conflicts they face—especially with Erik's father who has very different ideas about a bride for his son. (The play was also very popular in Swedish-America.)

Sweden has produced a number of internationally recognized opera singers including sopranos Jenny Lind (1820–87), Kristina Nilsson (1843–1921),

Birgit Nilsson (1918–2005), and Anne-Sofie Taube (1955–); tenor Jussi Björling (1911–60); and baritone Håkon Hagegård (1945–)—all of whom toured in the United States or performed with American companies.

Stockholm's opera house is not the only truly magnificent venue for opera and ballet. Among many others one of the most notable is the Göteborg Opera, which opened in 1994. This spectacular building, located on the edge of one of the canals that help define that city, was designed by Göteborg native, Jan Izikowitz, who sought to make the building fit with the dominant shapes of the waterfront area. One of the most technologically advanced theater spaces in all of Europe, the main hall seats just over 1,300 while a separate small theater seats 230.

Music

As with every other performing art in Sweden, variety helps define what is currently available for music lovers, and "something for everyone" certainly holds true. World-class professional, internationally and nationally recognized, institutional and organizational ensembles and solo performers, and thousands of just-for-fun bands and individuals populate the Swedish music landscape. Some of the music performed is distinctly Swedish, drawn from history or newly composed; some is in one or another global genre. On any given day in almost any given city, one can listen to live classical and modern symphonic, religious and secular choral, folk, country, rock, rap, blues, jazz, and ethnic music. Swedish musical tastes are broad, and the main differences tend to be, not surprisingly, between generations.[8]

If one takes what used to be considered high culture first, one encounters symphonic music, old and contemporary, performed by an range of ensembles that runs from the elite (Stockholm's Royal Philharmonic Orchestra, the orchestras of the established opera companies, or the Swedish Radio Orchestra), to smaller professional groups, to amateur orchestras of communities and regions, to the ensembles of gymnasia that specialize or offer extensive programs in music like those in Danderyrd, Växjö, or Falun. In addition, there are what most Americans think of a bands, which in Sweden are called "wind orchestras." These are not brass bands whose repertoires are dominated marches, but concert ensembles that play diverse repertoires that include both older and contemporary works either composed or adapted for this type of ensemble.

The venues for these groups range from superbly designed, dedicated concert halls to sport arenas, school auditoria, and churches. Among the first group are Stockholm's *Konserthus* (home of the Royal Symphony) and

Berwaldhallen (home for the Swedish Radio Orchestra and Choir), Göteborg's Concert Hall (home for the Göteborg Symphony Orchestra), and the Helsingborg Concert Hall (home of the Helsingborg Symphony Orchestra). What these buildings and many others illustrate, beyond their architectural and technical qualities, is the commitment in Sweden not only to encouraging the development of the performing arts through public funding, but also the commitment to providing excellent facilities.

A number of very fine composers have been part of the orchestral, symphonic, and choral music scenes in Sweden. Among these are:

- Franz Berwald (1796–1868), perhaps the best known member of one of Sweden's leading musical families. His works include four symphonies.
- Wilhelm Peterson-Berger (1867–1942), known best for his piano and choral compositions.
- Wilhelm Stenhammar (1871–1927), whose works include two symphonies, two operas, and a variety of pieces for chamber orchestras and piano.
- Hugo Alfvén (1872–1960), a composer of works for voice and orchestra, and best known for his Swedish Rhapsody No. 1, *Midsummer Vigil.*
- Ingvar Lidholm (1921–), known for his orchestral and choral works, some of which are highly experimental in sound.
- Sven-David Sandström (1942–), an orchestral and choral conductor and composer of the opera *Jeppe: The Cruel Comedy,* a piece based on Ludvig Holberg's eighteenth-century comedy.
- Fredrik Sixten (1962–), an organist and church music composer.
- Lars-Erik Vilner Larsson (1908–86), a composer principally of symphonic music.
- Allan Pettersson (1911–80), whose 17 symphonies have earned him a place as one of Sweden's finest and most productive composers. About his work he once said that he sought "to recover the songs once sung by the soul."

Folk music occupies a special place in this review. Just as in so many other places around the world, a culture of people's music or music of the commoners has existed for centuries. None of the celebrations of the rural communities of the country would have been the same without the songs and dances that went with them, played by local musicians on traditional instruments that are still used today. In the early nineteenth century, efforts were made to collect some of these as part of the broader work of defining Sweden and making the people Swedes. The preservation and celebration of folk culture was woven into one of the popular movements of the late nineteenth century, illustrated in the Nordic Museum and its outdoor adjunct, Skansen, as well as in the displays and performances at the 1897 Stockholm Exposition. Although interest waned in the early third of the last century, it returned following World War II, and today the playing of Swedish folk music either in concert venues or at dances and other celebrations is one of the most vital aspects of the music scene in Sweden. Literally hundreds of local folk musician organizations (*spelmanslag*) are spread across the country. Several national umbrella organizations help organize programs, including the National Association for Folk Music and Dance/*Riksförbundet för folkmusik och dans* and the Swedish Folk Dance Circle/*Svenska Folksdansringen.* The former has more than 15,000 members.

Traditional instruments are also important in this genre. The fiddle, accordion, and some variant of the guitar or mandolin (stringed and fretted) are common. Occasionally, a clarinet is used, and there are several types of Swedish bagpipes. Most interesting of all is the *nyckelharpa* or, literally, the keyed harp. Related distantly to the hurdy-gurdy, its roots appear to go back to the fourteenth century in Sweden. Looking something like a violin, a common version has four melody strings and a dozen sympathetic or drone strings. Several rows of keys are used to select or dampen combinations of strings (a la an autoharp), while the sound is produced by bowing the strings. The sound is unique with aspects of violin, the Norwegian Hardanger fiddle's drone strings, and even the harpsichord.[9]

Mention Swedish pop music to anyone over 30, and the immediate response is likely to be something about ABBA, the quartet of Benny Andersson, Björn Ulvaeus, Anni-Frid (Frida) Lyngstad, and Agnetha Fältskog that entered the music scene in the early 1970s. For a decade this group enjoyed enormous popularity and was one of Sweden's main exports. By some counts they are the second largest selling group in history after The Beatles, and they continue to sell several million records each year. Their songs, such as "Dancing Queen," "Take a Chance on Me," "Mamma Mia," and "Voulez Vous," stay in your head for years. ABBA's enduring popularity has been helped by new works from the ever-creative team of Andersson and Ulvaeus, such as the worldwide stage hit and 2008 film *Mamma Mia!* and the Swedish stage hit *Kristina från Duvemåla*—the latter based on Vilhelm Moberg's emigration novels.

The pop music scene in Sweden in the first decade of the twenty-first century is much more diverse than 20 years ago, populated by dozens of groups with primarily a Swedish following and by several with international recognition and broad international touring experience. The latter includes the team of Per Gessle and Maria Fredriksson in Roxette, the band The Cardigans, and solo performer Robyn. Gessle and Fredriksson began work together in the late 1970s, and the group took its name in the mid-1980s. As of 2007, they had produced seven major albums over the years. Among their best-known singles are "The Look," "Listen to Your Heart," and "Joyride." They are also featured on the soundtrack for the film *Pretty Woman* with the song "It Must Have Been Love." The Cardigans came together in 1992 and achieved real recognition with their second album, *Life*, from 1995. Over the years, and in spite of several extended breaks, they have produced seven albums, the latest being a "best of" from 2008. Among their better-known songs are "Erase/Rewind," "My Favorite Game," and "Love Fool." Robyn is a U.S. Grammy-nominated solo vocalist and songwriter. She began her career at 13 and moved into pop in the early 1990s. Since then, she has continued to evolve within the genre and has produced four major albums plus two "best of" compilations. Twenty of her singles have been successful in Sweden and/or internationally. Among her best known are "Do You Really Want Me," "Be Mine," and "With Every Heartbeat." In 2009, she received a Swedish Grammi (equal to an American Grammy) as Best Live Act for 2008.

Among the other popular music genres and a few of the artists are:

Soul

- Kaah, who performs in Swedish; Salem Al Fakir whose father is Syrian and mother Swedish, winner of four Grammis in 2008; Stephen Simmonds.

Rock, Punk Rock, and Heavy Metal

- Dungen—a Stockholm quartet that mixes various influences and styles and performs in Swedish.
- In Flames—a Göteborg group (with lots of member turnover) that has produced nine albums since the early 1990s.
- HammerFall—another Göteborg band with eight albums to its credit since its debut in 1993.
- Hellacopters—produced seven albums before its breakup in the fall of 2008.

Hip Hop, Rap, and Reggae

- Sons of Soul, The Latin Kings, and Just D were among the pioneering groups of the 1980s.
- Snook—a Stockholm duo who perform in Swedish and won the 2006 Grammi for Best Hip Hop Act.
- Adam Tensta—the son of a Gambian father and a Swedish-Finnish mother who grew up in the heavily immigrant Stockholm suburb of Tensta—hence his performer identity. His debut album, *It's a Tensta Thing*, won him the 2007 Grammi for Best Dance/Hip Hop/Soul recording.

- Timbuktu (Jason Michael Robinson Diakité)—born in Lund, has an American father, has lived in the United States, and performs mainly in *skånska* (Scanian Swedish). He has produced seven albums and won five Grammis.
- Interestingly, these genre seem to be particularly suited to the growing cultural heterogeneity of Sweden. Although many artists perform in English, some use Swedish and dialects like *Rinkebysvensk* (see above) that mix Swedish with one or another of the immigrant languages.

Pop

- A rising star in 2009 was Lykke Li. Born in the southern city of Ystad, she spent parts of her growing up years in many places, including Portugal, India, and the United States. Her breakthrough album, *Youth Novels*, came out in 2008. Performing in what has been labeled indie pop, she has developed a wide audience, especially among young people.

Then there is jazz, a musical form with both devoted audiences and a distinguished list of superb performers in Sweden. Although its roots are older, jazz historian and record producer Lars Westin believes that the essential takeoff point for this genre was in the fall of 1933, when Louis Armstrong gave six concerts in Stockholm. It has been live and well since. In a sequence of generations, individual artists and the bands in which they performed have explored and developed the medium, all the while open to the incorporation of new forms and sources of inspiration—such as Swedish folk and rock. Until the advent of rock and roll in the 1960s, the venue for jazz was often the dance hall. Swing and big band styles gave ample places for artists like bassist Thore Jederby, singer Alice Babs, clarinettist Åke Hasselgård, pianist Bengt Hallberg, and baritone sax player Lars Gullin. Although the performance opportunities and audiences narrowed in the 1960s, artists of a new generation of players that included Bernt Rosengren (tenor sax), Maffy Falay (trumpet), Eje Thelin (trombone), Christer Boustedt (alto sax), Jan Johansson (piano), and Monica Zetterlund (voice) carried on. The legacy of these and many other performers continues in the work of artists like trumpeter Göran Kajfes. He and an ensemble of superb collaborators including Per "Texas" Johansson, Jesper Nordenström, Johan Bertling, Mattias Torell, Jonas Kullhammar, Davor Kajfeš, Timbuktu, and David Österberg created the 2004 Grammi-winning album, *Headspin*, which has been described as "an exciting and unexpected mix of electronica, afrobeat, Miles-colored mystique, dub and Balkan-swing, enough to make you all floored."[10] Also vital to the contemporary jazz scene was the Esbjörn Svensson Trio (EST), that won the 2005, 2006, and 2008 Grammis for best jazz album. (Tragically, Svensson died in a diving accident in mid-2008.)[11]

As has already been noted, a gauge of the popularity of current music groups in Sweden are the Grammis, awarded annually in January and based on jury evaluations and (now) popular votes via the Internet. Among there winners for 2009 (awarded in 2010) were:

- Best Album. The punk rocker Joakim Thåström for *Kärlek är för dom som har tur/Love is for the Lucky Ones.*
- Best Artist. Singer and songwriter Lars Winnerbäck for his album *Tänk om jag ångrar mig och sen ångrar mig igen/What if I Change My Mind and then Change It Again.*
- Best Children's Album. Bröderna Lindgren/The Lindgren Brothers for their album *Presenterar meningen med livet! Presenting: The Meaning of Life.*
- Best Dance Band. Larz-Kristerz for their album *Hem till dig/Home to You.*
- Year's Best Folk Music. Sofia Karlsson for her album, *Söder om kärleken/South of Love.*
- Year's Best Hard Rock. The heavy metal band Mustasch for their album *Mustasch.*
- Year's Best Jazz. Singer, composer, and lyricist Jeanette Lindström for her album *Attitude and Orbit Control.*
- Year's Best Classical. Sonanza Chamber Ensemble for their album *Unheard of—Again.*
- Year's Best Club/Hiphop. Rapper Mårtin Edh, known as Promoe, for his album *Kråksången/Song of the Crow.*
- Year's Best Composer. Amanda Jenssen and Pär Wiksten for their album *Happyland.*
- Year's Best Female Artist. 2007 TV4 Idol runner-up Amanda Jenssen for her album *Happyland.*
- Year's Best Male Artist. Lars Winnerbäck for his album *Tänk om jag ångrar mig och sen ångrar mig igen.*
- Year's Best Newcomer. 22-year-old singer-songwriter Erik Hassle for his album *Hassle.*
- Year's Best Rock. Sweden's most popular and most awarded rock band, Kent, for their album *Röd/Red.*
- MTV's Prize for the Best Video. Rapper Jason Michael Robinson Diakité, known as Timbuktu for *Välj mej.*[12]

A number of factors have contributed overall to the liveliness of the music scene in Sweden. One has been the Social Democrats' proactive cultural policies, which provided financial incentives as well as greater educational opportunities. Another has been the development of new recording and listening technologies including stereophonic extended play and longplaying 45 and 33 rpm records, the transistor radio, digital recording technologies, the CD, and now MP3/iPod players, Internet download sources, and YouTube. A third is the growth of urban club cultures in venues like Stockholm's *Stampen*. Fourth is the advance of the large audience concert and the tour culture. Fifth is the development of venues that include huge halls like Stockholm's *Globen*, a host of outdoor stadiums, and countless city and town concert halls such as the charming center in the south central village of Aneby, population 6,700. A sixth is the growth of genre-specific music clubs across the country and the national associations that encourage local musicians as well as arrange concerts by local and touring artists. Seventh is the impact of demographic heterogeneity, which is exemplified in both the ethnic music of the new Swedes and in their contributions to old and current music genre. Finally, there are the forces of Americanization, the British "invasion," the European Union, migration, and globalization that have helped create an incredibly dynamic environment.

Film

Sweden has been developing a film culture since the late nineteenth century. The earliest examples were made under the auspices of the pioneering French film company, *Société Antoine Lumière et ses Fils*. They all ran for about one minute, and themes included King Oscar II's arrival at the Stockholm Exposition (*Stockholms utställning*) on May 15, 1897, and panoramas of various Stockholm sights. Most were directed by Alexanxdre Promio, from France, but a Swede, Ernest Florman (1862–1952), soon became involved. By the early years of the twentieth century, there were theaters for cinema productions in many of the country's cities, and a film industry based largely on the company *Svensk Filmindustri AB*/Swedish Film Industry, Inc., developed. It churned out literally dozens of silent pictures; most of which were soapy romances, melodramatic adventures, or comedies. A few, some drawn from classic works of Swedish literature, were extraordinary for their direction, costumes, cinematography, and acting. A good example is *Gösta Berlings Saga* from 1924. Based on Selmar Lagerlöf's epic novel, it was directed by Mauritz Stiller and featured Greta (Gustafsson) Garbo (1905–90). Mauritz (1883–1928) and Victor Sjöström (1879–1960) were Sweden's leading filmmakers during the silent movie era, and they did much to help establish Sweden's reputation and export market. Both began their careers as actors, moved into directing, were briefly enticed away to Hollywood in the 1920s, and returned to Sweden. Stiller died shortly after his return. Sjöström continued to act, and his last role was as Dr. Isak Borg, the central character in

Ingmar Bergman's *Wild Strawberries* from 1957, a part he especially enjoyed because he got to work with Bibi Andersson, who was 22 at the time!

By most accounts Swedish film in the 1930s, the first decade of talkies, left much to be desired. Audiences declined because of the Depression, tastes turned to the lighthearted, and Sweden lost its edge in the international film market, which was increasingly dominated by Hollywood. Sweden's greatest asset was Garbo, and she remained in America to make a series of films including *The Grand Hotel*, (1932), the historical drama *Queen Christina* (1933), *Anna Karinena* (1935), and *Ninotchka* (1939) until she dropped out of filmmaking in the early 1940s. During World War II, many of the films made were "preparedness movies"—propaganda films designed to increase public awareness to the dangers and national needs during the war. One of the best of these, *Första division*/The First Division, was the work of Hasse Ekman (1915–2004), who was involved in more than 50 films during his career. (He is best known for his 1950 film, *Flicka och hyacinter*/Girl with Hyacinths. Despite the troubles the war imposed on Sweden and the use of film for propaganda purposes, some serious films were produced. Among these was the screen adaptation of Vilhelm Moberg's *Rid i Natt* (1942), directed by Gustaf Molander. It was a thinly veiled critique of the government's neutrality policy that, at the time and for quite good reasons, favored the Germans. Also, Alf Sjöberg (1903–80), whose long career included acting, stage director at *Dramaten*, and filmmaking, directed a number of films based on earlier novels such as *Himlaspelet*/Celestial Drama or Way to Heaven, by Swedish author, director, and actor Rune Lindström (1916–73). At the close of the war he directed *Hets*/Torment. This dark drama was written by Ingmar Bergman and dealt with the tyranny of school teachers and the inability of the education system to deal with students who were different.

After the war, a new generation of filmmakers and actors, increasing government support for film as one aspect of the Social Democrats's larger cultural policies, and growing international opportunities reflected in the success of art film theaters and film festivals helped nurture a renaissance in Swedish film that continues to this day. During this period Swedish film developed and excelled in a number of areas including feature film, documentary, film for children and young people, and television productions. Swedish films were successful in international festival competitions and earned a well-deserved international reputation for quality in every aspect of the genre. While many might typify Swedish films as dark, depressing, and excessively introspective, this assessment is short-sighted and ignores their tremendous range.

The giant in this period was (and in ways still is) Ingmar Bergman (1918–2007). He was a truly extraordinary figure, not just in the history of

Swedish film, but in the history of modern Swedish literature, international film, and live theater in Sweden. His film career began with the screenplay for *Torment* in 1944 and ended with *Saraband* in 2003—more than 60 films. His theater directing career began with *Outward Bound* in 1938 and closed with Henrik Ibsen's *Rosmersholm* in 2004—more than 170 productions in all. In addition, he was an author of screenplays, essays, articles, and monographs including two autobiographic works, *Laterna magica*/The Magic Lantern from 1987 and *Bilder*/Images: My Life in Film from 1990. Among his best known films are: *Summer with Monika* (1953), *The Seventh Seal* (1957), *Wild Strawberries* (1957), *The Virgin Spring* (1960), *Persona* (1966), *Cries and Whispers* (1973), *The Magic Flute* (1975), and *Fanny and Alexander* (1982). Down to the mid-1980s, all of his films were made with Sven Nykvist as his cinematographer, and many featured an ensemble of actors that included Max von Sydow, Bibi and Harriet Andersson, Erland Josephson, Ingrid Thulin, and Liv Ullmann. Dark, brooding, foreboding, existential, frightening, and depressing are words often used by viewers to describe his work, and one cannot resist thinking that Nykvist should have opened the aperture on his camera in many of the black and white films from the 1950s and 1960s. Of course, these reactions are what Bergman sought to arouse as he addressed themes such as the existence of God, trust, redemption, loyalty and betrayal, the meaning (or meaninglessness) of life, angst, love, sexuality, and passion—themes that are broadly part of the human condition and not uniquely Swedish.[13]

Although Bergman was the giant (or the elephant) in the room in post–World War II Swedish film, there are many others who have made films both popular and important to the medium. A small sampling includes Bo Widerberg (1930–97), Mai Zetterling (1925–94), Lena Einhorn (1954–), Roy Andersson (1943–), Jan Troell (1931–), and Lukas Moodysson (1969–).

Widerberg's works include the beautifully filmed romantic tragedy *Elvira Madigan* (1967) about the doomed love between a Danish tightrope walker and a Swedish army officer, and two fine historical dramas: *Ådalen 31* (1969) about the labor unrest in northern Sweden's paper pulp industry and the workers' march to Lunde that was met by soldiers wholly untrained in managing such events and who killed four marchers and an innocent bystander, followed by *Joe Hill* (1971) about the Swedish immigrant labor organizer in America and his tragic end. These films were followed by a couple of mysteries including Sjöwall and Wahlöö's *Mannen på taket*/Man on the Roof (1976). His last film, *Lust och fägring stor*/All Things Fair (1995), was nominated for an Oscar. Set in World War II Sweden, it was a brilliant look at adolescence and an impossible relationship between a teenage boy, played by Widerberg's son Stig, and a teacher.

Mai Zetterling was one of Sweden's leading actresses—both at *Dramaten* and in film. She turned to filmmaking in the 1960s and made a number of highly acclaimed documentaries and three sensual, women-centered productions: *Älskande par*/Loving Couples (1964), *Natt lek*/Night Games (1966), and *Flickorna*/The Girls (1968).

Lena Einhorn is a physician, writer, filmmaker, and producer. She is best known for her 2005 film *Ninas resa*/Nina's Journey. Shot on location in Poland, it is based on Einhorn's August Prize winning book of the same title that tells the story of her mother's life as a young women who survived the Warsaw Ghetto. It took the honors as Best Film and Best Script in the 2005 *Guldbagge*/Golden Beetle competition.

Roy Andersson, once described as a "slapstick Ingmar Bergman," debuted in 1970 with *En kärleks historia*/A Love Story, an intimate and, at the same time,

The Guldbagge/Gold Bug award. Designed by Karl Axel Pehrson (1921–2005), these statues have been awarded by the Swedish Film Institute since 1964. (Courtesy of Swedish Film Institute.)

humorous look at teenage romance and emerging sexuality. His second film, *Giliap* from 1975 was a disaster, and he took over 20 years off from filmmaking to produce critically acclaimed video commercials. His return to film in 2000 with *Sånger från andra våningen*/Songs from the Second Floor was well received. In 2008, he won the Nordic Council Film Prize for his 2007 movie *Du levande*/You, the Living—which also won three 2007 *Guldbagge* for Best Film, Best Director, and Best Script. In making the award the selection jury wrote:

> In the brilliant film *You, the Living*, Andersson focuses on life, death and the fragile yearnings of mankind. With its unique visual style and narrative rhythm this everyday symphony challenges our preconceived attitude to film at the same time as it makes us use our senses in a new way. Instead of telling just one story in a conventional linear style, *You, the Living* is made up of carefully composed sequences from a bizarre world which is simultaneously sad and surrealistically funny. These humorous and tragic tableaux show our best and worst sides, make us laugh and force us to think. In brief, *You, the Living* reminds us of the opportunities that the film media holds for powerful personal experiences.

And Andersson said about the honor:

> The Nordic Council Film Prize is one of the best prizes in the world to win, because it emphasizes that film is not just entertainment, but also an important part of culture. My films are very universal in their own way but they also convey a Nordic mood which helps to create their special expression.[14]

Jan Troell debuted in 1966 with *Här har du ditt liv*/Here is Your Life, based on the great twentieth-century Swedish author Eyvind Johnson's autobiography. Although well received, his reputation rested more on his film versions of Vilhelm Moberg's four historical novels about nineteenth-century emigration to North America. These appeared as *Utvandrarna*/The Emigrants (1971) and *Nybyggarna*/The New Land (1972). Filmed in Sweden and the United States, they masterfully captured the complex story Moberg had labored so long to tell of mid-nineteenth-century emigration to and settlement in North America. Interestingly, Troell stopped making dramatic films for nearly three decades and turned to documentaries. He reappeared in 2001, with *Så vit som en snö*/As White as a Snow, about Sweden's first woman pilot, Elsa Andersson. Set on a train, it was built around a series of flashbacks that delved into Andersson's life. Renewed critical success came in January 2008, when his *Maria Larssons eviga ögonblick*/Everlasting Moments (2007) won five *Guldbaage* including Best Picture. Based on interviews with a daughter of the central character, it was set in the early twentieth century and revolved around the life of a working class wife burdened with too many children and an abusive husband who discovered another side of her world through a camera she won in a drawing. Once again this master of the historical film captured a compelling story from the past—an opinion expressed also by reviewer Astrid Söderbergh Widding when she wrote in the newspaper *Svenska Dagbladet:*

> But, above all, there is something that at base unites Maria Larsson and Jan Troell. That is the fascination for the everlasting moment, the fleeting instants that photography and film capture, the entrances of the past into an eternal present.[15]

Parenthetically, one of Sweden's younger filmmakers, Tomas Alfredson (1965–), also known as a comedian in the popular group *Killinggänget*/ Killing's Gang, won Best Director for *Låt den rätte komma in*/Let the Right One In. This film, which also won five Guldbagge, is based on a very popular Swedish vampire novel by John Ajvide Lindqvist (who also wrote the screen play), but Alfredson turns the focus away from the more ghoulish aspects of vampirism to look at the relationship that develops between Oscar, an isolated, bullied, and teased 12-year-old, and Eli, a vampire trapped eternally in an 12-year-old's body.

Lukas Moodysson's debut film, *Fucking Åmal*/Show Me Love (1998), was set in Åmål, a small city of about 13,000 on the western shore of Lake Vänern. Mixing comedy, youth culture, and pop music, it focused on the development of a lesbian love between two teenagers and how difficult and isolating it is for young people to be different. The film was enormously successful in Sweden and won four Guldbagge including Best Film, Best Director, Best Actress (shared by the two leading players), and Best Script. His second success was the documentary-style film *Tillsammens*/Together (2000), which explored life in a commune in the Stockholm in the mid-1970s. Although the tone of the film was relatively light, Moodysson managed to explore serious subjects including spousal abuse, alcoholism, the impact on children of parental conflicts, sexual identity, and mainstream society's intolerance of people who are different. The film was also highly praised for its accurate portrayal of the period in set, costume, music, ideals, and lifestyles. Subsequently, Moodysson's films turned increasingly dark as he explored some of the problems that face Sweden and the world, including child neglect and abuse, teenage prostitution, international trafficking in prostitution, exploitation of women and children, and suicide. These included *Lilya-4-ever* (2002), *Ett hål i mitt hjärta*/A Hole in My Heart (2004), and *Container* (2006).

His most recent film, *Mammut*/Mammouth (2008) was international in character—its language was English; its cast came from the United States, the Philippines, Mexico, and Sweden; and it was shot in the United States, the Philippines, Thailand, and Sweden. Several layers of story ran through the film as it dealt with issues of child loneliness, career obsessions, conflicted individuals living behind facades of material happiness, poverty, and personal sacrifice.

How or through what auspices have the hundreds of films made in Sweden over the last century been made, paid for, staffed, and the like? For seven decades one company dominated both filmmaking and the theaters in which they were seen: *Svensk Filmindustri AB*/Swedish Film Industry, Inc., established in 1919. In 1983, the company was purchased by the Bonnier investment group and split into *SF Bio AB* (theaters) and *Svensk Filmindustri AB* (filmmaking). A second company, *Europafilm AB*, was in the business between 1930 and 1984, when it, too, was bought by Bonnier and merged with *SF AB*.[16] Between 1920 and 1969, the center of Swedish film production was at a studio complex in Råsunda in the Stockholm suburb of Solna. Called *Filmstaden*/Film City, it included studios, set and costume facilities, film labs, and relaxation areas. Some 400 films came from this facility. Today, *Svensk Filmindustri AB* has only its administrative headquarters there, and the old buildings house offices, shops, studios, and restaurants. New, modern apartment complexes surround the old film city.[17] Although Stockholm remains a hub for filmmaking, several other centers have developed in recent years, including three major regional ones: *Film i väst*/Film West, based in Trollhättan near Göteborg and established in 1992; *Film i Skåne*, based in Ystad and established in 1995; and *Filmpool Nord*, based in Luleå and established in 1992. Each of these serves several functions—mainly as funding sources, production facility centers, and promoters of the genre and of cooperation within Sweden, the Nordic region, and Europe. European Union policies, programs, and funding have aided these groups in recent years, too. In addition to filmmaking involvement, they sponsor film festivals and educational programs. Collectively, they have had a hand in hundreds of productions including feature length films, documentaries, television programs, and animations. One or more of them were important in the production of Jan Troell's *Maria Larssons eviga ögonblick*, Alfredson's *Låt den rätte komma*, and Moodysson's *Mammut* in 2007–8.[18] Finally, the Swedish Film Institute, founded in 1963, is an important aid in funding and promoting film in Sweden, and Swedish Television, which has produced hundreds of single and multiepisode films over the years, is important as a source of films.

Two other indicators of the vitality of Swedish film are the *Guldbagge*/Gold Bug Awards and the 30 or more film festivals held in the country annually.

The *Guldbagge* have been presented by the Swedish Film Institute since 1964 (Ingmar Bergman won the first for *Silence*) and are based on votes by a nominating jury, with final decisions by a winners jury of seven. For works seen in 2009, the winners included:

- Best Film. *Män som hatar kvinnor*/Girl with the Dragon Tattoo (The film version of the first in Stieg Larsson's Millennium Trilogy).
- Best Director. Lisa Siwe for *I taket lyser stjärnorna*/Glowing Stars.
- Best Actress in a Leading Role. Noomi Repace for her role as Lisbeth Salander in *Girl with the Dragon Tattoo.*
- Best Actor in a Leading Role. Claes Ljungmark in *Det enda rationella*/The Rational Solution.
- Best Supporting Actress. Anki Lidén in *Glowing Stars.*
- Best Supporting Actor. Kjell Bergqvist in *Bröllopsfotografen*/The Wedding Photographer.
- Best Screenplay. Ulf Malmros for *The Wedding Photographer.*
- Best Cinematopgraphy. Hoyte van Hoytema for *Flickan*/The Girl.
- Best Foreign Language Film. *Das weiße Band—Eine deutsche Kindergeschichte*/The White Ribbon—A German Children's Story.
- Best Short Film. *Skrapsår*/Scratches by Gabriela Pichler.
- Best Documentary. *Ebbe—the Movie* by Karin af Klintberg and Jane Magnusson.
- Lifetime Achievement. Waldemar Bergendahl, a producer of more than 50 films since 1985.
- Best Achievement. Malte Forssell for work on *Mammouth.*
- The Gullspira (a prize awarded for extraordinary contributions in films for children). Maggie Widstrand, the casting director of some five dozen films.
- The Audience Award. *Girl with the Dragon Tattoo.*[19]

Among the country's film festivals, many of which have a unifying theme or concentrate on a type of film, are:

- Malmö *BUFF/Barn och ungdoms film festival*/Children's and Young People's Festival. The International Female Film Festival (IFEMA).
- Trollhättan *November festivalen*—features newcomers or debut artists.
- Lund *Fantastisk Filmfestival*/Fantasy Film Festival.
- Stockholm International Film Festival Includes feature, short, and documentary films.
- *0-budgetfestivalen*/The Zero Budget Festival For animated, short subject, and underground films.

- Eksjö Animation Festival.
- Göteborg International Film Festival. This claims to be Sweden's largest. From modest beginnings in 1979, its annual program has mushroomed. In recent years its two-week schedule has included the showing of more than 400 productions. As an indicator of its importance, the Ingmar Bergman International Debut Award has been presented there since its introduction in 2007.

In spite of what some might say about Swedish films being dark, brooding, depressing, emotionally intense, or totally devoid of humor, these and other similar descriptions do not apply to the vast majority of Swedish films. That being the case, is there yet something uniquely Swedish about Swedish film? In certain instances, yes; but in many the answer is no or only in some small ways. Of course, films based on specific historic events, processes, or individuals like *Ådalen 31, The Emigrants*, or *Everlasting Moments* certainly are Swedish. Geographic setting, lighting, costuming, musical score, mood, the ways in which characters think and act, or a particular camera style may also give a film its Swedishness. An interesting example to consider is Bent Hamer's film, *Salmer frå Kjökkenet*/Kitchen Stories (2003). A cooperative Swedish-Norwegian project, it poked fun at the often-cited stereotype of the taciturn, unemotional, silent, rational Scandinavian male—albeit in highly exaggerated form—and there were critics who argued that only a Scandinavian (or Scandinavian American) could understand or enjoy it.

An important aspect of contemporary Swedish film appears to be to make films that are global in their themes. The settings may be Swedish, but the issues are international. In part the motivation is financial. Most filmmaking is expensive. Recouping costs means winning audiences. Although Swedes love film and go out to movies often, the competition from other media is intense. Making films with European, American, and global audience appeal is good business. But there are good artistic reasons as well. Love, death, anxiety, frustration, sexual identity, crime, drugs, gender exploitation, racism, child abuse, immigrant ghettoization, career problems, and the like are human issues, not just Swedish ones. Just as theater, music, and literature have become increasingly international, so, too, has film.

Notes

1. See *Kulturrådet*/The Culture Council at http://www.kulturradet.se/. Accessed July 22, 2009. English option.
2. An outspoken critic of the Swedish welfare state is Roland Huntford. See *The New Totalitarians*.
3. See: http://www.sweden.gov.se/sb/d/11266/a/120332 and http://www.culturalpolicies.net/down/sweden_042009.pdf. Accessed April 5, 2010.

4. Ingrid Luterkort, *Om igen, herr Molander! Kungliga Dramatiska teaterns elevskola 1787–1964* (Stockholm: Stockhomia förlag, 1998).

5. In English, see Harry G. Carlson, "Riksteatern: The Swedish National Provincial Theatre," *Educational Theatre Journal*, 15(1), March 1963, 39. See http://riksteatern.se/default____12.aspx. Accessed July 22, 2009. English option. One of the best sources at the *Rikstearn*'s Web site is the 2007 annual report, *Det..här är Riksteatern: Samt årsredovisning för 2007.*

6. From "Vårt uppdrag" at http://www.sodrateatern.com/. Accessed July 22, 2009.

7. A good source of information about dance in Sweden is at http://dansportalen.se. Accessed July 22, 2009.

8. See http://sweden.se/eng/Home/Lifestyle/Culture/Music-room/. Accessed July 22, 2009. This Web site, which is part of the Swedish Institute's, includes print information and audio options that allow one to hear contemporary Swedish music in various genres!

9. A good history of the nyckelharpa is at http://www.nyckelharpa.org/resources/history.html. Accessed July 22, 2009. Details and images can be found at http://www.nyckelharpa.org/pdfs/tenor-harpa.pdf. Accessed July 22, 2009. One of Sweden's leading "folk" groups today is Väsen, a trio that is pushing the traditional envelope (s) to include more contemporary musical genre.

10. See http://www.dotshop.se/ds/browse.php?lid=323. Accessed July 22, 2009

11. For an excellent brief history of jazz in Sweden, see Lars Westin, "Jazz in Sweden" at http://www.visarkiv.se/en/jazz/index.htm. Accessed July 22, 2009. Westin is the editor of the Swedish jazz magazine *Orkester journalen.*

12. About the Grammi awards, see http://www.grammis.se/. Accessed April 5, 2010.

13. See http://www.ingmarbergman.se. This site is not just about Ingmar Bergman. Much of it is in English, and search options allow a very wide range of information to be accessed. See also Birgitta Steene, *Ingmar Bergman: A Reference Guide* (Chicago: University of Chicago Press, 2006).

14. The line "slapstick Ingmar Bergman" is from J. Hoberman, "Suspended Animation," *The Village Voice*, July 2, 2002. This includes a review of *Songs from the Second Floor.* See http://www.villagevoice.com/2002-07-02/film/suspended-animation/1. Accessed July 30, 2009.

15. See *Svenska Dagbladet*, September 28, 2008, at http://www.svd.se/kulturnoje/nyheter/artikel_1772249.svd. Accessed July 30, 2009.

16. A good, short history can be found at http://www.ingmarbergman.se/universe.asp?guid=80DE3ED1-50CF-4277-966C-12013C779021.

17. See http://www.gamlafilmstaden.se/. Accessed July 22, 2009.

18. On *Film i Väst*, see http://filmivast.se; on *Film i Skåne*, see http://www.filmiskane.se; and on *Filmpool Nord*, see http://www.fpn.se/site/. Accessed July 30, 2009. English options.

19. About the Swedish Film Institute, see http://www.sfi.se/en-gb/. On the Guldbagge see: http://www.sfi.se/en-gb/Swedish-Film/The-Guldbagge-Award/. Accessed April 6, 2010. In English.

8

Art, Architecture, and Design

SWEDEN'S CULTURE in terms of the arts, architecture, and design have long histories and many elements, and, as with other aspects of the nation's culture, there is a canon of works and artists that are familiar to many. Included in these are the artifactual remains of the material cultures of the prehistoric periods, the folk arts of the rural population down to the early twentieth century; the art of the church, court, nobility, bourgeoisie, and contemporary society; the architecture of the church, crown, nobility, rural folk, towns, and cities; and the objects of everyday life, both historical and contemporary. In virtually every one of these genres, the uniquely Swedish and the influence of foreign ideas, styles, and experts often merge.

Before examining the arts of the historical period, a few words about the much longer and older prehistoric era, c. 10,000 BCE to 1000 CE, are in order. The mute physical record from this period in Sweden is composed of literally thousands of objects accumulated mainly over the last 400 years or so, augmented by new discoveries and new techniques of analysis. It includes carved amber amulets, decorated pottery, images carved on stones, rings, bracelets, neck collars and necklaces, armbands, harness ornaments, elaborately decorated weapons and helmets, objects of everyday life such as combs and game pieces, picture stones, and runestones. According to the traditional chronology, they are the work of Old and New Stone Age, Bronze Age, Iron Age, Migration Period, and Viking Age peoples. Many of the objects are strikingly beautiful and reflect great skill and creativity in their execution. Some bear evidence of foreign influences, some a mixture of foreign and native. Many are uniquely original.

Swedish authorities have long sought to protect and preserve artifacts from this ancient past—even before they had any real idea of what they had discovered. Gustavus Adolphus established the Office of State Antiquarian/*Riksantikvarie* in 1630. One of the oldest laws on ancient monuments was enacted in mid-1660s, and an Antiquarian Institute was created at Uppsala in 1666.

Picture stone from Ardre on the island of Gotland. Some 300 of these have been found on the island. They date from the Migration and Viking Periods (c. 400–1100 CE). The Ardre stone depicts elements of Norse pre-Christian mythology. Originally located at special sites across the island, many of the stones are now housed in the Gotland Museum in Visby. (Photo courtesy of Brian Magnusson.)

A 1684 law protected finds of ancient artifacts, especially coins, and new monument laws were added in 1823 and 1867. Today, Sweden's National Heritage Board/*Riksantikvarieämbetet* maintains a registry of ancient sites and finds, and works with museums across the country.[1] The primary repository of finds is the Swedish Museum of National Antiquities/*Historiska Museet* in Stockholm, but there are many regional and local museums that hold some of these treasures, such as the historical branch of Gotland's County Museum in Visby.[2]

PAINTING

The body of art in paint media is extensive and highly varied. The oldest extant works date are from the Middle Ages (c. 1100–1500) and include depictions of biblical stories and religious figures on the walls and ceilings of churches and on wooden panels that hung in many churches. They also include painted sculptural works. The styles mirror those of the Continent, and the artists are largely unknown.

One of the most famous and best-known medieval work is the painted wooden statue of *Sankt Göran och draken*/Saint George and the Dragon, which stands in Stockholm's *Storkyrkan*/Great Church. It was executed by the north German artist, Bernt Notke, in the late fifteenth century. Based on the legend of St. George's rescue of a princess from the jaws of an insatiable beast, it commemorates the Battle of Brunkeberg, fought between the Danes and the Swedes in October 1471, and is a central image in the development of Sweden's national identity, both in the late Middle Ages and in the nineteenth century.

The growth of the state, external influences drifting north from Renaissance Italy, the Low Countries, and the German states, and the Reformation led to increased secularization in art, especially in the sixteenth century. Particularly important during this so-called Vasa Renaissance was the production of a large group of royal portraits. One of the most interesting works from the period is *Vädersolstavlan*/The Weather Sun Scene/The Sun Dog Scene. It depicts the city of Stockholm in April 1535, and shows the unusual halo effects that filled the sky on that date. Understood today to have been the result of particular weather conditions, the phenomenon was then believed to be an omen of bad times coming. The original was executed by *Urban Målare*/City Painter, and the extant copy is considered to be a copy done in the 1630s.

The most important period in early modern Swedish art history falls between about 1630 and 1792, with a break in the early eighteenth century. Roughly the first half of this parallels Sweden's so-called Age of Greatness,

Saint George Slaying the Dragon. Located in Stockholm's *Storkyrkan*, this painted wood statue was done by Bernt Notke in the late fifteenth century, probably to celebrate Sweden's victory over the Danes at the Battle of Brunkeberg (1471). (Photo courtesy of the Church of Sweden and the *Storkyrkan*.)

a time when the country was a major player in European and especially Baltic affairs. As will be seen below, it was also a period of great building activity, and the arts were fully engaged at the same time. The principal genre was portraiture. The style was Baroque. Among the leading figures were David Klöcker Ehrenstrahl, David Beck, and Jacob Elbfas. The more important, Golden Age came after 1730 or so, as Sweden recovered from the military defeats of the early eighteenth century. With support from the crown (especially Gustav III) and the nobility, some superb painters were active during this period, including Per Hilleström, Per Krafft, Gustaf Lundberg,

Elias Martin, Carl Gustaf Pilo, Lorens and Ulrika Pasch, Alexander Roslin, and Adolf Ulrik Wertmüller. Their works varied in style from late Baroque to Rococo to *Chinoisierie* to Neoclassical. Most excelled as portraitists, but some, like Hilleström, also produced landscapes and scenes from everyday life. Many of their paintings are now on display in the National Museum in Stockholm.

One of the best-known pieces in this group is Roslin's *Lady with the Veil*—a strikingly beautiful painting of his strikingly beautiful wife, Marie-Suzanne Giroust. Roslin (1718–93) was a leading portraitist of the eighteenth century. Born in Malmö, he learned his craft mainly in Stockholm. In 1745, he left Sweden and settled in Paris seven years later. It was there he executed works that included portraits of many of the Swedish nobility who visited (or lived in) the city, French nobles, and even the French royal family. He spent two years in the mid-1770s back in Sweden, where he worked on a number of portraits including ones of King Gustav III and the botanist Carl von Linné/Linnaeus.

Just as there was a relative decline in the arts in the early eighteenth century, there was a similar decline between about 1790 and 1820. Again, Sweden suffered from losses in war and the accompanying economic ills. However, recovery did come, and the country entered an extended period of important changes and growth. (See Chapter 1.) For all of the arts, urbanization, printing techniques that allowed for easier duplication of works, the growth of a middle class interested in art, a more dynamic and complex consumer market, and the commercialization of art helped drive developments. Also important was the founding of museums (National Museum, 1866), galleries, new schools, and international art movements and training centers. Stylistically, the century bore witness to great variety, ranging from Neoclassicism and Romanticism in the early decades to National Romanticism, Realism, Naturalism, and Impressionism at its end. Thematically, portraits continued in popularity across the period (especially among the growing bourgeoisie), but landscapes, depictions of historically important people and events, and "snapshots" of everyday life became increasingly the focus of the country's best artists.

In the late nineteenth and early twentieth centuries, Sweden produced a group of artists of enormous talent and lasting importance. Among these were Anders Zorn (1860–1920), Carl Larsson (1853–1919), Bruno Liljefors (1860–1939), and Johan Bauer (1882–1918). Zorn was in many ways the most international of this group. One would not, however, have expected the future he made for himself given his origins. A native of Mora in the province of Dalarna, an area many view as the heart (or soul) of Sweden, he was the son of an unwed working woman. Yet, by the time he was 15 he was a student at the school of the Royal Academy of Fine Arts (*Kungliga Akadamien för de fria konsterna*, an organization whose roots go back to 1735 in Stockholm) and within a few years had established a reputation as a watercolorist and portraitist.[3] His extensive travels and stays abroad began in 1881, continued for more than 20 years, and included time in France, England, and the United States. Summers, however, were almost always spent in Sweden, mainly at *Zorngården*, the residence he built in Mora. It was there that he and his wife, Emma, developed a museum for his collections and *Gammelgården*, a site dedicated to Swedish farm building traditions and other aspects of rural life. As an artist Zorn was an accomplished painter in both watercolors and oils, an etcher, and a sculptor. His works include commissioned portraits of many leading figures of his day in Europe and America, voluptuous nudes often set in the outdoors, and scenes depicting aspects of everyday life in Sweden.[4]

Carl Larsson also came from a background set in poverty, although this time in Stockholm. His artistic talent was spotted early on, however, and

Portrait of the French politician and journalist, Antonin Proust by Anders Zorn, c. 1888. An artist with wide and varied international contacts, this painting reflects his mastery of the art of portraiture. (© The Trustees of the British Museum/Art Resource, NY.)

he, too, received his formal training at the Royal Academy. He also spent several years abroad, mostly importantly at Grèz-sur-Loing near Paris. It was there that he painted many fine works, and it was where he met and married Karin Bergöö. In 1888, he and Karin were given a small residence, *Lilla Hyttnäs*, in Sundborn, near Falun. Over the next several decades, it became a center for the couple's artistic work, the family home, and eventually the lasting monument to their legacies. In both Sweden and abroad, Larsson is usually remembered for the wonderful watercolor paintings of the life of his family, domestic life at *Lilla Hyttnäs*, and the natural and material culture worlds that surrounded him. These images, reproduced today on seemingly every imaginable surface, are what many take to be the quintessential visual definers of *Swedishness*.

Larsson was not just an artist of family/folk life. He was also a muralist and a painter of history. Many of the works he believed to be his most significant were done for schools and museums. Several depictions of important moments in Swedish history are in the stairwells of the National Museum in Stockholm. One, however, *Midvinterblot*/Midwinter Sacrifice, a depiction of the sacrifice of the (mythical) pre-Christian king Domalde, became the center of a major controversy and was not given a place in the National Museum until 1997, more than 80 years after its completion.[5]

Although similar to both Zorn and Larsson in terms of his use of techniques, mediums, and some of the leading stylistic trends of the period (e.g., Impressionism), Bruno Liljefors's subject matter was very different. He was a naturalist, student of animal behavior, hunter, and keeper of a kind of zoo of the animals he often depicted. Among his internationally recognized works are strikingly accurate depictions of animals, their habitats, and the oftentimes harsh realities of nature. In addition to his paintings, he produced the earliest diorama scenes for the displays in the Biological Museum in Skansen, Stockholm.

John Bauer grew up in Jönköping, where his father ran a small specialty meat shop. As was typical of so many of his contemporaries, he studied art at the Royal Academy's school in Stockholm and spent a number of years abroad. Also, as with Larsson, his wife, Esther Ellqvist, was an artist. Bauer is best known for the illustrations he did for *Bland tomtar och troll*/Among Elves and Trolls (1907–10 and 1912–15), an especially important publication for young people that has appeared annually since 1907 and has contained stories by many of the country's best-known authors. These illustrations, like so many of Larsson's paintings, are seen by many as quintessentially Swedish—in this case because they depict the folkloric world of elves, trolls, giants, and heroes. They are often reproduced both in Sweden and abroad. But Bauer, too, had other sides. After 1915, he turned to a

Carl Larsson self-portrait from 1906. This work was executed at Sundborn, the family home near Falun in the province of Dalarna. It shows both the idyllic setting that surrounded the artist and the style for which he is so well known. (Scala/Art Resource, NY.)

variety of new genre including large works such as the fresco of "St. Martin and the Beggar" in the Odd Fellows Lodge in Nyköping and the sets for a ballet based on the legend of the Mountain King. Sadly, Bauer's life, along with the lives of his wife and son, was cut short in November 1918, when they all perished in the sinking of the small Lake Vättern ferry *Per Brahe*.[6]

Art in the twentieth and early twenty-first centuries in Sweden was and remains linked with and to some extent driven by international developments, and especially those in France, Germany, Russia, and the United States. At the same time, this has been a period rich in originality and variety. Virtually every major school of painting and/or *ism* of the period has had its practitioners and its audiences. The following list offers but a sampling of these along with the names of a few of the artists associated with the various schools:

- Fauvism: Isaac Grünewald (1889–1946), Sigrid Hjertén (1885–1948) (Grünewald's wife), and Leander Engström (1886–1927). These and others are also often listed as pupils of Henri Matisse and as the 1909-ists.
- Cubism: Georg Pauli (1885–1935), Siri Derkert (1888–1973), Otto Sköld (1894–1958)
- Naivism: Hilding Linnqvist (1891–1984), Eric Hallström (1893–1946)
- Colorism: Carl Kylberg (1878–1952)
- Surrealism: Erik Olson (1901–86), Stellan Mörner (1896–1979), Esias Thorén (1901–81), and the "Halmstad Group"
- Expressionism: Sven Erixsson (1899–1970), Bror Hjorth (1894–1968), Vera Nilsson (1888–1979)
- Concretism: Otto G. Carlsund (1897–1948), Olle Bærtling (1911–81), Pierre Olofsson (1921–96)
- Neo-Surrealism (the "Imaginists"): Max Walter Svanberg (1912–94), C. O. Hultén (1916–)
- Neo-Realism: Otto Sköld (1894–1958)
- Psychoanalytic: Lena Cronqvist (1938–)
- Postmodernism: Ernst Billgren (1958–)
- Contemporary

Also important in understanding this period is the fact that art itself has undergone repeated and/or ongoing redefinition. New media including film, video, and digital technologies have been important to this process. So, too, have questions about the place of the artist and audience in the context of work, performance as art, and mixed media art.

Sculpture

No survey of Swedish art would be complete without mention of several highly talented and internationally known sculptors. Among these are Johan Tobias Sergel (1740–1814), Carl Eldh (1873–1954), Carl Milles (1875–1950), and Axel Petersson (*Döderhultarn*) (1868–1925).

Sergel is Sweden's foremost pre-twentieth century sculptor. Trained in Paris and Rome, he was active between about 1780 and 1814. Among his best-known works are the statue of Gustav III that stands outside the National Museum in Stockholm and a stunning set of classic-motif pieces, several of which can be seen in the Gothenburg Museum Art. Eldh rose from relative poverty to study in Paris. Working mainly in Stockholm, he produced important architectural sculptures, a number of freestanding pieces including several of August Strindberg and a monument centering on Hjalmar Branting, one of Sweden's early Social Democratic leaders, located adjacent to the headquarters of the Swedish Federation of Trade Unions near *Norra Bantorget*. Eldh's contemporary, Milles, came from the Uppsala area. He, too, was trained in Paris, where he worked in the studio of Auguste Rodin. In the early years of the twentieth century, he and his wife, Olga, built a residence and studio on the island of Lidingö overlooking Stockholm. In 1931, he left to take a position as sculptor in residence and teacher at what became the Cranbrook Academy of Art in Bloomfield Hills, Michigan. During his nearly 20 years in America, he taught and inspired many promising sculptors and completed a number of major commissions for American buyers, including "Meeting of the Waters" in St. Louis. Since 1936, his Lidingö home has been a public facility and many of his sculptures are on display there. His signature works, like the "Poseidon Fountain" in Göteborg, often combined masterfully executed human or animal forms with both pools of reflective standing water and fountains.

Axel Petersson, who took the name *Döderhultarn* (after his home parish in Småland), was a very different kind of sculptor, but he is perhaps better known than any of the others mentioned above, both in Sweden and abroad. He was a wood carver who produced a series of about 200 "Scandinavian flat plane style" painted statues that depicted the lives of common folk of his area around 1900. His work first received wide attention when it was exhibited in Stockholm in 1909. Today his technique and the style in which he worked are much copied, and a museum and the building that was his home and shop in Oskarshamn are maintained as symbols of his importance.

Folk Arts

The folk arts (including spinning, weaving, knitting, clothing making, wood carving, cabinetmaking, furniture building, metal working, glass blowing, pottery making, and painting) occupy special places in Sweden's cultural heritage and life. Most originated far back in the country's history, when self-sufficiency, handcrafts, and the like were essential parts of both rural and town everyday life. Two important aspects of all the folk arts are that significant regional and local styles developed in many of them and that they were important elements of people's identities. For example, *dalmålning* was a genre of painting that was popular between about 1750 and 1830 in the province of Dalarna. It involved the depiction of stories from the Bible such as Jesus's entrance into Jerusalem or aspects of human existence such as the "cycle of life" from birth to maturity to old age to death in a primitivist or naive style with characters in contemporary folk dress. Paintings in this style were often executed on the walls of rural homes in the province and were signs of real or pretended affluence.

In the nineteenth century, the folk arts were threatened by industrialization and urbanization, and many feared that the old ways would vanish. In response, a broad-based and extensive folk movement developed that took several directions. One was aimed at the preservation of local history, customs, material artifacts, and sources of information. It resulted in the formation of local societies/*Hembygdsföreningar* and the founding of the national umbrella organization, Sweden's Union of Local Societies/*Sveriges Hembygdsförbund/SH*, in 1916. Today, overall membership totals more than half a million, which is distributed among 26 *SH*-affiliated regional organizations, which in turn serve as umbrellas for local societies. For example, in the western Swedish county of Bohuslän, some 95 local groups belong to Bohusläns *Hembygdsförbund*, which has a total membership of more than 35,000!

Another direction this movement took concentrated on the preservation of specific crafts, designs, patterns, and the skills they involved, as well as upon ongoing efforts to market handcraft products. Here one result was the founding of handcraft-focused groups called *hemslöjdförening*. They created a national organization, The Swedish National Union of Handcraft Associations/*Svenska Hemslöjdsföreningarnas Riksförbund/SHR*, in 1912. Today *SHR* has more than 15,000 members and works with about 70 local and 24 county associations. There are three national organizations affiliated with it and 23 affiliated shops that feature handcraft products. *SHR* also has published the journal *Hemslöjd* since 1933. A second important national organization dedicated to the preservation of a craft is The Association of Friends of the Textile Arts/*Handarbetets Vänner/HV*. It was founded in 1874, and today maintains a center in Stockholm that houses an extensive studio dedicated to the textile arts (*HV Atelje*), offices, an exhibition area, a shop, and *HV Skolan*/HV School.

A third direction for this movement involved the preservation and practice of folk music and dance. For example, players, called *spelmän*, formed local and regional associations, and today there is a national organization, *Sveriges Spelmäns Riksförbund*, based in the idyllic Dalarna town of Rättvik.

Also important in the development of this folk movement were the previously mentioned efforts in the late nineteenth and early twentieth centuries to define Sweden and the Swedes in terms of national identity. The folk arts, along with other elements such as history, customs, dialects, and folklore, were important parts of the constructed identity that developed. Artur Hazelius and his Nordic Museum played a central role in this, as did the state via the growing public education system, the military, and encouragement of expositions such as the one held in Stockholm in 1897. Today, the Department of Culture/*Kulturdepartmentet* plays a leading role in folk art preservation, and each county has at least two handcrafts consuls/*hemslöjdkonsulenter* who are responsible for maintaining awareness of the handcrafts, encouraging activities in them, and fostering commercial opportunities. In order to qualify for a position as a handcrafts consul, individuals must complete a two-year course at the Friends of the Crafts School/*HV skolan* in Stockholm.

Architecture

Sweden's surviving architectural history begins around the twelfth century. Only archeological ruins—posthole locations, soil indicators of ancient structures, and stone foundations—survive as records of earlier structures. Interestingly, even such fragmentary evidence does allow for some measure of imaginative reconstruction, such as efforts to "build" the grass huts of New Stone Age farmers or the longhouses of the Vikings. As with the visual arts, it was the conversion to Christianity, the development of an increasingly permanent political state, and the growth of towns such as Visby (on the island of Gotland), Stockholm, and Uppsala that gave rise to the buildings—churches, monasteries, and castles—that are the oldest pieces in Sweden's architectural legacy.

Parish churches collectively make up one of the most important parts of this history. Väversunda Church, located a few miles south of Vadstena on the east side of Lake Vättern, is one of the oldest examples. Probably built on the site an earlier wooden church, it is a small Romanesque style crucifix-form structure in limestone and dates to between c. 1160 and 1300. Carefully restored in the late 1940s, the interior is especially rich and includes both twelfth- and seventeenth-century wall paintings (murals), the original thirteenth-century baptismal font, two medieval crucifixes—one a copy and the other original—and an elaborately decorated wood and iron door (likely the original), signed "Asmund made this door" in runic characters and illustrating the merging of earlier (Viking) and Christian motifs. Although not all of Sweden's hundreds of parish churches are as old or as rich in their artistic heritages, many illustrate the development of architectural styles and church art, as well as the history of organ building in Sweden.

Because several historically Danish areas in far southern Sweden were annexed to the country in the seventeenth century, Sweden has two archdiocesan cathedrals, Uppsala and Lund. Although significantly different in style and building materials and having undergone several "restorations," each is a magnificent example of medieval church architecture and a repository for important works of religious art.

An archbishopric for Sweden was established at Uppsala in 1164, and a Romanesque cathedral was built at "old" Uppsala. This church was destroyed

Väversunda Church near Vadstena on the east side of Lake Vättern. Built between about 1160 and 1300, this is one of Sweden's oldest parish churches. Romanesque in origin, it has been carefully maintained and restored. (Courtesy of Brian Magnusson.)

by fire in the early thirteenth century. Its replacement, in the heart of the present-day city, was constructed over the course of the next two centuries—progress often being interrupted by epidemics, political turmoil, and (no doubt) lack of funds. The basic plan is French Gothic, and takes the typical cross or basilica form of the period; the style of the building is described as "north German Baltic brick Gothic." The inner and outer walls include glass clearstories, and several small chapels punctuate the perimeter around the nave. The primary construction material was brick, and masons from many locations in Europe apparently were recruited to work on the building.

What the original church looked like is difficult to determine exactly because of two major restorations. The first occurred after fire destroyed much of Uppsala and severely damaged the church in 1702. The architect Carl Hårlemann directed this restoration, and he essentially converted the building to match the late Baroque tastes of the period. For example, the tall Gothic spires were replaced by much lower Classical towers. The second major restoration came in the late nineteenth century, under the direction of the architect Helgo Zettervall (1831–1907). A leading figure of his time,

Uppsala Cathedral exterior. Romanesque in style and primarily of brick, construction began in the late twelfth century. Several renovations have altered its basic appearance. (Photo courtesy of Glenn Kranking.)

he was involved in a number of important restorations that included the cathedrals in Lund, Skara, and Linköping. Often criticized for his work, he was inclined to force ideals on his projects rather than search for historical authenticity. To his credit, Zettervall returned the church to its Gothic origins and appearance—albeit with some of the excesses of nineteenth-century neo-Gothicism and the use of more modern materials and techniques. He even installed decorative elements made of concrete, which did not last very long. A third restoration was discussed in the 1970s, but (luckily?) only important preservation repairs were actually carried out.

As important as the building are its interior elements that include the Vasa, Jagellonica, Sture, Finsta, and Peace Chapels; stained glass windows; the early-eighteenth-century grand pulpit; the remains of Sweden's national saint, Erik; the graves of Gustav I Vasa and his three wives, John III, the botanist Carl von Linné/Linnaeus, the eighteenth-century scientist-mystic Immanuel Swedenborg, and many of the country's archbishops; three organs; and a carillon.

Lund Cathedral Interior. Construction of the original church began around 1150. The present structure is largely the result of an early-sixteenth-century restoration effort and three subsequent projects. The interior is a treasury of important works of design and art including the famous clock, Horologium Mirabile Lundense.

This list is a mere sampling of the richness of the architectural achievement and the quality of the stonework, painting, metal work, textiles, and other decorative arts that are contained there. Also, because of the way the city has grown up around it, it is almost impossible to get a view from the outside that encompasses the grandeur of this church. A full appreciation for the richness of the exterior and interior can only be gained by repeated visits.

Lund Cathedral, which was consecrated in 1145, was the central church of Denmark and only became a Swedish church when the territory in which it is located on the southwest coast became part of Sweden in 1658. It is a sandstone structure in Romanesque style. Like Uppsala Cathedral, it experienced serious damage by fire (in 1234) and has undergone several transformational renovations. The one that altered the look of the building the most was apparently the one undertaken by Helgo Zetterval between 1860 and 1880. He sought to model the building in a neo-Romanesque style and gave it the two bell towers and entrance that exist today. The interior is magnificently decorated and particularly known for the twentieth-century mosaic in the choir section, the hand-carved choir benches, a late-fourteenth-century altar triptych, and the largest church organ in Sweden. One of the best known and perhaps most interesting pieces in the church is "Horologium Mirabile Lundense," an early-fifteenth-century clock that displays the movement of the heavens, announces the time, and serves as a calendar. It is a truly remarkable piece.[7]

One of the most interesting "modern" churches is in Kiruna, the northern iron mining city. Completed in 1912, it was built by the mining company *LKAB* (*Luossavaara-Kiirunavaara Aktiebolag*) and designed by Gustaf

Kiruna Church. Designed by architect Gustaf Wickman and completed in 1912, this church reflects the blending of architectural styles common to the early twentieth century. It is made mostly of wood and painted with the traditional Falun Red paint. The interior contains the works of a number of important early twentieth-century designers and crafts people. (Photo courtesy of Valerie McCluskey.)

Wickman, whose other works include the Swedish Pavilion for the 1893 Chicago Worlds Fair and a building at the 1897 Stockholm Exposition. Stylistically, it is a mixture of neo-Gothic, National Romantic, and *Jugend Stil*. Some say its basic form is patterned after the four-sided *Sami* hut or *lappkåtan* so common in the region. The altar painting is by Prince Eugen, and other artists involved in the decoration of the church included Albert Engström, Christian Eriksson, and Ossian Elgström. Strikingly beautiful both outside and in, it is constructed almost entirely of wood and painted in the very traditional Swedish color, Falun red. In 2001, it was judged "the all-time best building built before 1950" in Sweden.[8]

The buildings belonging to the crown, the nobility, and the state also comprise important parts of Sweden's architectural legacy. Among the oldest are the royal fortresses of the late medieval and early modern periods, including those at Gripsholm, Kalmar, Vadstena, and Vaxholm. In the seventeenth and eighteenth centuries, the relative prosperity and the real or perceived importance of the country, as well as the need on the part of both the crown and nobility to build residences that displayed their positions in the society resulted in a group of remarkable buildings in terms of their designs, settings, and furnishings.

Two outstanding examples among the relatively large number of surviving royal palaces and/or castles are the Royal Palace (*Kungliga slottet*) in Stockholm and Drottningholm Palace. Both were and remain important symbols of the state and monarchy, and parts of them are open and accessible to the public. For several centuries the crown's main residence in the capital was the Tre Kronor/Three Crowns castle—an interesting building but one that had become a hodgepodge of pieces and designs. The fire that destroyed it in 1697 created a much-appreciated opportunity to construct an "appropriate" royal palace. This is the building that stands today as a primary residence of the royal family and as the site of three museums. Designed by Nicodemus Tessin the Younger, the exterior dates mainly from the first half of the eighteenth century. Tessin envisioned a magnificent Baroque building with an equally impressive interior filled with the finest art, furniture, and other items of interior decoration of the times. Following his death in 1728, he was succeeded by Carl Hårleman, who made important changes to the interior, which became Rococo in style. Progress on the construction of the building was slow, and it was not ready for use until 1754. As a symbol of the monarchy and the state, it was certainly a success. The core of the palace is a multistory square with an open central courtyard. Wings extended from this core to the east and west, and there is an addition formal courtyard on the west side. There are some 600 rooms in the palace, many of which met Tessin's hopes in terms of their elegance.

Stockholm Royal Palace. This is the primary residence of the Swedish royal family. The exterior design is chiefly the work of Nicodemus Tessin the Younger. Carl Hårleman is responsible for much of the interior design. Construction dates between 1697 and 1754. (Photo courtesy of Glenn Kranking.)

Drottningholm, which lies outside of the bustle of Stockholm and is also a primary residence of the royal family, is a strikingly appealing place in a wonderful, almost idyllic, setting. It (along with the other buildings on the grounds) was designated a UNESCO World Heritage site in 1991. The entire complex was described by that organization as follows:

> The Royal Domain of Drottningholm stands on an island (*Lovön*) in Lake Mälar in a suburb of Stockholm. With its castle, perfectly preserved theatre (built in 1766), Chinese pavilion, and gardens, it is the finest example of an eighteenth-century north European royal residence inspired by the Palace of Versailles.[9]

Prior to the building of the present palace, several Swedish monarchs had used the location as place close to but away from the noise, dirt, distractions, and dangers of the capital. John III built a small palace there for his wife in the late sixteenth century. Construction of the current building began in the late seventeenth century. Designed by Nicodemis Tessin the Elder (1615–81),

The Chinese Pavilion on the grounds of Drottningholm Palace. Designed by C. F. Adelcreutz, it was completed around 1769 and reflects the influence of Chinese art and design popular at the time.

it was the residence of Hedwig Eleonora, widow of Karl X. Executed in the Baroque style of the day, the main building was three stories. Two-story wings and extensions were added to each end. One side of the palace faced the lake, the other the elaborate Baroque gardens designed by Tessin's son. The Chinese Pavilion was added in 1769 and reflects the fascination of Europeans with things Chinese. The present version of the Court Theater, designed by Carl Fredrik Adelcrantz, opened in 1766. Largely ignored in the nineteenth century, it was restored in the 1920s and today offers a series of productions in the summer.

Many of the remaining palaces of Sweden's once powerful nobility date from the seventeenth century, Sweden's Age of Greatness. Within the city of Stockholm there is, for example, the palace of Axel Oxenstierna, who served as chancellor to both Gustavus Adolphus and Christina. Commissioned just before his death in the mid-1650s, it was designed by Jean de la Vallee (1620–96) as one element in what was planned to become a set of palaces adjacent to the royal residence. Oxenstierna died before the building was completed, and it was never occupied by the family. For a time (1668–80) it was used to house *Sveriges Riksbank*/The Swedish National Bank and subsequently other government offices. Two important palaces belonged to

Carl Gustaf Wrangel, one of the most extraordinary military leaders of the period. The first was his city home, Wrangel Palace in Stockholm. Working on an older structure, it was redone under the direction of Nicodemus Tessin the Elder. Sufficiently elegant for more important residents, it served as the royal palace for many years after the 1697 fire and now houses the Swedish Court of Appeals (*Svea hovrätt*). The second was *Skokloster*, built between 1654 and 1676. Located northwest of Stockholm on the shores of an arm of Lake Mälar, it is the largest surviving private palace in Sweden. Also located on the great lake that extends far into Sweden from the capital is *Tyresö*. Southeast of the capital, it was constructed mainly in the 1630s and was the country home of Gabriel Gustafsson Oxenstierna, another leading noble of the mid-seventeenth century.

Then there is *Läckö*, which is situated on a bay in Lake Vänern north of Lidköping in western Sweden. Its history dates back to the late thirteenth century, when the first fortress was built on the site by the Bishop of Skara. The crown took possession in the early sixteenth century, and it was given to the de la Gardie family in 1615. Many renovations and additions changed the nature of the place, the most far-reaching coming under Magnus de la Gardie after about 1650. A former favorite of Queen Christina and head of the regency that ran Sweden during Karl XI's minority, he was arguably the richest and most powerful man in Sweden in the 1660s and early 1670s. His properties were spread across the entire country. His Stockholm residence, *Makalös Palace*, was the most elaborate of the day. Ultimately, his ego got the better of him, he lost the favor of the young king, and was stripped of most of his wealth. Lastly, there is *Finspång Palace*, the home of Louis de Geer the Younger, son of the Dutch entrepreneur who did so much to expand Sweden's economy in the seventeenth century. The palace was built in the late seventeenth century and lies close to the cannon industry center developed by his father. Today these buildings are either the property of the state or have been converted to privately owned commercial sites. Most are open to the public, and they certainly stand as reminders of the wealth and power of Sweden and a few Swedes.

The nineteenth century and the first two decades of the twentieth was a period of vitality, variety, and imitation. The architectural styles of the period tended to be backward looking, with labels that include Neoclassic, Renaissance, Neo-Gothic, National Romantic, and Historical. Designers borrowed from the past, mixed styles, and wove foreign and Swedish elements into their designs. As the country changed and became increasingly urban and industrial, Sweden's cities became perpetual construction sites. (Between 1800 and 1900, Stockholm's population grew from around 75,000 to more than 300,000, and Göteborg's from around 13,000 to more than 130,000.)

Gothenburg Opera House. Completed in 1994 and designed by Jan Izikowitz at the firm of Lund & Valentin. Inspiration for this stunning building came from both the world of opera and from it setting adjacent to the harbor of Sweden's second largest city. (Photo by Kjell Holmner. Courtesy of Väst Sverige/West Sweden. Image Bank Sweden.)

The new factories, shops, government and public buildings, schools, apartments, villas, parks, and street plans gave ample opportunities to architects and urban designers. Some of the country's best-known buildings help define this period. Among these are the National Museum, Nordic Museum, Royal Opera House, *Dramaten*, *Riksdag*/Parliament Building, *Nordiska Kompaniet*/*NK* department store building, headquarters of *Svenska Handelsbanken*/Swedish Bank of Commerce, Stockholm Central Railway Station, Stockholm City Hall, and the Svea Life and Fire Insurance Company building in Göteborg (now the Elite Plaza Hotel).

One of the most interesting and symbolically important of these buildings is the Nordic Museum (*Nordiska Museet*). Today the country's principal ethnographic center, it and the adjacent folk park, *Skansen*, are largely the results of the work of Artur Hazelius (1833–1901), a man driven to preserve the material record of the cultures of Sweden's people in the face of the corrosive

Nordiska Museet/Nordic Museum in Stockholm. Design for the building began under Magnus Isaeus, but was completed by Isak Gustaf Clason and Gustaf Amén. It opened in 1907. (Photo courtesy of Henrik Nordstrom.)

affects of nineteenth-century modernization. The building was designed principally by Gustaf Clason and is described as Danish Renaissance in style—with plenty of National Romantic elements drawn from Sweden's past. Gingerbreadist might be a way to describe this rather eclectic building intended to stand as a symbol of Sweden's people and history. It was completed in 1907.[10]

While the leading design styles of the nineteenth and early twentieth centuries tended to be backward looking and designers took their inspiration from the past, Swedish architects in the twentieth century sought to create a new style based on different materials (mainly steel, glass, concrete, and engineered wood) and different ideals about the fundamental appearance of a building. A style variously labeled Modernism, Functionalism (*Funkis*), and Swedish (Scandinavian) Modern predominated between about 1930 and 1960, and remains popular today. It was characterized by simplicity, cleanliness of line, the absence of add-on decorative elements, and no attempts to imitate some earlier design style. The beauty of a building or other structure lay in its design—that was to reflect its function—and in the materials used.

Although there were earlier steps in this move to Modernism, a key moment for Sweden came in 1930, when Stockholm hosted an exhibition (*Stockholm utställning*) dedicated to Modernity and *funkis*/Functionalism.

The lead architect for this was Gunnar Asplund, whose Stockholm City Library forms a kind of bridge between the old and new. His design for the main exposition building, with its walls of glass suspended in a steel frame, epitomized the new direction. So, too, did the other exhibition buildings and the model apartments and houses on display. Concurrently, the housewares (furniture, kitchenware, etc.) utilized at the site and even the advertising posters and other graphic works were in the new style.

For much of the remainder of the twentieth century, Swedish designers, along with their colleagues in the other Nordic countries, enjoyed great influence, and Scandinavian Modern became both a defining element of cultures of all the Nordic countries and a commonly used international term. One should note, however, that this shift in design was not solely the work of Swedes or Scandinavians. This was, for example, the era of the Bauhaus in Germany and of Frank Lloyd Wright and many other modern architects in America. The development of Modern architecture was an international process. It is also important to keep in mind the connections this new architecture had with other aspects of the 1930s. This was the decade in which the Social Democrats gained a near majority in the parliament and were able to begin serious efforts to build the people's home (*folkhemmet*). It was an era of great faith in people's ability to engineer the good society—in politics, social programs, education, the arts, and architecture.

The Swedish modernists fundamentally altered the look of the architectural landscape. Their work included housing projects based upon affordable small, single family houses and multistory apartment complexes, bridges such as *Västerbron*/West Bridge and road complexes like the tangled web that straddles *Slussen* in Stockholm, subway stations, office buildings like *Wenner-Gren Center* or the Cooperative Society's *Glashuset*/Glass House, and public or government buildings like *Riksbankhuset*/The National Bank Building. The last of these opened in 1976. Designed by Peter Celsing, it has a cold, imposing, some believe even sterile, black granite exterior. (The intention was to convey a sense of solidity and safety—appropriate for a bank.) The interior is much warmer and lighter, and spaces are filled with superb examples of Swedish interior design.

Some of the best (and most controversial) examples of Swedish functionalism are the suburban apartment complexes designed and built in the 1960s under the so-called *Million Programme*/Million Program—a successful effort to create 1 million new housing units to meet a pressing need in many Swedish cities. These complexes, such as Tensta, Rinkeby, and Skärholmen in Stockholm, Hammarkullen in Göteborg, and Rosengård in Malmö, were designed as self-contained suburbs that included a number of multistory apartment buildings (both high-rise and lower, three-to-five story units),

The Rosengård Housing Development in Malmö. Built in the 1960s as part of the Million Program that aimed to provide a million new housing units. Today the area houses more than 20,000 people, many of whom are new Swedes. (Courtesy of Kurt Ive Kristoffersson.)

shopping centers, public services, recreational facilities, and transportation connections with the larger city. Malmö, Göteborg, Stockholm, and many of Sweden's smaller metropolitan areas were sites for these projects. At the time of their building, they generally looked good and seemed like wonderful solutions to the country's housing problems. Over time they proved less than ideal, and today many of them have become suburban ghettos for ethnic minorities.

In recent decades Swedish architecture has turned at least partially away from the cool, undecorated aspects of functionalism toward the more decorative, eclectic, varied, even risky elements of Postmodernism. Examples of this shift include the works of Gert Wingårdh (1951–), who is often mentioned as Sweden's leading contemporary architect. Among them are *Universum* (a science center in Göteborg), the control tower at Arlanda Airport, and the House of Sweden (Embassy) in Washington, D.C. *Globen*/*Ericsson Globen*/The Globe, the spherical sport arena on Söder, Stockholm's south island, is another example. Designed by *Berg Arkitektkontur*/Berg Architectural Offices, it opened in 1989. Surrounding the arena is a complex of shops, restaurants, and the like called "Globe City," which is in part the work of Ralph Erskine (1914–2005).

Erksine, who is considered one of the most important architects of the twentieth century, was born in England, but spent most of his professional life in Sweden. He was important both as a designer and as advocate of some of the fundamental ideals of his adopted country, and because of both, the Swedish Association of Architects/*Sveriges Arkitekter* has awarded a prize in his honor since 1988. The following comments from the organization say much about Erskine and Sweden:

> Ralph Erskine has had an immense influence on the Scandinavian architectural debate. He has been faithful to his belief in the development of a good and equal society and he has, without compromises, pledged and fought for the need for social and political awareness in the built environment.
>
> Ralph was a true humanist. His buildings radiate optimism, appropriateness and wit, which endear them to many. His philosophy of work accommodated the climate and the context together with the social and humanistic needs of people. He was concerned that the expression of buildings should engage the general public interest, generate a sense of ownership and appeal to genuine participation.[11]

Finally, there are two fascinating projects that reflect the new and the old in the architectural styles at play in Sweden. Representing Postmodernism is The Tenants Savings Bank and Building Society's *Hyresgästernas Sparkasse-och Byggnadsförening (HSB)'s* Turning Torso tower in Malmö. This 54-story residential complex was designed by the Spanish architect Santiago Calatrava, and it gets its name from the way in which the building twists 90 degrees around its central core like a corkscrew as it rises.[12] It is anything but a simple, functional rectangular solid.

Representing the successful merger of the early Functionalism of Gunnar Asplund with a very contemporary new building is the winning design by Germany architect Heike Hanada for the addition to the Stockholm City Library. Picked from a field of more than a thousand submissions, Hanada's Delphinium is actually based on two buildings. One is a translucent, white multistory block that would actually reveal what was going on inside the building. The other is a low, single-story unit that would connect the new and the old buildings. The design was praised for its cleverness, beauty, sensitivity, clarity, and iconic qualities. In a 2007 report from the competition jury, it was noted how "its idiom is clearly related to Asplund's own language of design in the form of clear and simple geometric shapes and subtle details. As of early 2010, the project has been put on hold. In part this was because there was considerable criticism of any design that might compromise Asplund's original building. More importantly, the planning group decided that spending a huge amount of money on an addition that would further

Turning Torso in Malmö. Designed by Spanish architect Santiago Calatrava and completed in 2005, this 54-story apartment complex illustrates the drift away from the functionalism that characterized much of modern Sweden's architecture. (Courtesy of Kurt Ive Kristoffersson.)

concentrate Stockholm's library facilities in a single place was not a good investment in times of tight budgets and changes in the nature of reading materials and how people access them.[13]

Brief mention ought also be made of folk architecture. This is embodied in the buildings of Sweden's rural society and includes mainly houses and storage buildings. Here fundamental designs date from the Middle Ages or even earlier. Basic house plans, such as the so-called *parstuga*, in which a centrally located entrance area opens onto rooms to the left and right, have been passed down for centuries. So, too, have basic farm building arrangements including the relatively scattered pattern of northern Swedish farms and the tight, enclosed courtyard layout of buildings common in the far south. The materials used in these buildings have generally depended upon what is close to hand. Obviously, in a country as heavily wooded as Sweden, timber has been primary. The ways in which it has been used have varied widely, however. Log, sawn timber, and daub and wattle building techniques predominate in highly predictable patterns, as do specific building forms and even the colors of the paint used on them. One of the best places to see the variety of rural buildings is at the open-air folk museum, *Skansen*, in Stockholm, where about half a dozen farms and a number of related rural buildings have been reconstructed and preserved.[14]

An interesting look at what some Swedes believe to be important architectural structures in their country and, thereby, what they believe represents their architectural culture was provided by three surveys conducted in 2007 and 2008; one by the newspaper *Aftonbladet*/The Evening News, a second by a division of Swedish Radio, and a third by the magazine of the national cement industry *Betong*/Concrete. In each case audiences were asked to select from a list what they believed to be the "seven wonders of Sweden" (*Sveriges sju underverk*). Here are the results:

Aftonbladet's list, based on 80,000 votes:

- Göta Canal, 1832
- Visby's ring wall, late thirteenth century
- The warship *Vasa*, c. 1630
- The Ice Hotel in Jukkasjärvi, since 1990
- Turning Torso, 2005
- The Öresund Bridge, 2000
- Globen, 1989

Swedish Radio's list, based on 4,000 votes:

- Göta Canal, 1832
- Ale's Stones, a stone "ship" monument in southern Sweden, c. 500 CE
- Malmö Mosque at Rosengård, 1984
- Lund Cathedral, early twelfth century
- Karlskrona, the naval city on the south coast, founded in 1680
- Visby's ring wall, late thirteenth century
- The Bronze Age rock carvings at Tanum, c. 1500 BCE

Betong's list, based on 3,000 votes:

- The Öresund link/The bridge and connecting elements, 2000
- Sandö Bridge in northern Sweden, 1943/2003
- Turning Torso, 2005

- Arlanda Airport Control Tower, 2001
- *Svampen*/The Mushroom, a water tower and café in Örebro, 1958
- Svinesund Bridge on highway E6 linking Norway and Sweden, 2005
- *Kaknästornet*, the broadcast hub Swedish Radio and Television in Stockholm, 1967.[15]

The results are, of course, far from scientific. *Aftonbladet*'s and Swedish Radio's listeners self-selected, but they did opt for a range of historical and contemporary structures. *Betong* has a small and prescriptive readership, and, not surprisingly, all of their choices were modern structures that made extensive use of concrete.

Design

The last of the arts to be considered here is design. In Sweden its components form a long list that includes textiles, clothing and fashion, glassware, ceramics and pottery, graphic arts, domestic appliances, automobiles, packaging, furniture, housewares, etc. As with the other areas of the arts, design has two main streams, historic and modern. The former can be divided into the design of the upper classes and folk design—although there are links between the two. The latter is more "democratic" and encompasses mainly the last 110 years or so.

The design history of the upper classes, which survives in the objects and decorations in the palaces, country homes, manor houses, apartments, and urban villas of Sweden's nobility and nineteenth-century bourgeoisie reflects mainly the artistic and architectural styles that defined the years between about 1500 and 1900. It is embodied in furniture, housewares, interior decorative elements, utilitarian objects like tiled heating stoves (*kakelugnar*), and fashions. All of the royal and noble palaces mentioned earlier were (and some remain) filled with period material culture objects. Some of these were obtained from abroad, but many were the work of either immigrant (sometimes recruited) or native artisans and often had uniquely Swedish aspects such as native materials, colors, decorative patterns, and techniques to them.

Folk design includes a similar range of categories but was different. While keeping up appearances may have been the driving force for the upper classes, utility was a primary factor for the common people. Furniture, housewares, clothing, and the like were first useful and purposeful. This does not mean, however, that these things were without esthetic value or beauty. The products, for example, of domestic woodworkers, weavers, smiths, or potters were often superbly executed and decorated. Traditional weaving patterns executed on multiharnessed looms included complex rosepath designs, wooden tableware might have intricately carved decorative elements, and cabinets and chests might be elaborately painted. Often both the basic design of objects and their decorations had very old origins. Sometimes, however, attempts were made to copy elements of the styles of upper classes. To an extent this can be seen in some of the surviving folk dress costumes worn today on special occasions by men and women or by folk dance groups or folk musicians.

Although it began earlier, industrialization made great headway in the nineteenth century and had a number of impacts on design in Sweden. For one, it resulted in a kind of freezing of folk designs. Second, it became a key force behind the development of the folk arts movement and efforts to define Sweden's national identity. As part of the folk arts, traditional design became the domain of preservationists and museums. Today, folk design remains important to what many consider to be Swedish, both in Sweden and abroad. Tourist shops across the country stock carved and painted Dalarna horses, rag rugs, straw Christmas ornaments, knitwear, and the like alongside contemporary fine crystal, jewelry, ceramics, stainless steel kitchenware, and moose decals.

A third impact of industrialization was that design was professionalized and moved into the factories that over time produced more and more of the furniture, housewares, clothing, etc. of most Swedes. In response, *Svensk Slöjdföreningen*/The Swedish Crafts Association was founded in 1845. (Today this organization is *Svensk Form*/Swedish Society of Crafts and Design.) Its initial purpose was to advocate for craft-produced goods and maintain quality standards. In the early twentieth century, the mission of the organization came to focus on the ideal that beautiful things are important to the quality of individuals' lives and to society, and that this ideal can be achieved through cooperation between designers and industrial producers. This ideal was expressed by women's rights advocate Ellen Key in the 1899 book *Skönhet för alla*/Beauty for Everyone, by art critique and director of the organization Gregor Paulsson in his *Vackare Vardagsvara*/More Beautiful Everyday Things from 1919, and by the 1917 *Hemutställning*/Home Exhibition in Stockholm, at which the latest in furniture, kitchens, wallpapers, ceramics, and the like were featured in 23 room-like settings.[16] Exhibitions have been important in demonstrating design developments and providing broad public forums. As was the case with architecture, an important moment in the history of Swedish design was the 1930 Stockholm Exposition. Every building on the grounds was furnished and provided a venue for literally thousands of objects in the new style, including radios, record players, automobiles, telephone kiosks, clocks, tables, chairs, desks, cabinets, glassware, ceramics, graphic art, and light fixtures. Among the designers were Simon Gate (glass), Carl Malmsten (furniture), and Sigurd Lewerentz (an architect who designed the winged emblem of the exposition). In 1955, a major exhibition was held in the southwest coast city of Helsingborg. Called H-55, it featured the work of designers from the Nordic countries, England, France, West Germany, and Japan. More than a dozen Swedish designers participated.

In recent years *Svensk Form* has added ecological and sustainability concerns to its mission. In addition, it continues to publish *Form* (formerly *Svensk Slöjdföreningens Tidskrift*, begun in 1905), organize exhibits, work with affiliate groups across the country, and maintain two design centers—one under its own direction in Stockholm and a second run by its Skåne branch. It and several other organizations cooperate in educational programs, exhibitions, and competitions. Since 2006, *Svensk Form* and *Stiftelsen Svensk Industridesign (SVID)*/The Swedish Industrial Design Foundation have awarded prizes for the best designs in a nominated competition. The winners in 2008 included a line of special product containers, ergonomic stacking chairs, extruded aluminum jewelry "bangles," a mobile phone–music player device, an eco-friendly fluorescent light fixture, a line of geometric-shape clothing, a specialized electronic device for club DJs, a multipurpose extreme sports helmet, a carpet made from a specially developed snarled/felted wool, and "the world's thinnest tables" for use in offices.[17] In addition, the *Stora Designpriset*/The Outstanding Design Prize has been awarded annually since 2003. Here the cooperating organizations include *Svensk Design*, *SVID*, and *Teknikföretagen* (an interest organization based on technology companies). In 2009 the nominated designs included the DJ device mentioned above, an ice auger, motorcycle boots, and a medical laboratory machine. The winner was a web camera designed by Zenith Design Group of Malmö and manufactured by Axis Communications in Lund.[18] Previous winners have included Volvo's XC90, an Ericsson mobile phone, and a computer monitor.

For much of the twentieth century modern design dominated in Sweden and the other Nordic countries, and during this time the country became recognized internationally for its glassware, ceramics, furniture, textiles, lighting, housewares, automobiles, communication devices, etc. Companies such as Orrefors, Kosta Boda, Gustavsberg, Höganäs, Electrolux, Volvo, SAAB, and L. M. Ericsson came to be known worldwide for the quality of their designs. For many people, perhaps more outside of Sweden than in the country, Swedish design today is symbolized by IKEA, the global flat-pack furniture giant. (Some would even say that IKEA *is* Sweden in a representational sense.) It has intentionally and successfully developed product lines that reflect the fundamentals of Scandinavian/Swedish modern design—simplicity, clarity, functionality, beauty, and use of contemporary materials. And there is another aspect to this philosophy. Lars Engman, who worked with the company for more than 40 years and was recently its design director, pointed this out when he called the company's basic design philosophy "Democratic Design," the elements of which are "beautiful form, good function, and an affordable price, creating a better everyday life for as many people as possible."[19] Taking this a step further, Olle Wästberg, director of The Swedish Institute (2009), has argued that IKEA represents exactly what a number of organizations in Sweden are seeking to do, that, is to "brand" Sweden and thereby give it a place in the world economy based on a set of clearly defined traits. In the emerging model, Sweden is "progressive," and four fundamental words—innovative, open, caring, and authentic—are used to describe it further. About these Wästberg has written:

> Innovative means new ways of thinking. Seeing things from a new perspective. Seeing opportunities and solutions and having faith in a better future. Not allowing oneself to be limited by engrained opinions or traditions.
>
> Open means having a positive attitude toward free thinking and to differences between people, cultures and lifestyles. It involves being curious and sensitive to others as well as giving people space and creating exchanges; space for the ideas and views of individuals, as well as physical space to move freely without obstacles, fences or crowding in our readily accessible countryside, cities and places in between.
>
> Caring means safeguarding every individual. Providing safety and security as well as respecting and including all people. It means feeling empathy and sharing with those who are most vulnerable; becoming involved with others and trying to see to the needs of every individual.
>
> Authentic means being natural and unaffected. It means being reliable, honest and informal. It also involves being straightforward, unpretentious and clear, as well as standing up for one's values even when it is not very comfortable. To be authentic means to be in touch with your past and your roots and open to the future.[20]

MUSEUMS

Overall, Sweden has many excellent museums (by one count more than 280) that cover every theme imaginable from art and architecture to mining, money, steelmaking, sports, or water use. Although many of these are in Stockholm, Göteborg, or Malmö, one can also find them in smaller cities, towns, and the countryside.[21]

For the fine arts, the largest and one of the oldest is Stockholm's National Museum. Its origins lie in the collections of art developed by Swedish kings from Gustav I Vasa in the early sixteenth century onwards. A royal museum was established in 1792 in the Royal Palace, and from it the National Museum was established in 1866—the year in which the current building opened. The collection includes more than 16,000 paintings and sculptures, more than 30,000 objects, and some half a million drawings and sketches. A second very important center is the Göteborg Museum of Art/*Göteborgs konstmuseum*, founded in 1861. It, too, holds an extensive and highly varied collection that includes several pieces by the eighteenth-century Swedish sculptor Johan Tobias Sergel and paintings by the Göteborg colorists/*Göteborg koloristerna*, a group of "color poets" from western Sweden who were important in the 1930s. Also important are the Modern Museum (see below) and the Malmö Museum of Art/*Malmö konstmuseum*, which focuses in its collection policies on contemporary works. In addition, many of Sweden's smaller cities have museums that have smaller collections and serve as venues for both national and international exhibitions.

A vital center since 1958 for both modern and contemporary art in Sweden has been Stockholm's Modern Museum/*Moderna museet*. First housed in an old navy drill hall on Skeppsholm, today it occupies a recently renovated modern (and controversial) building that opened in 1998. In a short article on the vision of the museum, its director (in 2009), Lars Nittve, wrote insightfully about the dual roles the museum must play—as a center for collecting and displaying the defining works of modern art *and* as a place where contemporary art is both displayed and happens. Some of his more important comments were:

- "The past and present are inextricably interwoven; this is the lifeblood of the modern museum. Each new work re-invents art history, and forces us to see old works in a new light."
- Art is something that "comes into being in its encounter with the beholder" (borrowing from Marcel Duchamp).
- "Art no longer admits any limitations on legitimate techniques and materials."
- Art is no longer "a cultural category that [is] largely bound to one particular sense," but rather a "zone into which phenomena, actions, design projects and texts can be introduced."[22]

Illustrating the diversity of its offerings, in the summer of 2009, the museum's exhibits included one of the paintings of Clay Ketter, an American who has lived in Sweden since 1998 and is a leading figure in contemporary Swedish art; another of three large works based on photographs and text by the American feminist and social criticism artist, Barbara Kruger; and a third, titled "Back to Reality," of Swedish and American photographs from the 1970s, based on the museum's permanent collection.

For architecture, the buildings themselves are most important, but there also is *Arkitekturmuseet*/The Museum of Architecture in Stockholm. The National Museum, along with the organization centers mentioned above and a number of important galleries, such as *Designgalleriet* in Stockholm, are important for design.

Schools

There are a number of very fine preparatory secondary schools as well as colleges or academy schools that train artists, architects, and designers in Sweden. While none may be explicitly committed to a particular style or method, all of them have their missions and leave their marks on their students. The premier school for the fine arts is The Royal College of Fine Arts/*Kungliga konsthögskolan* in Stockholm. Its origins lie in the Royal Academy of Fine Arts, which maintained the school until 1978. There are similar colleges (*högskolor*) in Umeå, Malmö, and Göteborg. In architecture, the leading institutions are the Schools of Architecture at the Royal Institute of Technology (Stockholm) and Lund University and Chalmers University of Technology in Göteborg. The flagship schools of design, interior design, and the crafts are *Konstfack*, founded in the 1844, and *HV Skolan* in Stockholm. In addition, there are programs at Göteborg, Växjö, and Umeå.

Three examples of preparatory schools or focused program schools are the Mora Folk High School, established largely through the efforts of Anders and Emma Zorn in 1907/8. Among its principal curricular lines are programs in art, weaving, pottery, glassblowing, and handcrafts. Lunnevad Folk High School, located near Linköping in east central Sweden and founded in 1868 as one of the three earliest folk high schools in the country, has strong programs in art, design, dance, and music. Finally, there is *Capellagården* on the island of Öland off the southeast coast. It was founded by the great Swedish furniture designer Carl Malmsten in 1960. Four programs dominate its offerings: textiles, furniture design, ceramics, and gardening. In a comment that tells one much about the spirit of arts education at the school and in Sweden in general, Malmsten once said:

> My vision was to create a school for both the body and the spirit, a meeting place for young people from across the country, animated by a desire to merge beauty and function into their handcrafted work.[23]

To conclude, brief attention ought be given to some of the factors that influence Sweden's arts culture today. First, as with so many other aspects of Sweden today, globalization and ethnic diversification are evident in virtually every genre of the arts. In the folk arts, new traditions are being added to the mix in the areas of textiles, painting, furniture, interior decor, and the like. In the fine arts, ethnic styles, methods, and themes are being woven into what many see as the more usual Swedish forms. Interesting also, is that in some cases arts that were considered fine in an immigrant's homeland are regarded as folk arts in Sweden (and elsewhere). This, along with other issues, adds a new layer of complexity to the perennial question—what is art?[24]

A second factor is the impact of new mediums and technologies. In the visual arts, for example, paint, photography, computer graphics, digital devices, video, and performance elements are often mixed. Architecture is affected by new materials and growing ecological and environment concerns, while design faces many of these pressures as well as the constant drive for innovation.

Finally, government policies and financial support are also important to the arts in Sweden. State resources have long been committed to all of the arts, and the Ministry of Culture is charged with several missions here. The following is a description of some of these:

> The objectives of national cultural policy include: taking action to enable everyone to participate in cultural life, to experience culture and to engage in creative activities of their own; promoting cultural diversity, artistic renewal and quality; enabling culture to act as a dynamic, challenging and independent force in society; preserving and making use of our cultural heritage; promoting a thirst for learning, and promoting international cultural exchange and meetings between different cultures in the country.
>
> Cultural policy covers issues concerning archives, museums and the cultural environment; theater, dance and music; architecture, form, design and the visual arts; burial and cremation services; libraries, literature and cultural publications; payments and grants to artists; film and video; handicrafts; religious communities; research and development in the field of culture; access to cultural activities for people with disabilities: culture for national minorities; culture for children and young people; culture in working life; culture and the popular movements: support for regional cultural activities; and the interaction between cultural policy and other policy areas.[25]

In order to accomplish its mission, the ministry works with other government agencies and a range of organizations, many of which have been mentioned above. In this context, it is worth remembering that there is an ongoing debate over the extent to which government ought be involved in the arts. How much of a role it ought play in leadership or administration and how much it ought to spend are two issues at the center of this debate. Another concern is over the impact government influence has on taste, on defining what is good and not good in the arts. Many critics have long felt that Sweden's governments have had too much influence in this area and thereby have contributed to a kind of boring uniformity in place of genuine creativity. Given the changes that appear to be taking place in the distribution of power among the old political parties of the country, the drift to more conservative governments, and the ideals set forth in the 2009 Cultural Commission's report, changes are likely in this area.

In general, all of these factors support one of the fundamental ideals of the "people's home" —that beautiful things, including works of art in a wide range of genre, are important to the individual and to the society as a whole. Consequently, Sweden is a place where artists, architects, and designers receive significant private and public support and where educational opportunities and public venues in which to experience the arts abound. It is also a place where public and private buildings are often, in and of themselves, works of art, interiors are furnished and decorated with beautiful things, and the products of industry are both functional and attractive.

Notes

1. See http://www.raa.se/cms/extern/index.html. Accessed July 15, 2009.
2. See http://www.historiska.se and http://www.lansmuseetgotland.se/1322. Accessed July 24, 2009.
3. The academy maintained the school until 1978, when it became The Royal University College of Fine Arts/ *Kungliga konsthögskolan*. It also maintains its own collection, library, and archives. It facilities are located in the Sparre Palace in Stockholm.
4. An excellent source is at http://www.zorn.se/engmain.html. Accessed July 30, 2009.
5. See http://www.clg.se/start.aspx. Accessed July 30, 2009. This site is in Swedish or English and very informative and visually rewarding.
6. See http://www.johnbauersmuseum.nu/. Accessed July 30, 2009. This is the best site in Swedish about him and his work. On the sinking, see http://www.faktaomfartyg.se/per_brahe_1857.htm. Accessed July 30, 2009.
7. On the Uppsala Cathedral, see http://www.uppsaladomkyrka.se/setupups/engelsk/default.asp?orgID=464. Accessed July 27, 2009. On the Lund Cathedral, see http://www.lundsdomkyrka.org/index.shtml. Accessed July 24, 2009. English options.
8. See "Kiruna kyrka utsågs av Arkitektriksdagen 2001 till 'alla tiders bästa byggnad, byggd före 1950' i Sverige" at http://www.kommun.kiruna.se/upload/3697/Broschyren%20Byggnader%20i%20centrala%20Kiruna%20f%C3%B6r%20webb.pdf. Accessed July 27, 2009. There is a wonderful image of the church at this site, too.
9. See http://whc.unesco.org/en/list/559. Accessed July 27, 2009. A video program of the site is available here, too. In English.
10. See the Nordic Museum's Web site http://www.nordiskamuseet.se/. Accessed July 14, 2009.
11. See http://www.arkitekt.se/s16091. Accessed July 6, 2009.
12. See http://www.designbuild-network.com/projects/turning-torso/. Accessed July 13, 2009.

13. See *Asplund. Architectural Competition. The Stockholm City Library. Excerpt from the Jury's Report*. 2007 may be found at www.arkitekt.se/s28227/f4552/asplund_jury_report_shorty.pdf. Information on the project may be found at http://www.nyttstadsbibliotek.stockholm.se/ and at http://www.nyttstadsbibliotek.stockholm.se/Sve/Sidor/Bilder/f5069.pdf. Accessed April 6, 2010.

14. See http://www.skansen.se/pages/?ID=260. In English. Accessed July 25, 2009.

15. There is an article on this at http://sv.wikipedia.org/wiki/Sveriges_sju_underverk. Accessed July 24, 2009. Each of the survey sources has its own Web site information.

16. See Creagh, Lucy, et al. *Modern Swedish Design. Three Founding Texts*. New York: The Museum of Modern Art, 2008. This book contains three works viewed by many as essential in the development of modern Swedish design: Ellen Key's "Beauty in the Home" (Beauty for All) from 1899, Gregor Paulsson's "Better Things for Everyday Life" (More Beautiful Everyday Things) from 1919, and *acceptera* (Accept), by Gregor Paulsson, Uno Åhrén, Gunnar Asplund, Wolter Gahn, Sven Markelius, and Eskil Sundahl—all of whom were involved in the 1930 Stockholm Exposition.

17. See http://www.swedishdesignaward.se/page/241. Accessed July 27, 2009.

18. See http://www.storadesignpriset.se/. Accessed July 27, 2009.

19. See http://www.d-vision.co.il/151721&set=0. Accessed July 14, 2009.

20. See http://www.wastberg.se/viewtext.php?tid=263. Accessed July 27, 2009. This article appeared originally in the Summer 2009 issue of the journal *Public Diplomacy*, which is available in print.

21. See http://www.museums.dk/sweden.html, for example. Also useful is http://www.visitsweden.com/sweden/Attractions/Culture/Museums-of-Sweden/. Accessed July 30, 2009.

22. See http://www.modernamuseet.se/en/Moderna-Museet/About/Vision/. Accessed April 7, 2010.

23. See http://www.capellagarden.se/index.asp?visa=13. Accessed July 8, 2009. About Carl Malmsten see http://www.c.malmsten.se/. Accessed July 30, 2009.

24. See Owe Ronström, "The Forms of Diversity: Folk Art in Multicultural Sweden" in Barbro Klein and Mats Widbom, eds., *Swedish Folk Art: All Tradition Is Change* (New York, NY: Harry N. Abrams, 1995), pp. 175–79.

25. See http://www.sweden.gov.se/sb/d/8371/a/74122. Accessed July 27, 2009.

Bibliography

Ahlstrand, Kajsa, and Göran Gunner, eds. *Guds närmaste stad? En studie om religionernas betydelse i ett svensk samhälle i början av 2000-talet.* Stockholm: Svenska Kyrkan and Verbum Förlag, 2008.

Andersson, Daniel, and Åke Sander, eds. *Det mångreligiösa Sverige: ett landskap I förändring.* Lund, Sweden: Studentlitteratur AB, 2005.

Roland Anderson. *Dalmåleri—dalmålarna, deras liv och verk.* Mora, Sweden: Dalarnas fornminnes—och hembygdsförbund, 2007.

Anwar, M., J. Blaschke, and Å. Sander, eds. "Muslims in Sweden," in *State Policies Towards Muslim Minorities. Sweden, Great Britain and Germany.* Berlin: Edition Parabolis, pp. 203–374. Available at http://www.islamawareness.net/Europe/Sweden/Muslims_in_Sweden.pdf.

Beckman, Svante, and Sten Månsson. *KultureSverige 2009: Problemanalys och statistik.* Linköping: SweCult at Linköping University, 2009.

Bengtsson, Eva, ed. *Media Developments 2006.* Swedish Radio and TV Authority, 2006. (This is a comprehensive survey of the media—press, radio, television, film—in Sweden for 2005. A newer version may be available.) Published in print and pdf versions. Online at http://www.rtvv.se/_upload/uk/download/MU_2006_eng.pdf. Accessed July 30, 2009.

Bentsson, Eva-Lena, et al. *Signums svenska konsthistoria. Konsten 1845–1890.* Lund: Bokförlaget Signum, 2000.

Berefelt, Gunnar. *Svensk konsthistoria.* Stockholm: AWE/Geber, 1977.

Berggren, Henrik, and Lars Trägårdh. *Är svensken människa?* Stockholm: Norstedts, 2006.

Berlin, Peter. *Xenophobes Guide to the Swedes*. UK: Oval Books, 1994.

Caldenby, Claes, and Olof Hultin. *Architecture in Sweden 1995–1999/Arkitektur i Sverige 1995–99*. Stockholm: Arkitektur förlag, 2000.

Childs, Marquis. *Sweden: The Middle Way*. New Haven, CT: Yale University Press, 1980. First published in 1936.

Childs, Marquis. *Sweden: The Middle Way on Trial*. New Haven: Yale University Press, 1980.

Cowie, Peter. *Scandinavian Cinema*. London: The Tantivy Press, 1992.

Creagh, Lucy, et al. *Modern Swedish Design. Three Founding Texts*. New York: The Museum of Modern Art, 2008. (Note: This book contains three essays viewed by many as essential in the development of modern Swedish design: Ellen Key's "Beauty in the Home" from 1899, Gregor Paulsson's "Better Things for Everyday Life" from 1919, and "Acceptera," which was written by Paulsson and Uno Åhrén, Gunnar Asplund, Wolter Gahn, Sven Markelius, and Eskil Sundahl—all of whom were involved in the 1930 Stockholm Exposition.)

Curry, Andrew, with Carsten Snejbjerg, photographer. "Raiders or Traders." *Smithsonian*, 39:4 (July 2008), 24–30. (This deals with Viking ships and a voyage by a reconstruction from Denmark to Ireland.)

Dahlberg, Marie, Lena Koller, and Marie Ravegård. *Amazing Sweden*. Sweden: Snowfling Media, 2008. (This is a lavishly illustrated work that covers many of the topics in this book.)

Daun, Åke. *Swedish Mentality*, translated by Jan Teeland, foreword by David Cooperman. University Park: Pennsylvania State University Press, 1996. First published as *Svensk Mentalitet* in Sweden in 1989.

Downman, Lorna, Paul Britten Austin, and Anthony Baird. *Round the Swedish Year*. Stockholm: Swedish Institute with Bokförlaget Fabel, 1967.

Frängsmyr, T., translated by Judith Black. *Alfred Nobel*. Stockholm: Swedish Institute, 2004.

Grate, Pontus, ed. *Treasures of Swedish Art: From Prehistoric Age to the 19th Century*. Malmö: Allhem Publishers, 1963.

Grive, Madeleine, and Mehmed Uzun. *Världen i Sverige: En Internationell Antologi*. Stockholm: En bok för alla, 1995.

Hadenius, Stig, Lennart Weibull, and Ingela Wadbring. *Massmedier Press, radio och tv i den digitala tidsåldern*. Stockholm: Ekerlids, 2008.

Hadenius, Stig, and Lennart Weibull. "The Swedish Newspaper System in the Late 1990s," *Nordicom Review*, 20:1 (November 1999), 129–152.

Hagens, William, and Willow Hagens. *Zorn in America: A Swedish Impressionist of the Gilded Age*. Chicago and Minneapolis: The Swedish-American Historical Society and The American Swedish Institute, 2009.

Hagstrom, Jerry. *To Be, Not to Be Seen—The Mystery of Swedish Business*. Washington, DC: The George Washington University School of Business and Public Management, 2001.

Hellberg, Thomas, and Lars Magnus Jansson. *Alfred Nobel*. Stockholm: Alno Production, KB, 1984 and Karlshamn, Lagerblads Förlag, AB, 1986. English version.

Holkers, Märta. *Den svenska målarkonstens historia*. Stockholm: Bonniers, 2001.

Huntford, Roland. *The New Totalitarians*. New York: Stein & Day, 1972.

Ingebritsen, Christine. *The Nordic States and European Unity*. Ithaca, NY: Cornell University Press, 2000.

Jones, Michael, and Kenneth R. Olwig. *Nordic Landscapes. Region and Belonging on the Northern Edge of Europe*. Minneapolis: University of Minnesota Press, 2008. See section on Sweden (Chapters 6–10).

Kent, Neal. *A Concise History of Sweden*. Cambridge Concise Histories. Cambridge, UK: Cambridge University Press, 2008.

Klein, Barbro, and Mats Widbom, eds. *Swedish Folk Art: All Tradition Is Change*. New York: Harry N. Abrams, 1995.

Larson, Göran, researcher. *Muslims in the EU: Cities Report: Sweden*. Open Society Institute, EU Monitoring and Advocacy Program, 2007. See http://www.eumap.org/topics/minority/reports/eumuslims/background_reports/download/sweden/sweden.pdf.

Lindqvist, Herman. *A History of Sweden*. Stockholm: Norstedts, 2006.

Loughran, Kim. *The Year in Sweden*. Stockholm: Bokförlaget Max Ström, 2009.

Löfgren, Lars. *Svensk Teater*. Stockholm: Natur och Kultur, 2003.

McIlroy, Brian. *World Cinema 2: Sweden*. London: Flicks Books, 1986.

Miles, Lee. *Fusing with Europe? Sweden in the European Union*. Farnham, UK: Ashgate, 2005.

Misgeld, Klaus, Karl Molin, and Klas Åmark. *Creating Social Democracy. A Century of the Social Democratic Labor Party in Sweden*. University Park, PA: Pennsylvania State University Press, 1992.

Myrdal, Alva. *Towards Equality: The Alva Myrdal Report to the Swedish Social Democratic Party*, Stockholm: Prisma, 1971. (This report is the result of the Working Group on Equality established by the party and Sweden's National Association of Trade Unions/*Landsorganisationen* in 1968.)

Nestingen, Andrew K. *Crime and Fantasy in Scandinavia: Fiction, Film, and Social Change*. Seattle: University of Washington Press and Copenhagen: Museum Tusculanum Press, University of Copenhagen, 2008.

Nordic Literature. This was an annual publication from the Nordic Council. Published from 1993 through 2006. (It included articles and book reviews on a wide range of topics related to Nordic literature.)

Nordin, Dennis Sven. *A Swedish Dilemma: A Liberal European Nation's Struggle with Racism and Xenophobia, 1990–2000*. Lanham: MD: University Press of America, 2005.

Nordstrom, Byron. *The History of Sweden*. Westport, CT: Greenwood, 2002.

Plath, Iona. *The Decorative Arts of Sweden*. New York: Scribners, 1948 and Dover Publications, 1960.

Popenoe, David. *Disturbing the Nest: Family Change and Decline in Modern Societies.* New York: Aldine De Gruyter, 1988. (See especially Part II, "The Case of Sweden," 85–258).

Popenoe. "Marriage and Family: What Does the Scandinavian Experience Tell Us." *2005: The State of Our Unions.* The National Marriage Project at the University of Virginia. (See: http://www.virginia.edu/marriageproject/ and http://www.virginia.edu/marriageproject/annualreports.html).

Roald, Anne Sofie. *Women in Islam: The Western Experience.* New York and London: Routledge, 2001.

Robinowitz, Christina Johansson, and Lisa Werner Carr. *Modern Day Vikings: A Practical Guide to Interacting with the Swedes.* Yarmouth, ME, Intercultural Press, 2001.

Rudberg, Eva. *The Stockholm Exhibition, 1930: Modernisms Breakthrough in Swedish Architecture.* Stockholm: Stockholmia förlag, 1999.

Statistiska Centralbyrån. *Barn och deras familjer 2006.* Demografiska Rapporter 2007:4. Stockholm, 2007. Available at http://www.scb.se/Pages/Publishing CalendarViewInfo____259923.aspx?PublObjId=5393. Accessed April 14, 2010.

Stegeby, E. Kenneth. "An Analysis of the Impending Disestablishment of the Church of Sweden," *Brigham Young University Law Review,* 1999 (2), 703–749.

Svanberg, Ingvar, and David Westerlund. *Blågul islam? Muslimer i Sverige.* Nora, Sweden: Bokförlaget Nya Doxa AB 1999.

Svensson, Sonja. "Four Centuries of Children's Books in Sweden." (This is an eight-page survey of the history of Swedish literature in Sweden.) It is available as a pdf file at the Web site of the Royal Library of Sweden. See: http://www.sbi.kb.se/Documents/Public/Utgivning%20och%20f%C3%B6rmedling/FOUR%20CENTURIES%20OF%20CHILDREN.pdf.

Sveriges National Atlas/National Atlas of Sweden. 19 volumes. Leif Wastenson, ed. Stockohlm: Almqvist & Wiksell, 1990–Present. Available in Swedish or English, in print or CD/DVD. (See also http://www.sna.se/webbatlas/index.html.)

Swahn, Jan-Öyvind. *Maypoles, Crayfish, and Lucia: Swedish Holidays and Traditions.* Stockholm: Swedish, 1999.

The Swedish Institute. http://www.sweden.se. (This is an excellent place to begin a search about almost any topic related to Sweden. Print and pdf versions of what are called factsheets are available on a wide range of topics.)

Thente, Jonas. "Literary Perspectives: Sweden. Beyond crime fiction, handbags and designer suits." *Eurozine,* September 23, 2008. Online magazine at www.eurozine.com/articles/2008-09-23-thente-en.html. Accessed July 30, 2009.

Tranströmer, Tomas, translated by Robert Bly. *The Half-Finished Heaven.* Minneapolis, MN: Greywolf Press, 2001.

Wadbring, Ingela. *En tidning i tiden? Metro och den svenska dagstidningsmarknaden* (A Paper for Its Time? *Metro* and the Swedish Newspaper Market). Göteborg

University, Department of Journalism and Mass Communication, Doctoral Dissertation, 2003.

Waern, Rasmus, ed., and A. E. Lindman, photographer. *Gert Wingardh*. New York: Birkhauser; 2001.

Waern, Rasmus, ed. *Guide to Swedish Architecture*. Stockholm: The Swedish Institute, 2001.

Warme, Lars, ed. *A History of Swedish Literature*. Lincoln: University of Nebraska Press, 1994.

Widenheim, Cecilia, ed. *Utopia & Reality. Modernity in Sweden. 1900–1960*. New Haven: Yale University Press, 2002. (This book covers an exhibit of the same title shown at Bard Graduate Center for Studies in the Decorative Arts, Design, and Culture in 2002.)

Wendelius, Lars. *Den dubbla identiteten: Immigrant- och Minoritetslitteratur på svenska 1970–2000*. Sweden: Uppsala University, Center for Multi-Ethnic Studies, 2002.

Wikan, Unni, Translated by Anna Paterson. *In Honor of Fadime: Murder and Shame*. Chicago: University of Chicago Press, 2008. (Originally published as *For ærens skyld: Fadime till ettertanke*. Oslo: Universitetsforlaget, 2003.)

Index

About the Author

BYRON J. NORDSTROM is professor emeritus at Gustavus Adolphus College in St. Peter, MN. Dr. Nordstrom is the editor and compiler of *Dictionary of Scandinavian History,* and author of *Scandinavia since 1500* and *The History of Sweden*. In addition, he has published many articles on Swedish-American history and is currently the editor of *The Swedish-American Historical Quarterly.* In 2008, Dr. Nordstrom received the Order of the Polar Star, Commander rank, from King Carl XVI Gustaf of Sweden for his work furthering knowledge and understanding of Sweden.

Recent Titles in Culture and Customs of Europe

Culture and Customs of Germany
Eckhard Bernstein

Culture and Customs of Italy
Charles Killinger

Culture and Customs of the Baltic States
Kevin O'Connor

Culture and Customs of Ireland
Margaret Scanlan

Culture and Customs of the Czech Republic and Slovakia
Craig Cravens

Culture and Customs of Ireland
W. Scott Haine

Culture and Customs of Ukraine
Adriana Helbig, Oksana Buranbaeva, and Vanja Mladineo

Culture and Customs of the Caucasus
Peter L. Roudik

Culture and Customs of Serbia and Montenegro
Christopher M. Deliso

Culture and Customs of Turkey
Rafis Abazov

Culture and Customs of Greece
Artemis Leontis

Culture and Customs of the Netherlands
John B. Roney